Cayman Islands

THE BRADT TRAVEL GUIDE

THE BRADT STORY

The first Bradt travel guide was written by Hilary and George Bradt in 1974 on a river barge floating down a tributary of the Amazon in Bolivia. From their base in Boston, Massachusetts, they went on to write and publish four other backpacking guides to the Americas and one to Africa.

In the 1980s Hilary continued to develop the Bradt list in England, and also established herself as a travel writer and tour leader. The company's publishing emphasis evolved towards broader-based guides to new destinations – usually the first to be published on those countries – complemented by hiking, rail and wildlife guides.

Since winning *The Sunday Times* Small Publisher of the Year Award in 1997, we have continued to fill the demand for detailed, well-written guides to unusual destinations, while maintaining the company's original ethos of low-impact travel.

Travel guides are by their nature continuously evolving. If you experience anything which you would like to share with us, or if you have any amendments to make to this guide, please write; all your letters are read and passed on to the author. Most importantly, do remember to travel with an open mind and to respect the customs of your hosts – it will add immeasurably to your enjoyment.

Happy travelling!

Hilary Bradt

Hilary Bradt

19 High Street, Chalfont St Peter, Bucks SL9 9QE, England
Tel: 01753 893444; fax: 01753 892333
Email: info@bradt-travelguides.com
Web: www.bradt-travelguides.com

Cayman Islands

THE BRADT TRAVEL GUIDE

Tricia Hayne

Bradt Travel Guides Ltd, UK
The Globe Pequot Press Inc, USA

First published in 2001 by Bradt Travel Guides Ltd,
19 High Street, Chalfont St Peter, Bucks SL9 9QE, England
web: www.bradt-travelguides.com
Published in the USA by The Globe Pequot Press Inc, 246 Goose Lane,
PO Box 480, Guilford, Connecticut 06437-0480

Text copyright © 2001 Tricia Hayne
Maps copyright © 2001 Bradt Travel Guides Ltd
Illustrations © 2001 Individual photographers and artists

The author and publishers have made every effort to ensure the accuracy of the
information in this book at the time of going to press. However, they cannot accept any
responsibility for any loss, injury or inconvenience resulting from the use of information
contained in this guide.

British Library Cataloguing in Publication Data
A catalogue record for this book is available from the British Library
ISBN 1 84162 039 4

Library of Congress Cataloging-in-Publication Data applied for

Photographs
Front cover Tricia Hayne
Text Cayman Islands Tourist Board (CITB), Tricia & Bob Hayne (TH);
Karen & Ian Stewart (KS)

Illustrations Carole Vincer
Maps Alan Whitaker

Typeset from the author's disc by Wakewing
Printed and bound in Italy by Legoprint SpA, Trento

Author

Tricia Hayne joined Bradt Travel Guides in 1993 and is now editorial director. She has travelled widely in North America and to many island destinations worldwide. A watersports enthusiast, she enjoys swimming, diving and sailing, as well as walking and generally exploring new places. She has had articles published in various national and local magazines and newspapers, including *The Bookseller* and *The Independent on Sunday*.

FEEDBACK REQUEST

Any book about the Cayman Islands is necessarily a snapshot in time. New restaurants open, hotels change hands, dive operators come and go. The material in this guide was accurate at the time of research, but by the time you visit there will inevitably have been changes. Do drop me a line, whether it's to pass on details of a new venue, or to tell me about that wonderful meal – or indeed to share any negative experiences. All correspondence will be personally answered, and will help to ensure that the next edition of this guide will reflect the findings of a far wider group of people.

I look forward to hearing from you. In the meantime, have a great trip!

Bradt Travel Guides,
19 High Street, Chalfont St Peter, Bucks SL9 9QE, England
Tel: 01753 893444; fax: 01753 892333;
email: tricia_hayne@bradt-travelguides.com;
web: www.bradt-travelguides.com

Contents

LIST OF MAPS

Acknowledgements

This book would never have been written without the support of Don McDougall at the Cayman Islands Tourist Board. To him, and to Sarah Sheehan, Natasha Earl and – most of all – Jonathan Sloan for their help in so many ways, I am very grateful. Thanks, too, to Angela Martins, Director of Tourism in Cayman, for her enthusiasm and encouragement.

Countless people and organisations have helped in numerous ways with advice, recommendations and suggestions. More specifically, I am indebted to the following, every one of whom has made a significant contribution to this book:

In Grand Cayman: Martyn Court, Judith Burt and her mother, Margaret, for countless insights into the Cayman Islands from the inside; David Martins for his help with the cultural perspective; Rod McDowall of the Cayman Tourism Alliance Watersports Committee for help with the text, and organising our first dives in Cayman waters; Gina Petrie at the Department of Environment; Philip Pedley at the Cayman Islands National Archive for his advice on the history; David Carmichael of Cayman Islands Sailing Club for suggestions on the text; Will Kelly for taking the time to wade through his slide collection; Fred Burton and Wendy Moore at the National Trust; Andrew Guthrie at Queen Elizabeth II Botanic Park; Patricia Bradley for looking over the information on birds; Geddes Hislop for showing us the secrets of the Mastic Trail; and Nicky for introducing us to the natural beauty of West Bay, and her tales of Cayman past and present.

On the sister islands: Marc and Sabine at Paradise Villas; Diana Scott, for her stories of life on Cayman Brac, and Genevieve Robbins for hers on Little Cayman; the staff at Reef Divers; John Byrnes for his hefty input on climbing; and Ian and Karen Stewart for help with matters photographic.

In the UK and elsewhere: John Moody of Stanley Gibbons for his contribution on philately/stamps; Jim Stevenson of the RSPB; Frank Lepore at the National Hurricane Center, Miami; Guy Marriott; Mary Chandler-Allen at the government office for kindly wading through statistics; and Alan Whitaker for his infinite patience faced with impossible maps.

To Hilary Bradt, whose knowledge of travel and travel writing I could never hope to emulate, thank you for the opportunity to see the other side of the coin. And finally, to my husband Bob – researcher extraordinaire – this is for you.

Introduction

The Cayman Islands are one of the remaining 14 outposts that comprise the British Overseas Territories. On the surface, there is an American gloss about the place, with luxury hotels and shops geared totally to the well-heeled tourist. Dig a little deeper, though, and you'll find a whole new world, where Britain meets the Caribbean, and relaxation is the key.

The approach to Seven Mile Beach from Owen Roberts Airport does not bode well. A sinking feeling dispels the Caribbean glow instilled by the airline's complimentary rum punch as the scene unfolds into a sprawl of wide roads seeded with anonymous warehouses and downtown US fast-food outlets.

But first impressions are deceptive. Just a few minutes' drive from the airport and you could be sipping that rum punch, watching the sun set over the Caribbean from a pure white sandy beach. Or selecting from an almost bewildering choice of restaurants in George Town, where the atmosphere is more that of an old-fashioned market town than an international financial centre. Or dipping into an underwater world whose wonders bring divers back year after year. A little further afield, and you'll discover small sandy coves washed by a turquoise sea, or tortuous rocky shores which reward those who brave them with extraordinary coral formations and the coastline at its wildest. Better still, you will catch intriguing glimpses of an island culture founded on the sea, a proud people determined not to lose touch with their heritage.

They say that 'duppies' can only be seen by those with time to look. Perhaps the same could be said of the true Cayman Islands. So do give yourself time. Take a walk beyond your resort. Visit another island. Stop and talk to people. These islands have a story to tell, if you slow down and listen.

NOTES ABOUT ADDRESSES

Cayman addresses feature post office box numbers rather than street names, which are a recent addition to the Cayman Islands. In many cases, the box number bears no relationship to the physical location of an address – thus, for example, Morritt's Tortuga in East End has a George Town box number. Wherever possible, I have given the street name and/or location, as well as the box number. This means, for example, that where a place is on West Bay Road, this will be stated rather than Seven Mile Beach, which may be the post box code but which runs parallel to the road.

Many of Cayman's restaurants, shops and services are located in small shopping malls and plazas set back from West Bay Road or in similar locations. Rather than put every such venue on the maps, which would make them too crowded to be of use, the name of the mall or plaza has been given, so readers should check the address when looking for a place on the map. Thus, for example, for Edoardo's in Coconut Place, find Coconut Place on the map and you have effectively pinpointed Edoardo's.

Part One

General Information

Tarpon

CAYMAN ISLANDS AT A GLANCE

Islands Grand Cayman, Little Cayman, Cayman Brac

Location In the Caribbean Sea, approximately 640km (400 miles) south of Florida, 268km (167 miles) northwest of Jamaica

Size Grand Cayman 76 square miles (197km^2); Little Cayman 10 square miles (26km^2); Cayman Brac 14 square miles (36km^2)

Time GMT –5 (USA Eastern Standard Time). No daylight saving time.

Electricity 110 volts; 60Hz

International telephone code + 1 345

Status British Dependent Territory

GDP US$30,120 per capita (1998)

Currency Cayman Islands dollar (CI$)

Population (1999) 39,020 (Grand Cayman 37,083; Little Cayman 115; Cayman Brac 1,822)

Economy Major earners are tourism and banking

Capital George Town (1999 population 20,625)

Language English, with some regional dialects

Religion Christian

Flag Light blue background; Union flag top left corner; Cayman Islands coat of arms on white circular background

National anthem 'God Save the Queen'

National song 'Beloved Isle Cayman'

National emblem Giant turtle

National flower Banana orchid

National bird Cayman parrot

National tree Silver thatch palm

Background Information

HISTORY
with Bob Hayne, and with particular thanks to Philip Pedley of the Cayman Islands National Archive

> He hath founded it upon the seas
>
> Cayman Islands motto (Psalm 24:2)

Looking out to sea from George Town, it takes little to imagine a renegade Spanish ship of the line hobbling into the safety of this natural harbour, its desperate crew both hungry and thirsty. In those days turtles were abundant on Seven Mile Beach, especially in May, June and July, their eggs and meat providing much-needed succour. But sailing in these waters has its dangers, and many a vessel has foundered here or on one of the many reefs that encircle these small islands.

The first recorded sighting of the Cayman Islands was not in fact of Grand Cayman, but of the Lesser Caymans, or sister islands. During Christopher Columbus' fourth and final quest in search of the New World in 1503, while en route from Panama to Hispaniola, he sailed past the two islands now known as Cayman Brac and Little Cayman. His young son, Ferdinand, described them as 'two small and low islands, full of tortoises (as was all the sea about, insomuch that they looked like little rocks), for which reason these islands were called Tortugas'. Presumably they stuck in Columbus' memory as a good place for provisions, for the turtles were collected in large numbers, effectively a living larder for the sailors.

The Turin map of 1523 showed all three islands in roughly the right position and called them Lagartos, meaning 'alligators' or 'large lizards'. The eventual name Cayman seems to have stuck around 1540, derived from a Carib word for the crocodile family, *caymanas*: the islands evidently once abounded with marine crocodiles.

Over 80 years after Columbus' sighting, when Sir Francis Drake's fleet passed within sight of the islands in 1586, they were still uninhabited. Drake anchored for two days off Grand Cayman, surrounded by crocodiles, alligators, iguanas and turtles. The lure of fresh water and turtle meat meant that the island became a regular port of call for European ships in these waters well into the 19th century.

3

Pirates and profiteers

Although the islands were isolated, the lack of reliable charts at the time meant that they were on one of the standard sailing routes through the Caribbean. Ships heading east towards North America and Europe found it quicker and safer to sail west at first, with the wind behind them, travelling as far as the western end of Cuba before turning east for Europe, with the aid of the Gulf Stream. It's not surprising, then, that the eastern tip of Grand Cayman, with an almost unbroken reef and a prevailing easterly wind, came to be labelled the 'graveyard of the Caribbean', not least as a result of the almost legendary Wreck of the Ten Sails (see page 167). Conversely, the rich pickings from shipwrecks may well have served as an attraction to privateers, who sailed under royal patronage, or renegade pirates and freebooters.

In 1670, the Treaty of Madrid was signed by England and Spain, in an attempt to bring peace to the region. Under the terms of the treaty, it was declared that the Cayman Islands, along with Jamaica and several others, would officially belong to England. Pirates were not to be dissuaded from their prize by a mere treaty, however, and ships in the Caribbean continued to sail in fear. It is even said that Blackbeard 'took a small turtler' off the islands, though this was a time upon which story books are based and such things are almost certainly the stuff of legends. In reality, the Cayman Islands were more frequently a staging post for merchant or naval ships than threatened by pirate invasion.

THE BLACKBEARD LEGEND

Blackbeard's reign of terror in the Caribbean in fact lasted less than two years, until his demise in November 1718 at the hands of jealous pirates. Yet his colourful character and bloodthirsty exploits have become legendary, outshining the feats of more successful rivals and securing his place in the annals of history.

Born of either British or Jamaican parents (no one is quite sure), Blackbeard's real name is usually given as Edward Teach, but Tach, Tatch, Thatch or Tache have all been put forward – as indeed has Drummond! With a long, thick black beard covering most of his face, and twisted into Rastafarian-style locks, his very appearance was awesome. He wore pistols over his shoulders like bandoliers and was reputed to stick slow-burning matches under his hat to increase his look of ferocity. His mastery of his 'craft' went well beyond his appearance, of course. Once, in an idle moment in his cabin, he took out a pair of pistols, blew out the candle, crossed his hands and shot under the table at the ship's master, one Israel Hands, apparently as a random gesture to reinforce his authority in the eyes of the crew in general. Hands, lamed for life, nevertheless went on to achieve immortality as the blind Pew in Stevenson's *Treasure Island*.

Settlers and slaves

The origin of the first settlers on Cayman is uncertain. It is possible that they were deserters from the British army in Jamaica in the mid 17th century, one surnamed Bodden. It is more likely, however, that they were small-time planters or loggers from Jamaica, who had begun to arrive in small numbers by about 1700.

Grants of land issued by the governor of Jamaica from 1734 encouraged settlers to bring their servants and slaves to the island and become planters. By 1773, there were 39 families on Grand Cayman, many of them descendants of the original Bodden, including his grandson, Isaac. Slaves at this time made up at least half of the population of 450 people, shipped out to the islands from Jamaica in increasing numbers. And when, in 1781, the slave ship *Nelly* was wrecked off the coast of Grand Cayman, several slaves were sold to the islanders in return for 'salvage and other expenses'. Other settlers were fugitives of one sort or another from Jamaica, while yet more wound up on the islands as a result of shipwreck.

When Edward Corbet visited Grand Cayman in 1802, on a fact-finding mission for the governor of Jamaica, he found a total population of 933 inhabitants, of whom 545 were slaves. Yet slavery here, with no major plantations, was not the business that it became on other Caribbean islands. Most households had fewer than ten slaves, whereas in Jamaica at the same time the norm was nearer a hundred. The relative isolation of Cayman also meant that the relationship between slaves and their owners was far more relaxed than elsewhere. Indeed, even before the release of slaves following the 1834 Abolition Act, the occasional slave owner was married to a former slave. While many of the freed slaves moved to the northern parts of Grand Cayman, others eventually emigrated to the Bay Islands off Honduras.

Trade

With the growth in population at the end of the 18th century, trade became more important to the region. Initially, merchant vessels were few, carrying cotton, turtles and timber to Jamaica, and returning with such essentials as rum, flour, candles, soap, canvas and, inevitably, slaves. In spite of such legitimate trade, not a few islanders are reputed to have continued in 'the wrecking business', profiting from the spoils salvaged from ships that foundered on the reef.

By early in the 1800s, the stock of turtles in the seas around the islands was sufficiently depleted that they ceased to be of use to visiting ships seeking provisions, and the turtlers were forced to journey further afield to Cuba and beyond for their catch. With the need for larger vessels to undertake these longer voyages, shipbuilding became more important, taking advantage of the abundance of local timber. The majority of the craft constructed were schooners, primarily intended for the turtling industry, but later, sloops were built as well.

Social change

With changes in society – and particularly the emancipation of slaves – during the 1800s, came changes in the way that the islands were governed. In 1831, a

TURTLING AND THE CATBOAT

D is for danger we fear in the night

from 'The Turtlers' Alphabet' in
Traditional Songs from the Cayman Islands

One of the mainstays of the Cayman economy was for centuries the turtles surrounding the islands. Originally seen as a means of survival for ships in Cayman waters, the turtles experienced a rapid decline as a result of over-collection. At the beginning of the 19th century, turtlers turned their attention to the fishing grounds of Cuba, bringing their catch back to Cayman to be kept in sea pens until sold to visiting ships or transported on to Jamaica.

As the fishing grounds were further extended to the Nicaraguan cays, many Caymanian seafarers eventually settled on the mainland. In an interesting instance of reverse immigration, there are today numerous people from Central America living and working in the Cayman Islands, quite possibly some of them direct descendants from those 19th-century Caymanians who sought prosperity overseas. Trade in turtles continued until turtling was made illegal in 1970, following an international ban on turtle products in the 1960s.

At the very heart of the turtling industry from the early 1900s was the boat that took the fishermen to sea, the Caymanian catboat. In fact, the catboat was an important form of transport until the middle of the 20th century, a small boat used not just for work but for pleasure as well. A stable, single-sailed vessel, of wooden construction – usually mahogany – it was developed by seamen on Cayman Brac. It has no keel or centreboard, making it ideal for movement in shallow waters. With a crew of up to four men, it was usually 22ft (6.7m) overall. Over the years, though, catboats of different sizes have been built, such as the 14ft (4.3m) example on display upstairs in the museum in George Town.

While sometimes the boats sailed alone, at others they would be taken out to the fishing grounds on board large, ocean-going schooners or sloops. Here, eight to 12 boats and their crew of two 'rangers' would be offloaded and left to make their catch, then collected up on the schooner and returned to the island. The round trip took about eight weeks. The catch was split between the crew of the catboat and the schooner by prior agreement.

A recent revival has seen catboats being retrieved from old boathouses and restored to seaworthiness. First raced in Cayman Brac around 1905, today they take part in the occasional regatta in Grand Cayman, held under the auspices of the newly founded Cayman Catboat Club.

small body of local people met at Pedro St James near Savannah, and in a historic move set about forming an elected assembly. It was not until 1863, however, that this assembly was recognised by Britain, when Cayman was officially declared a dependency of Jamaica. The three islands retained their separate administrations until 1877.

Although numerous sailing ships visited Cayman from Jamaica, Tampa or Cuba in the early 20th century, their visits were irregular and the islands remained somewhat cut off from the outside world, Then in May 1927 came the launch of the *MV Cimboco* (an acronym for the Cayman Islands Motor Boat Company). For the next 20 years, the motorised sailing ship became the islands' lifeline, plying once a month between Grand Cayman's East End, Cayman Brac and Jamaica, carrying the all-important post, as well as passengers, food and other goods between the three. During the 1930s, the 72ft (22m) sailing schooner, *Goldfield*, began its monthly passage between Tampa and Grand Cayman, a journey of six days that brought the first regular link with the American mainland. The arrival of one of these two ships was such an event on Grand Cayman that word would be passed round and a celebratory picnic held to welcome it into harbour.

Shipping notwithstanding, the real breakthrough in communications came with the introduction of the radio station in 1935, a joint venture between the Cayman Islands and the Cuban government. Visitors remained rare, however. Indeed, in 1939 Robert Fuller, author of *Duppies Is*, was told that he was only the twelfth American citizen to set foot on the islands.

Not surprisingly, the majority of the menfolk remained reliant on work at sea for their livelihood, particularly in the US merchant marine, and many of them spent long periods of time away from the islands. During World War II, their seamanship proved invaluable to Britain, with around a thousand Caymanian men serving in either the British Royal Navy or the merchant navy.

By the 1940s, many of the islanders, who until then had been living very much hand to mouth, found themselves with a little spare cash – a result of income earned by seamen working abroad – and the opportunity, however meagre, to invest in the government savings bank. Inevitably, this new-found wealth brought change, and with it the chance to buy such luxuries as a car. An air link between Tampa and Grand Cayman was established, the route plied by a seaplane until 1953, when an airfield was opened on Grand Cayman. At that time, though, there were few hotels for visitors. One that did exist then was the Seaview, just to the south of George Town, and today a popular dive lodge.

When Jamaica opted for independence in 1962, the Cayman Islands elected to remain under the British Crown, with their own administrator reporting direct to Westminster. The year 1966 saw the introduction of landmark legislation to encourage banking and duty-free trade, and the boom years began. As tourism gained a hold, development began to gather speed and air traffic to Grand Cayman increased. Yet even in 1971 there were only three incoming flights a week, swelling the local population of 12,000 by a further 22,000 visitors a year.

The intervening years have seen an increasing reliance on both the tourist industry and offshore banking. Today, cruise ships and aeroplanes between them bring nearly 1.5 million visitors a year to a group of islands whose population is around 40,000. While nobody would deny that the islands have gained immeasurably in financial terms, the changes wrought in the last years of the 20th century have had a social impact far greater than any of those who brought the first cars to the island could possibly have imagined.

GOVERNMENT AND POLITICS

The Cayman Islands, one of the last 14 British Overseas Territories, have experienced democratic government since 1831. The titular head of state is HM Queen Elizabeth II, represented by the governor, currently John W Owen, who is appointed by the British government. The governor, who has overall responsibility for defence, external affairs and internal security, including the police, oversees a democratically elected Legislative Assembly which incorporates a nine-member Executive Council. The 1972 Constitution was amended by the Crown in 1994.

There are no political parties as such. Elections to the Legislative Assembly are fought every four years between independent candidates or loose groupings. At the last elections, held in November 2000, around 50 candidates stood for the 15 places on the Legislative Assembly. Once elected, these members then vote to allocate the five ministerial positions on the Executive Council. The remaining members of the council are the speaker, chief secretary, financial secretary and attorney-general. The latter three are civil servants, appointed to the post by the governor, who also appoints the speaker on the basis of recommendations received. There is no overall leader of the assembly. The Legislative Assembly is based in George Town, opposite the law courts, while the executive council meets at the government administrative building, known locally as the Glass House, in Elgin Avenue.

The islands are divided into eight districts, mostly synonymous with the relevant town or island: West Bay, George Town, Savannah, Bodden Town, East End, North Side, Cayman Brac and Little Cayman. On the sister islands, the governor is represented by a district commissioner.

Major issues facing the government today are Cayman's role as a financial centre, together with immigration and the status of expatriate workers. There is also a growing unease in some quarters at the lack of voice held by Cayman within the British governmental system on issues that have a direct bearing on the islands.

Legal system and the police

Cayman's legal system is based on English common law. There are two courts: the Grand Court of the Islands (from which appeal may be made in the first instance to the Court of Appeal in Jamaica, and in the second instance to the Privy Council in London), and a lower Summary Court, as well as a Juvenile Court.

Policing is the responsibility of the Royal Caymanian Police, which has 130 officers on Grand Cayman, eight on Cayman Brac and one on Little Cayman. A number of British police officers are seconded to the island's force.

SILVER THATCH ROPE

In modern terms, the silver thatch palm, now designated the national tree of the Cayman Islands, could be seen as something of a money tree. Not that it gave up its rewards lightly. Until the late 1940s, rope woven from its leaves formed the basis of the Cayman Islands' economy, used by the islanders to purchase everyday goods from shopkeepers, who in turn traded it for imported goods from Jamaica. Extremely durable in water, silver thatch rope was valued by seamen both in the Cayman Islands and far beyond.

Once a week, two or three 'tops cutters' would head into the dense forest of the interior to crop the leaves from the top of the tree, leaving them to dry in situ for a week before hauling them back for the women to start work. Each top was stripped into strings then woven into strands, which were in turn split into groups of three and stretched out. Each set of three strands was then attached to a winch, and coiled as the handle was turned to make the final length of rope. A standard length, measuring 25 fathoms (150ft/45m), was made up of around 30 leaves.

ECONOMY

Cayman has one of the highest standards of living in the Caribbean, with GDP per capita standing at US$30,120 in 1998. The annual growth rate had slowed slightly to 4.6% by 2000, with a rate of inflation of just 2.3% at the end of 2000. There is no minimum wage, but the average hourly wage for an unskilled worker in 2001 was between US$5.60 and $9.35. Unemployment is low, at around 4.4%; in fact, there is a considerable deficit of skilled workers, particularly in the field of tourism, and in 1997 expatriate workers accounted for some 39% of the labour force.

Until the early 1960s, the economy of the islands was based on fishing and farming. This can be pretty well narrowed down to fishing and rope, which was almost literally a cash crop at the beginning of the 20th century. Today, however, the major sources of revenue are tourism and the financial sector, with only a tiny proportion of the population engaged in agriculture and fishing.

The government has little influence on the economy, with policies formed through a partnership between government and the private sector via the Private Sector Consultative Committee.

Government revenue was estimated in 1998 to be a staggering CI$249.9 million (US$312.37 million), with expenditure at just CI$195.25 million (US$244.06 million). In 1995, the import/export balance was CI$332.5 million of imports against CI$3.4 million exports. Imports thus outstrip exports by about 100 to 1, but the visible trade gap is more than offset by invisible earnings from tourism and financial services.

The UK accounted for exports to the islands of £9.76 million in 1998, and in return received around £320,000 worth of imports. The islands receive no

TAX-FREE CAYMAN

The chances are that those who don't know the Cayman Islands as a holiday destination have heard of it as a Caribbean tax haven, and they'd be right. The fifth largest offshore financial centre in the world, after London, Tokyo, New York and Hong Kong, it is also the second largest captive insurance centre. By the end of 2000, there were 580 banks and trust companies registered, and 545 licences granted under insurance law. By the end of 2000, 59,922 companies were registered in the Cayman Islands Registry of Companies, to which users can today gain electronic access.

Broadly, there is no direct taxation – no taxes on income, profits, capital or capital gains, property or inheritance. Companies have flocked to take advantage of the islands' current tax laws and confidentiality legislation, particularly in the light of a 30-year government guarantee against any direct taxation. In addition, and in order to encourage development, building materials and equipment, machinery and tools are exempt from tax at present.

The downside of all this, of course, is that there is a significant level of indirect taxation, with prices on the islands some of the highest anywhere in the world. A 20% import duty is levied on most imported goods, licence fees are payable on bank and trust licences, and there is stamp duty on all documents.

direct financial aid from Britain, although the Overseas Territories Department supports a number of public service projects including, in recent years, two initiatives involving the police.

Tourism

From its infancy in the 1960s, tourism has developed to become central to Cayman's booming economy. Today, it accounts for around 70% of the islands' GNP. Indeed, the price of land facing the sea on Seven Mile Beach ranks among the highest in the world, a direct result of Cayman's popularity as a holiday resort.

While the vast majority of visitors come from the US, around 8% originate in Europe, mostly from the UK. The number of visitors grew strongly throughout the 1980s and 1990s, but in the last couple of years numbers have stabilised, with a total of 406,620 visitors in 2000. By comparison, 1970 saw just 22,891 visitors to the islands. The cruise-ship market is also significant, bringing a massive 1,030,900 passengers into George Town during 2000. This actually represents a slight downturn on the previous year, because several ships were diverted from the islands as a result of bad weather. There are over 10,800 visitor beds (including those in condominiums) on the islands, most of them on Grand Cayman.

Tourism-related projects have brought other rewards, too, with the erection of hotels, a new cruise-ship facility at George Town docks and high-quality residential development giving a boost to the construction industry.

Financial services

In recent years, numerous financial institutions have been attracted by the islands' tax-friendly status, making Cayman an international offshore finance centre of world renown.

Several regulatory bodies have been set up to control the financial sector, and the Chamber of Commerce has been encouraging investment since its inception in 1965. In 1996, the two financial authorities were amalgamated to form the new Financial Services Supervision Department and Currency Board, and the following year saw the inauguration of the Cayman Islands Monetary Authority and the Cayman Islands Stock Exchange.

Agriculture and fishing

Outside of tourism and banking, most of the local population are employed in the traditional areas of fishing, shipbuilding and farming, while turtle farming is also significant. Exports, all marine based, include green turtles and turtle shells, lobster, finfish, and fish for aquariums.

The size and isolation of the islands and their relative prosperity linked to tourism means that they are heavily dependent on imported foodstuffs, a situation that the government is keen to reverse. Inevitably, such hopes are limited by a lack of water and relatively infertile soil, but by the end of 2000 the islands were self-sufficient in crops such as mangoes and green bananas, while improvements in the local production of pork and beef are having a positive effect as well.

Much of the fish consumed on the islands is caught within Cayman waters, although this is inevitably limited by marine parks regulations, and fish sold in supermarkets is rarely local.

CAYMANITE

Caymanite is a semi-precious gemstone, distinctive for its uneven bands of colour, that is specific to the Cayman Islands. Believed by geologists to have been formed millions of years ago from volcanic dust that drifted to the islands from neighbouring countries, it occurs in occasional outcrops in the bluff formation between layers of the dominant white limestone.

The colours of caymanite range from black and grey through rusty orange to light brown and cream, each the result of different metallic compounds. While the reddish colour results from a predominance of iron, it is manganese that causes the black layers, with copper, cobalt and nickel also present.

Polished caymanite jewellery can be seen in several shops on Grand Cayman, but it is illegal for visitors to take it away in its raw state.

A STORM BY ANY OTHER NAME?

Hurricanes are the revolving tropical storms peculiar to the Caribbean and the Gulf of Mexico. The name 'hurricane' derives from the Caribe Indian word, *huracán*, and is, simply, the local name for the tropical cyclones that hit this region in the summer months. In the Pacific, the same weather system is known as a typhoon.

The storms form over warm seas, around 79°F/26°C, during periods of high barometric pressure. A central area of calm, known as the 'eye', is characterised by clear skies and light winds, and may grow to as much as 30 miles (48km) across. Around this, violent winds revolve at speeds in excess of 155mph (248km/h), accompanied by torrential rain (sometimes as much as 1inch/25mm an hour) and thunder and lightning. A typical Atlantic hurricane is some 300 miles (480km) in diameter (Pacific storms may reach a staggering 1,000 miles (1,600km) across) and moves at a speed of between nine and 15mph (15–25 km/h) in the lower latitudes.

The National Hurricane Center (NHC) in Miami (www.nhc.noaa.gov/) tracks weather systems via satellite and reconnaissance aircraft. NHC issues a 72-hour forecast every six hours, at 5.00 and 11.00, both morning and evening. Hurricanes are categorised according to the Saffir-Simpson scale of one to five, with category five being the most serious. Between 1950 and 1952, hurricanes were given phonetic names, such as Able, Baker, Charlie, for ease of recognition and communication. Women's names were used exclusively between 1953 and 1979, but since then men's and women's names have been alternated. For the Atlantic, there are six alphabetical lists of 21 names, used on a rotating basis.

In the northern hemisphere, hurricanes move clockwise along a curving track from the mid Atlantic through the West Indies and into the southern

GEOGRAPHY AND CLIMATE

Located in the western part of the Caribbean Sea, the Cayman Islands are situated between 19°15' and 19°45' north, and 79°44' and 81°27' west, some 167 miles (268km) northwest of Jamaica, and approximately 480 miles (768km) south of Miami in Florida. The largest of the three islands, Grand Cayman, is around 22 miles (35km) in length. The sister islands, as they are known, lie 89 miles (143km) northeast of Grand Cayman, separated from each other by a channel of less than five miles (7km): Cayman Brac is 12 miles (19.3km) long, while the smallest of the islands, Little Cayman, is just 10 miles (16km) in length. The islands cover a total combined land area of almost 100 square miles (260km²).

The three islands are effectively the tips of the Cayman Ridge, a submarine range of mountains extending from southern Cuba. Imagine that you could see only the top floor of a 100-storey skyscraper, and you get some idea of the geology of each of these islands that effectively rise straight up from the sea bed. Forget all ideas of a mountainous environment, though. Neither Grand Cayman nor Little Cayman projects much above sea level, with the highest

USA, often leaving a trail of destruction in their wake. Worst-affected areas are low-lying coasts, which means that the Cayman Islands are highly susceptible to the havoc that can be caused by both winds and the accompanying tidal surges. The islands are theoretically at risk from June to November, when the conditions required by a hurricane are prevalent. It was close to the end of this period, in early November 1932, that Cayman was hit by the one of the worst hurricanes in living memory.

Although official records date only from 1886, information in the museum at Cayman Brac suggests that 17 hurricanes have been recorded on one or all of the islands since 1735, with no obvious pattern emerging. Indeed, in 1838 the islands were hit twice, and the years 1915–17 saw three successive hurricanes in this part of the Caribbean, whereas there have been periods of over 35 years without any direct impact. That said, on average a category one hurricane will pass within 60 nautical miles (or approximately 52 'land' miles) of George Town every five years.

The most recent hurricane to hit the islands, Hurricane Katrina, was in 1981, when a waterspout caused by the storm uprooted a sea-grape tree and hurled it into the bar of the nearby Brac Reef Hotel! Fortunately, the ferocious Hurricane Gilbert of 1988 passed just to the southeast of Grand Cayman, resulting in little or no damage to the island. Emergency hurricane procedures are in place on all three islands, with designated shelters in strategic points, including several schools. Even supermarkets produce leaflets on what to do in the event of a hurricane. Should there be a hurricane warning, tune to Radio Cayman (AM 1555 kHz and 1205 kHz; FM 105.3 MHz) for the latest information. Hurricane emergency enquiry numbers are as follows: Grand Cayman 949 6555; Cayman Brac 948 2523; Little Cayman 948 1051.

point on Grand Cayman just 60ft (18m). Even Cayman Brac, where the bluff runs most of the length of the island, has a high point of only 144ft (43.9m). Deep beneath the surface, between the Cayman Islands and Jamaica to the east, lies the narrow Cayman Trench, some 110 miles (176km) long and plunging to the sea bed well over four miles (25,198ft/7,680m) below.

Predominantly of coral formation, the islands also feature the older, very rugged, bluff rock both on Cayman Brac and on Grand Cayman. There are essentially two types of bluff limestone. Cliffrock, the basis of the evil-looking formations found at Hell on Grand Cayman, is dark grey in colour, caused by algae which live and feed off the limestone, while the lighter grey ironshore is softer than cliffrock and breaks more easily.

The islands have no rivers, any surplus water being absorbed into the porous limestone rock. The only natural water is in saline ponds, which become brackish after rain. Vegetation consists for the most part of scrub and mangrove swamp. In fact, at least half of the land area on both Grand Cayman and Little Cayman is made up of mangrove swamps, while on Cayman Brac mangroves are to be found at the western end of the island. The combination of low rainfall, relatively infertile soil and high labour costs means that the islands have little in the way of agriculture.

Climate

The Cayman Islands bask in a tropical climate cooled from November to March by the northeast trade winds. In the winter (December to March) there may be occasional 'nor'westers', strong winds which bring inclement weather as a result of frontal systems sweeping down from North America. May to October are warm and frequently wet, though brief showers are generally the norm; June to August can be extremely hot and humid. The average annual rainfall is around 50 inches (127mm), mostly experienced in short storms that last no more than a few hours at most. Nevertheless, flooding can occur, and it has been known for fish in the swamps to be found swimming among the trees or even down the road!

Although there is a risk of hurricanes from June to November, the Cayman Islands lie further west than the typical hurricane course, and there has been no widespread damage since Hurricane Allen hit Cayman Brac in August 1980.

NATURAL HISTORY AND CONSERVATION
Mangroves

Grand Cayman, Little Cayman and the western point of Cayman Brac were originally predominantly made up of mangrove swamps, the typical vegetation of coasts and estuaries in the tropics. The term 'mangrove' is actually a general term for fast-growing, salt-tolerant trees up to 120ft (40m) tall, with roots that are submerged at high tide. Mangroves have glands to exude excess salt, while specially modified roots provide support for the plant and act as breathing organs.

Mangroves are crucial to land stability, protecting inland areas from high winds and storm surges and helping to maintain areas of fresh water. As they grow, sediment becomes trapped between their roots, eventually creating new land with nutrient-rich soil that is in turn colonised by other species, such as palm trees. Additionally, fallen mangrove leaves decompose to form a complex food web that is vital for the survival of fish and other aquatic creatures. In spite of this, large tracts of mangrove swamp on the Cayman Islands are threatened with destruction by the pressure on land for development.

There are three types of mangrove found on the Cayman Islands. The red *Rhizophora mangle*, found right on the outer fringes of the swamps, has stilt or 'prop' roots, enabling it to grow in relatively deep water. The black *Avicennia germinans* grows inside, in shallower water. It has a dark-coloured bark and finger root projections, or pneumatophores, which work rather like snorkels to bring oxygen to the plants. The third, the white *Laguncularia racemosa*, with its pale trunk, prefers a drier environment.

Another plant to be found in the mangrove swamps is the gnarled buttonwood, *Concocarpus erectus*, a hardwood tree whose roots can tolerate the brackish water of this environment, while lower down, the swamp fern, *Acrosticum sp*, flourishes.

Plants

The islands have at least 24 endemic species of plants, many of them **orchids**, and all to be seen in Queen Elizabeth II Botanic Park on Grand Cayman. The native orchids, including the exquisite banana orchid, *Stromburgkia*, designated as the national flower, put on their display in June. There are actually two species of banana orchid. While both are tipped with a rich purple, the Grand Cayman species is predominantly white, occasionally with a yellow centre, while that found on the sister islands has a more yellowish hue. The ghost orchid, *Dendrophlax fawcetti*, may be found on exposed peaks of cliffrock. The yellow, purple and red colours of bromeliads, or airplants, are to be seen in trees right across the islands.

Among aquatic plants, there are two native species of **waterlily**, both white, one popularly known as the water snowflake.

Although agriculture plays an insignificant part in the economic success of the country today, most homes in the past would have had an area set aside for **crops** such as yam, plantain, sweet potato and cassava, with **fruits** including the soursop, avocado, tomato, mango and various citrus fruits also grown. Coconuts, too, were once an important cash crop, with all three islands dependent upon their yield throughout the 19th century. By the early 1900s, between one and two million fruits a year were exported, but by 1905 trade had peaked and, when disease struck, the industry was effectively wiped out.

Trees

Timber was once of major importance in the economy of the Cayman Islands, and many areas have been systematically stripped of trees. Most important in this trade was the mahogany tree, few of which remain although they are to be seen on the Mastic Trail (see pages 160–1).

No matter where you are, you can't help but see the attractive **red birch**, which grows readily throughout the islands. Known elsewhere in the Caribbean as the 'tourist tree', it is easily identifiable by its peeling red bark; islanders can have a cruel sense of humour! While the broad-leaved **sea-grape** tree, *Coccoloba uvifera*, has long adorned beaches throughout the islands, the graceful **casuarinas** that provide such valuable shade are not in fact native trees, having been imported from Australia. Along the roadside, the colourful yellow **elder** brightens up many a dull hedgerow around Christmas, while in the summer the vivid orange of the occasional **flame tree** comes into its own. And then there is that king of trees, the lofty **royal palm**, *Roystonea regia*. The favoured nesting site of the Cayman parrot, it is still to be seen in woodland areas in the interior. Since the leaves of a palm fall off twice a year, you can calculate the age of the tree by counting the outer rings on its trunk and dividing the number by two.

Several trees stand out as economically valuable to Caymanians over the years. The slim **silver thatch palm**, *Coccothrinax proctorii*, now designated the national tree, is endemic to the islands and in times past provided the raw material both for thatching and for the locally made rope. For a seafaring nation, this rope was once a major source of revenue, even acting as a form of currency when trading with other islands (see also page 9). Also of importance were the **coconut** palm, with coconuts a major source of revenue until the 1930s, and the **mahogany** tree, heavily felled for timber and boatbuilding, and now quite rare – its leaves are easy to spot with their uneven 'shoulders'. The **black mangrove** was invaluable in the construction of turtle-holding pens as its tough wood is water resistant. The rough leaves of the **broadleaf**, *Cordia sebestena caymanensis*, were used like sandpaper to polish turtle shells ready for export, while the waterproof latex from the **balsam**, *Clusia flava*, was used to seal the hulls of boats. Where pastures were abandoned over the years, the land was sewn with **logwood**, *Haematoxylum campechianum*, used initially for extracting indigo dye; as it took hold, however, it came to be considered a pest.

Watch out for the less friendly side of nature: Cayman has several **poisonous** native trees and shrubs. The maiden plum, *Comocladia dentata*, has dark green leaves that are not dissimilar to those of the mahogany tree. If touched by accident, the poisonous sap – which cannot be washed off with water – will cause blisters. So, too, will the sap of the manchineel, *Hippomane mancinella*. You can even be affected indirectly, since rain can wash the corrosive sap on to you if you're walking beneath the tree at the wrong moment. Also poisonous are the vine pear, *Selenicereus grandiflorus*; the lady hair, which has stinging hairs; the cow itch, *Mucuna pruriens*; and the leguminous vine, whose seed pods are covered in irritating hairs which blow in the wind when the pod dries and disintegrates. If you intend to wander in the forest, do ensure that you can identify these trees as, although they are rare, all grow wild.

An excellent book, *Wild Trees in the Cayman Islands*, is available at the National Trust in George Town and in local bookshops (see *Further Reading*, page 224).

Animals
Mammals
Nine species of **bat** are native to the islands. Of these, the most common is the Jamaican fruit bat, *Artibeus jamaicensis*, easy to spot in the caves at Cayman Brac. Much rarer is the velvety free-tailed bat, *Molossus molossus*, and the mosquito-eating Brazilian free-tailed bat, *Tadarida brasiliensis*, a small colony of which is to be found in the Salina Reserve (not open to the public).

The **agouti**, an introduced rodent that was hunted in the past for its meat, and is still the object of some poaching, is rarely seen except in captivity, although it is present in the botanic park.

Birds
Over 200 species of birds have been recorded in these islands, of which 17 are endemic subspecies. The only bird truly endemic to the islands, the Grand Cayman thrush, is now extinct.

Of course, the bird most widely associated with the Caribbean is the parrot. The **Grand Cayman parrot**, *Amazona leucocephala caymanensis*, is a gregarious and noisy bird with a wide variety of calls. Although an endangered species, the population of this parrot has stabilised since the introduction of controls on hunting, and the occasional glimpse of its distinctive red, yellow and green plumage may be caught as it flies high over the centre of the island. The **Cayman Brac parrot**, *Amazona leucocephala hesterna*, however, is reckoned to be the rarest parrot in the Caribbean, confined almost exclusively to the parrot reserve on the Brac. Considerably quieter than its larger cousin, it is also far more secretive in habits. Both parrots are unique to the islands. The Cayman Brac parrot nests high up in the hollows of old Indian cedar trees, while the Grand Cayman parrot favours both the royal palm and the ironwood, *Chionanthus caymanensis*. Seed-lovers all, they can be unpopular with farmers, but are equally attracted to almonds and the salty grapes of the sea-grape tree.

Easy to spot is the attractive little **bananaquit**, *Coereba flaveola sharpei*, a flower-piercing bird related to the tanager. The most common bird in the Caribbean, it feeds on nectar, insects and fruits; its black and yellow colouring brightens up many a picnic or woodland walk. The **stripe-headed tanager**, *Spindalis zena*, is another native, and you may also see the yellowish **vitelline warbler**, *Dendroica vitellina vitellina*, particularly in the botanic park. Another native to the islands is the **northern flicker**, *Colaptes auratus gundlachii*, a species of woodpecker that also breeds in the botanic park, as does the West Indian woodpecker. The woodland **Caribbean dove**, known locally as the white billy dove, has red legs and is quite tame, making it popular with birdwatchers – and poachers too.

Birds of prey include the **sparrowhawk** and the ghostly **barn owl**. Relatively common on Little Cayman, they are also to be found both on Grand Cayman and the Brac.

A small flock of **West Indian whistling-ducks**, *Dendrocygna arborea*, is to be found on ponds to the east of Little Cayman, and a second group has been re-established at North Side on Grand Cayman (see page 164). On Cayman Brac, the ducks are also to be found in the wetlands to the west. Whistling-ducks are nocturnal feeders, moving from their daytime home in the mangroves to freshwater ponds in order to feed. The only duck to breed in the islands, it is now protected under Cayman law.

A group of **cattle egrets** interspersed with the occasional **great egret** is a regular sight in the wetland areas of all three islands, while the **yellow-crowned night heron**, *Nyctanassa violacea*, and the **tri-coloured heron** are also common. **Black-necked stilts**, *Himantopus mexicanus*, with their white chest, long beaks and long red legs, wade through the shallow waters searching for food.

Of the seabirds, the large colony of **red-footed boobies**, *Sula sula*, on Little Cayman is pretty impressive, very much an ornithological success story. Both morphs (colorations) of the bird are to be seen here, the dominant brown representing some 90% of the total, with the rest white. Living in not such peaceful co-existence with the red-footed boobies is the **magnificent**

frigatebird, *Fregata magnificens*. The best time to see frigatebirds is during the mating season, from November to January, when the male flaunts his brilliant red chest in a bid to attract the female of the species. Known to locals as the 'man o' war', the frigatebird is the pirate of the skies, wheeling far overhead on watch for boobies returning from their fishing grounds. The man o'war's target is not confined to the red-foots, though, as a glance at the skies on Cayman Brac will testify. Here, high up on the bluff, lives a small colony of **brown boobies**, *Sula leucogaster*. Distinctive for its brown body and tail, with white underparts, the brown booby spends most of its waking hours out at sea, like its red-footed cousin, diving for fish. Threatened by encroaching development, Cayman Brac's resident population of brown boobies is slowly declining.

For details of birdwatching, see pages 108–9, 189 and 193–4.

Reptiles

Although crocodiles once abounded on Little Cayman (hence the name 'Cayman', from the Spanish *caymanas*), the native crocodiles, *Crocodylus rhombifer* and, to a lesser extent, *Crocodylus actutus*, are now locally extinct, although both species survive elsewhere, notably in Cuba.

There are still, however, 19 reptiles endemic to the Cayman Islands. Of these, by far the most numerous are the sea turtles (see pages 23–4). In addition, there are two subspecies of rock **iguana** which are the subject of a conservation programme under the auspices of the United Kingdom Overseas Territories Conversation Forum (UKOTCF), in conjunction with the National Trust. The territorial Grand Cayman blue iguana, *Cyclura nubila lewisi*, sleeps in holes in the ground, emerging during the day both to feed and to soak up the heat of the sun. The female, shorter than the male, lays 8–20 eggs in May or June in a large burrow in the sand. Iguanas eat plants and berries, with a particular fondness for wild plums. The grey iguana, *Cyclura nubila caymanensis*, is endemic to both Little Cayman and Cayman Brac, and is frequently to be seen on Little Cayman sunning itself on the road. The common iguana, a green species that is not a native, is becoming widely spread throughout Grand Cayman.

Geckos, too, abound, as do 'curly tails' – small lizards with tails curled right back on themselves that are fun to watch as they scuttle along the decking in the sun.

The freshwater **pond turtle**, *Trachemys decussata*, locally known as a **hickatee**, is common in fresh or brackish ponds on Grand Cayman, but less so on the sister islands. Hickatees grow to a length overall of 12 inches (0.3m), with the female longer than the male. There is a hickatee in captivity at the Turtle Farm on West Bay, but more happily a group has set up residence in a part of the botanic park.

Although there are six species of **snake** on the island, none is particularly big, and none is poisonous. Five of these reptiles are very shy, including the tiny Cayman boa constrictor, all of six inches (15cm) long, but the sixth, the aptly named racer snake, *Alsophis cantherigerus*, is often to be seen slithering rapidly after its unsuspecting prey. And if you're in the interior, keep an eye

MOSQUITOES

Until relatively recently, mosquitoes were the scourge of Caymanians and their animals. In particular, the black salt marsh mosquito, *Aedes taeniorhynchus*, was so prevalent that cattle would die from asphyxiation. Right up until the 1960s children and adults alike would take a smoke pan – a simple paint can filled with lighted coconut trash – or, on Cayman Brac, rosemary and dried cow dung – if they ventured out of doors after dusk.

Smokewood was burned on fires to help keep mosquitoes at bay. Interestingly, the 'smokewood' used by people who lived east of Bodden Town was in fact the black mangrove; it was only those who lived west of the town that burned the freshwater plant known today as the smokewood tree.

Nowadays, mosquitoes are the responsibility of the Mosquito Research and Control Unit. Established by the entomologist Dr Marco Giglioli, the unit keeps the insects under control by a combination of means. Canals or dykes have been cut through the mangrove swamps and these are flooded with sea water at strategic times to prevent mosquitoes breeding, while a second wave of control is provided by regular spraying on a rotational basis right across the islands.

open for the **Cuban tree frog**; its ability to 'mosaic' (change colour) through brown, green and yellow makes it quite a challenge to spot.

Insects and creepy crawlies

The one insect you are unlikely to avoid on the Cayman Islands is the **mosquito**. Once the scourge of the islands, it is now largely controlled (see box above). On a more benign note, there are numerous **butterflies**, including the zebra, *Heliconius charitonius*, which is almost always on the wing, and the Cayman swallowtail.

Land crabs, or soldiers, abound in the most unlikely places. Without their own natural protection, they forage along the seashore for temporary homes in the form of empty shells, discarding these like secondhand clothing as they outgrow them for more appropriate cover. Capable of climbing trees, they also inhabit caves and are often found on the road. If you disturb one unexpectedly, don't be surprised to hear it squeal!

Marine environment

The Cayman Islands were formed from coral, and the fringing reefs with their clear turquoise waters and myriad creatures are without doubt the greatest attraction for visitors. The sea bed at this depth is alive with extraordinarily colourful and bizarre formations – great barrel sponges that grow painstakingly slowly, bright yellow tube coral and swaying sea fans provide the backdrop for a range of creatures that is almost breathtaking.

Typically, a fringing reef is an uneven platform of coral separated from the coastline by a shallow lagoon, and with a steep slope on the seaward side. In Cayman waters, though, this 'steep slope' is effectively a wall, an almost vertical drop-off straight down into the abyss. The reef forms a natural protection for the island from the waves that relentlessly roll on to its shores, and is home to over a thousand different creatures that live together in complex harmony.

Life below the surface can roughly be divided up into four zones: the reef, down to 200ft (65m), features fish and coral, and is the limit of the area in which divers can move about. Below this on the wall, between 200 and 600ft (60–182m), are sponges, while deeper still, at 600–1,000ft (182–305m) is the realm of the sharks and starfish. Below 1,000ft (305m) is classified, quite simply, as 'the deep'.

The reef

Coral reefs are home to over a quarter of all marine life, and are among the most fragile and endangered ecosystems in the world. Cayman's reefs are composed of hard coral, gorgonians and algae – there is no soft coral growing here. Most **hard coral** grows at a rate of just half an inch per year (a little over one centimetre), with the living tissue on or very near the surface. Made up of living polyps, it is incredibly fussy, requiring clear, clean water to a maximum depth of 130ft (40m), which is the limit of sunlight penetration. And if that wasn't enough, it needs sea temperatures of 21°C or above in order to thrive, which effectively limits its range to 30° north or south of the Equator. If it is disturbed, or broken, it may never recover. If sand or other sediment is stirred up around it, the polyps can suffocate. Little wonder, then, that divers should treat this living 'rock' with such caution – the coral's life, quite literally, depends on it.

The evocative names of many of the corals make them easy to identify, even for the novice. The maze-like structure of the brain coral looks just like a human brain, its swirls and coils creating endless patterns. Similarly, tube corals are just that, tall narrow tube-like structures often in vivid colours, while plate coral has all the appearance of a badly stacked set of dishes after a hasty dinner party. And then there is the staghorn coral, clearly named for its resemblance to a stag's antlers. Less obvious, perhaps, is the pillar coral, one of the few corals to feed in the daytime. The distinctive 'fuzz' of its long fingers, pointing straight up by some 8ft (2.4m) or so, is actually the polyps extending to ensnare passing plankton.

The great barrel-like structures that perch atop the coral like some gargantuan drinking vessel are in fact **sponges**, which obtain nutrients by filtering them out of the water. Equally slow-growing, their size does not equate with toughness: even apparently superficial damage to the lip can result in permanent harm.

Gorgonians, although also a form of coral, look more like plants. Of these, the most in evidence is the purple common sea fan, which is to be found in shallow waters everywhere, its rather rigid structure waving back and forth with the relentless rhythm of the sea.

BLACK CORAL

Close to the depth limits of recreational diving, you may come across the rare black coral, the raw material for much of the jewellery sold in many of Cayman's tourist shops. This fragile and slow-growing creature is on the Convention on International Trade in Endangered Species (CITES) list and takes two or three years to grow just an inch (2cm). It has been illegal to take it from Cayman waters since 1978, so the coral for jewellery is imported – in theory under licence – from Nicaragua and Honduras.

The best black coral grows at depths of 100ft (30m) or more, with delicate fronds gracing a relatively thick stem. In the wild, it actually looks light brown or even white; it is only after hours of painstaking polishing that the shiny black colour is achieved.

Although coral has been used in jewellery for thousands of years, the art of black coral sculpture was unknown in Cayman until some 20 years ago. Artists uses the stem of the coral, which can be up to four inches (10cm) thick, for carving, but the technique is pretty wasteful, with a significant proportion of the coral harvested simply discarded.

Far faster growing than the surrounding organisms, **algae** can gain a hold on damaged coral and if not checked can eventually swamp its host, leading to permanent damage or death. It would be easy to cast algae as the bad guy, yet there is an interdependence between these two organisms that is essential to both. Oxygen, produced by algae through photosynthesis, is essential for the coral, which in its turn produces waste on which the algae feed. It is only when the delicate balance between these two is upset that lasting damage can occur.

Other marine life

Several species of **shark** may be seen either on the reef or farther out to sea. Most common is the nurse shark, *Ginglymostoma cirratum*, which grows up to 14ft (4.3m) long and is often to be seen resting beneath an overhanging rock. Hammerheads (*Sphyrna sp*), too, are occasionally spotted offshore, while small specimens of lemon shark, *Negaprion brevirostris*, are regularly attracted by food put out by local restaurants. The reputation of these creatures goes before them, yet for the most part it is unfounded, and one operator in Grand Cayman has even started a dive-research programme into the behaviour of Caribbean reef sharks. With a similarly bad reputation, and also an inhabitant of Cayman waters, is the **barracuda**, *Sphyraena barracuda*. Groups of youngsters are the most common, but the occasional adult is sighted as well. Divers who come across a barracuda can scare it off by swimming parallel, effectively proving that you're bigger than he is.

Another shade lover is the stunning silver **tarpon**, *Megalops atlantica*. Out in the open, though, it is spectacular, seemingly suspended motionless in the blue, as if posing to be captured on canvas by a portrait artist.

The **southern stingray**, *Dasyatis americana*, is the species to be found at Stingray City, the gentle rise and fall of their 'wings' moving them gracefully through the water. The larger **spotted eagle ray**, *Aetobatus narinari*, is more likely to be seen just off the wall.

One of several species of **grouper** that inhabit Cayman waters is the Nassau grouper, *Epinephelus striatus*, its white body patterned with irregularly spaced vertical bands in colours that it can change from brown through to dark green, almost at will. A lover of shade, it seeks out rocks and other outcrops on the reef where its body is well camouflaged. A slow-growing fish, it is now on the endangered list, a result of overfishing during spawning periods. All groupers start their adult lives as females, later becoming males.

Out on the reef, the kaleidoscope of colour created by so many fish is constantly changing. Several species of **parrotfish** contribute to the effect, the most common being the blue, yellow and green queen parrotfish, *Scarus vetula*. These fish, too, are hermaphrodites, starting as females but eventually ending up as males, each of a different colour. The parrotfish also has an unusual method of feeding, using its nose rather like a blunt chisel against the coral in order to extract the algae that is its food. Having helped to clean up the coral, it continues by excreting sand, thus completing the eco-friendly cycle.

Almost as colourful is the blue and yellow queen **angelfish**, *Holacanthus ciliaris*, although its handsome cousin, the black and yellow French angelfish, *Pomacanthus paru*, is far more distinctive In fact, the latter is distinctly nosy, swimming straight up to divers, its startling yellow eyes watching your every move. **Damselfish** have something of a reputation for curiosity as well, and may even be aggressive. At least one member of this family, the little sergeant-major fish, *Abudefduf saxatilis*, with its smart black-and-white bars, is instantly recognisable. The black durgon, *Melichthys niger*, is one of several **triggerfish** to inhabit the reef, the distinctive pale blue line that forms the meeting point between its fins and body making it easy to identify.

As **butterflyfish** and bright blue **tangs** dart in and out, shoals of blue and yellow striped **French grunt** swim lazily around the reef, as do any number of the larger **jacks**. The erect dorsal fin of the reddish-orange **squirrelfish** makes it look rather like a ship in full sail. Regularly seen in shallow waters, its large dark eyes are particularly noticeable. By contrast, the expert camouflage of the **flounder** makes its presence on a sandy floor very hard to detect.

Pufferfish are curious creatures, often seen at Stingray City trying to muscle in on a free lunch. When inflated, their almost spherical bodies are unmistakable. The not dissimilar **porcupine fish** is easily distinguished from the inflated pufferfish by the spines for which it is named. It is particularly important not to touch the porcupine fish – holding it in your hands removes the mucous film which helps to protect it from many of the surrounding corals. If it's curiosity you're after, look out for the fragile-looking **trumpetfish**, *Aulostomus maculatus*, its long, thin body almost transparent, and its tail flattened.

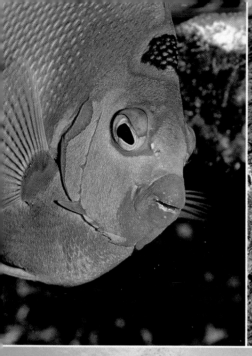

Previous page Spectacular yellow tube sponges at Grand Cayman's Orange Canyon (KS)

Above left Colourful queen angelfish, easily spotted in Cayman waters (KS)

Above right The extraordinary camouflage of a peacock flounder (KS)

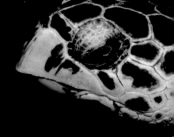

Above Hawksbill turtle, once coveted for its shell (KS)

Left A diver at the guns on the wreck of the Captain Keith Tibbetts (KS)

Sea urchins in these waters are much larger than their European cousins, their long black spines decorating many a rocky cove. The subject of a conservation programme since near total extinction in the 1980s, they are only now beginning to recover, and are once again active in controlling the spread of algae. Don't tread on them of course – the spines are painful and can cause infection. Watch out, too, for the **stonefish**, well camouflaged against the rocks; its sting is poisonous.

While several shellfish may be found around the islands, it would be hard to think of any more closely associated with Cayman than the **conch**. Conch shells, immortalised in *Lord of the Flies* for the trumpet-like noise achieved if you blow through them correctly, are to be found decorating sand gardens throughout the islands, as well as on the beaches. The queen conch, *Strombus gigas*, is a large, edible sea snail which lives in shallow waters. The female lays egg masses, comprising up to half a million embryos, which take five days to hatch into veligers. The snails are mature at three years, when they weigh around 2lb (0.9kg), with the shell measuring approximately eight inches (20cm) in length.

After dark, the underwater world takes on a different feel, as the world of the colourful reef fish is displaced by that of the night feeders. **Moray eels**, lurking in rocky crevices, await the arrival of the next meal to swim unsuspectingly past. The largest of the species in these waters, the green moray, *Gymnothorax funebris*, can be 6ft (1.8m) or more in length. Stories abound of morays making unprovoked attacks on humans, but contrary to popular myth they are not poisonous, though the bite may easily become infected. Interestingly, the moray can sometimes be attracted from its lair by a diver with food. The protected **spiny lobster**, *Panulirus argus*, may be seen hiding under rocks or in coral nooks almost anywhere on the islands, even in the daytime, so keep your eyes open for its long antennae. At night, though, this species is on the lookout for food, and much easier to spot. **Octopus** and **squid**, too, are nocturnal, both of them capable of fast movement which enables them to outwit enemies such as the scavenging moray. And so for the most part are the **corals**, which feed during the hours of darkness.

Sea turtles
Sea turtles are pretty well synonymous with the Cayman Islands, whose sandy beaches, ideal for nesting, and the abundant supply of sea grass or – as it is known here – turtle grass (*Thallasia testudinum*) are essential to their survival. But while threats of piracy may no longer be relevant, threatened the turtles remain, suffering today more from loss of habitat than from direct hunting. All seven species of sea turtle are protected under the Convention on International Trade in Endangered Species (CITES), with further protection afforded under Cayman's own marine conservation laws.

Turtles live largely in water, coming ashore only to nest. Unlike their landlubber cousins, sea turtles are unable to retract either their heads or their flippers into their shell for protection. The most common turtle around the islands is the green sea turtle, *Chelonia mydas*, so-called because its fat is a greenish colour. Also indigenous to these waters are the loggerhead turtle, *Caretta caretta*, named for its unusually large head, and the smaller hawksbill turtle, *Eretmochelys imbricata*. Regularly seen by divers and snorkellers, the hawksbill is smaller than its cousins. Its exquisite shell is the source of the traditional 'tortoiseshell', long coveted for ornamental purposes, but now outlawed in the Cayman Islands. Two of the other four sea turtles may also be found here, with Kemp's ridley sea turtle, *Lepidochelys kempi*, the smallest and most endangered species at around 150lb (66kg), and the leatherback, *Dermchelys coriacea*, the largest at up to 2,000lb (890kg).

Wild turtles still nest on Little Cayman, but on Grand Cayman loss of habitat and nesting sites through development of the beaches has seriously affected their numbers. Here, the wild population is enlarged by turtles released from Turtle Farm, although it is still too early to know if they will be able to breed successfully in the wild (see pages 152–3).

Conservation

The mangrove wetlands of the Cayman Islands give the area an importance for biodiversity much greater than their small area would suggest. Indeed, the islands will be the first British Overseas Territory to be covered by the protocol on specially protected areas and wildlife. Almost inevitably, pressure

GREEN SEA TURTLE

The green sea turtle lays between 300 and 540 eggs per season in the wild, nesting every three or four years, with the eggs hatching from May to September. In captivity, these figures increase, with up to 1,700 eggs in total laid over several batches in a season. In their first year, the hatchlings grow up to 6lb (2.7kg), and can be expected to weigh up to 52lb (24kg) by the time they are three or four. Turtles are cold-blooded animals, requiring warm water to survive. In fact, water temperature affects the sex of the hatchlings – at 82°F (28°C), a balance between male and female is to be expected; cooler than that and males will dominate; hotter and there will be a predominance of females.

Turtles do not nest until they are at least 25 years old, when they lay their eggs deep in the sand. The eggs take around 60 days to hatch, at which time the hatchlings make their way towards the sea, attracted by the play of moonlight on the waves. The abundance of artificially lit pools in Cayman has resulted in more than one group of hatchlings heading the wrong way and finding themselves on the way to the poolside bar!

The Turtle Farm on Grand Cayman serves as a breeding ground for the green turtle (see pages 152–3). After being bred and hatched on the farm, a number of the turtles are released into the wild, a policy that has led to an upturn in the previously declining sea turtle population.

on land in Grand Cayman has given rise to serious concern about the future of the island's mangroves. Although the Central Mangrove Wetland Area is in part designated as a Ramsar site (so named after the town in Iran where, in 1971, a convention met to discuss wetlands of international importance), the 8,500-acre site is still highly vulnerable, with only 592 acres secured under the ownership of the National Trust. More positively, the 623-acre Salina Reserve, towards the east of the island, is fully owned and protected by the Trust. This wetland area is surrounded by buttonwoods and mahogany trees, bordered to the north by a rocky ridge, whose dry forest is home to white-crowned pigeons and the Cayman parrot, while in the surrounding caves lives the endangered insect-eating Brazilian free-tailed bat. In the interests of conservation, neither area is accessible to the public.

Beach erosion has become a serious issue following the high level of building along Grand Cayman's Seven Mile Beach. Only a couple of years ago, the beach was 200ft (65m) wide all the way along. Now however, the southern end is reduced to almost nothing in the winter when the occasional storms have their most dramatic impact on the beaches. A beach erosion committee, established to monitor the situation, effectively has three options: to import sand into the area, to pump in sand from offshore, or to sculpt the beach by redistributing sand from the north along West Bay, where the beach used to be narrow but is now fairly wide. Only time will tell whether any of these measures will prove to be a success.

Marine conservation

To prevent damage from dive boats and visiting divers, marine parks have been designated throughout the islands. Yet the threat to Cayman's coral reefs is by no means limited to divers. Fishing, too, can take its toll, as can souvenir hunters and general boat traffic. And while pollution in these waters may be relatively insignificant, land reclamation is not, with the interference caused by dredging and infilling having inevitable consequences upon the surrounding ecosystems. As yet there is no legislation in place to address issues relating to development, including such matters as the construction of canals.

Marine Park Zones represent the most popular diving areas, including most of West Bay, and Little Cayman's Bloody Bay Wall, with fishing almost totally banned. Only line fishing is allowed, and this just from the shore. Boats wishing to moor outside the harbour area must use one of the 205 fixed moorings that have been placed around the three islands in order to protect the reef. These moorings, which are free of charge, are marked by white buoys with a blue stripe, to which are attached lengths of yellow rope. Boats up to 60ft (18m) may also anchor in sand, provided that there is no contact at any point with the coral.

In Replenishment Zones, such as shallow-water lagoons or sounds, line fishing is permitted, but a ban on taking conch and lobster allows these species to breed and reproduce freely.

An Environmental Zone has been established to protect the mangroves that fringe the eastern side of Grand Cayman's North Sound. Here, boats are

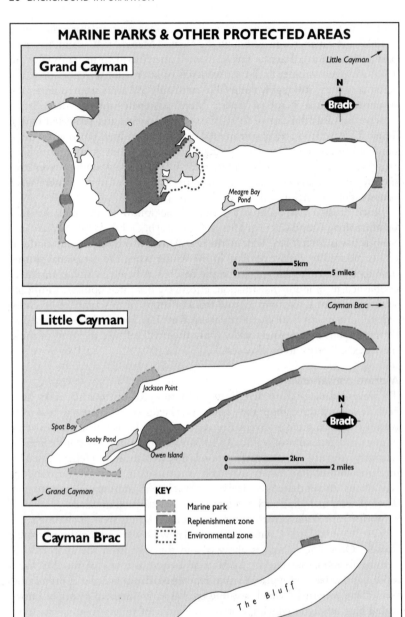

MARINE PARKS & OTHER PROTECTED AREAS

Grand Cayman

Little Cayman →

N

Bradt

Meagre Bay
Pond

0 ———— 5km
0 ———— 5 miles

Little Cayman

Cayman Brac →

Jackson Point

N

Bradt

Spot Bay

Booby Pond

Owen Island

0 ———— 2km
0 ———— 2 miles

← Grand Cayman

KEY

Marine park
Replenishment zone
Environmental zone

Cayman Brac

The Bluff

N

Bradt

White
Bay

West End

0 ———— 2km
0 ———— 2 miles

← Little Cayman

allowed at a maximum speed of 5mph (8km/h), but no in-water activity is permitted, nor any fishing or anchoring. This is particularly important as the sea grass grows in a peaty sediment that is very fragile. The protection of North Sound, however, is a thorny issue, with a considerable conflict of interest between conservationists, watersports enthusiasts and local people committed to traditional pursuits and native dishes such as conch stew.

The possession or use of spearguns by visitors is illegal anywhere in Cayman, and the Department of the Environment is working to impose an outright ban on both these and Hawaiian slings.

Three marine enforcement officers are employed by the Department of Environment to enforce the law. Infringements may be reported on VHF channel 17, or by telephoning the Department of Environment on 949 8469.

Conservation bodies

The **National Trust for the Cayman Islands** (PO Box 31116 SMB, Courts Road, Eastern Av, George Town; tel: 949 0121/0894; fax: 949 7494; email: ntrust@candw.ky; web: www.caymannationaltrust.org) is engaged in long-term projects to preserve the unique wildlife and flora indigenous to Cayman. Central to this is the creation of a system of nature reserves across the islands.

The **UK Overseas Territories Conservation Forum** (14 Goose Acre, Cheddington, Leighton Buzzard, Beds LU7 0SR; tel: 01296 661363; email: sara.cross@ukotcf.org; web: www.ukotcf.org) was founded in 1987 with the aim of raising awareness about the wealth of biodiversity in the UK Overseas Territories. Particularly high on the forum's current agenda is the threat to the central mangrove wetlands in Grand Cayman.

The work of the forum is supported by a number of conservation and scientific organisations, including the the National Trust for the Cayman Islands and the Royal Society for the Protection of Birds (RSPB, The Lodge, Sandy, Beds SG19 2DL; tel: 01767 680551; fax: 01767 683211; email: wildlifeenquiries@rspb.org.uk; web: www.rspb.org.uk).

To support the work of the forum, you can become a friend. Details may be obtained from Frances Marks, Forum Co-ordinator, at 15 Insall Road, Chipping Norton, OX7 5LF, UK; tel: 01608 644425; email: fmarks@ukotcf.org.

PEOPLE

The majority of the people live on Grand Cayman, whose population in 1999 was 37,083, more than treble its population just 25 years earlier. The islands saw a 52% growth in population during the early 1980s, but this has now slowed to around 5% per year.

The population of the islands is extraordinarily diverse. Statistically, around a fifth originated from Jamaica and North America, another fifth from Europe and a similar number from Africa, with the remainder of mixed race. According to one newspaper report, though, there are 'over 100 nationalities in these islands'. And that's without the large influx of expatriate workers in recent years which has led to Caymanians almost becoming a minority in their own country.

The majority of Caymanians (but less those on Cayman Brac), are employed in jobs that are for the most part unrelated to tourism. In addition to the local population, a significant number of expatriate workers live on the islands, employed in areas from tourism to construction and finance. Many of these workers originate from the UK, the US and Jamaica, with several Hondurans working on Cayman Brac.

Caymanians, long used to taking in newcomers from a variety of backgrounds and cultures, and with a seafaring history, are naturally tolerant and very welcoming. Nevertheless, the isolation of the islands over the years has meant that a few families dominate, and several names crop up time and again, in every aspect of society. Look out for Bodden, Ebanks and Scott, all of which are pretty commonplace, as are Walton and Tibbetts – the latter two particularly on the Brac – and Kirk or Kirkconnell.

Even those who have been afforded Caymanian status do not consider themselves to be truly Caymanian, which is effectively a birthright. In fact, there is a widely held view that you cannot be considered Caymanian if you haven't grown up in a world dominated by the sea, mosquitoes and conch stew!

EDUCATION

Education is compulsory for children aged 4–16, and is free for Caymanian pupils, although fees are payable for children of non-Caymanians. The curriculum is based on the British educational system, leading to CXC (Caribbean Examinations Council) exams, similar in standard to the British GCSE. After the age of 16, children may enrol at the Community College of the Cayman Islands or the International College of the Cayman Islands, or may opt to continue their studies overseas. In addition to the government schools, there are some fee-paying church schools, and others that are linked to the American educational system.

Cayman Brac has three primary schools and one high school, while on Little Cayman there are no schools at all. Until recently, children here had no choice but to attend school on Cayman Brac, but in a recent initiative a teacher is being flown in daily from Cayman Brac to work with two school-age children on the island.

LANGUAGE

English is spoken right across the islands, though the range of accents is broad, and it's close on impossible to work out whether or not you are talking to a Caymanian. Rumours that the Cayman accent is akin to Scottish or even Welsh do not appear to be founded in truth, at least not nowadays when the influence of the United States and other Caribbean islands on the local language is immense.

RELIGION

Caymanians are for the most part very religious, and there are churches throughout the islands. In 1831, responsibility for Grand Cayman fell to the bishop of Jamaica, who despatched the first Anglican clergyman to the island.

A few years later, the Presbyterian minister William Elmslie took up residence in George Town, where he built the church that still bears his name. Today, the people of Grand Cayman are predominantly Presbyterian – as typefied by the United Church in Jamaica and the Cayman Islands (UCJCI) – but various Anglican, Catholic and other denominational churches are represented as well. There are also a number of Afro-American spiritists and Rastafarians.

On the sister islands, the Baptist church is prevalent, a legacy of the arrival of the first Baptist minister on Cayman Brac in the 1880s.

CULTURE

It's only 30 years or so since the islands' economy was based on the sea, with no electricity on the islands and very little influence from the outside world. While most men were away at sea for long periods of time, it was the women who formed the backbone of society and held the family together, with little time or money for leisure. Games such as *waurie*, where two players compete to win each other's pieces, were the norm then, and can still be played in many homes and guesthouses, though watch out for local variations in the rules if you have played in other countries!

Although influence from the US on the local culture has been significant in recent years, it does not detract from the independence and natural tolerance of a nation whose small-town ethos makes the Cayman Islands rather different from the rest of the Caribbean. Indeed, faced with the relatively sudden influx of such strong influences from outside, many Caymanians are fighting to maintain their own cultural heritage, supported by the Cayman National Cultural Foundation and the National Trust for the Cayman Islands. The annual Cayfest (see page 57) does much to promote local culture, while Pirates Week incorporates district heritage days.

Art

Cayman art is just beginning to come to the notice of the outside world, aided by the formation of a Visual Arts Society. Native Son is a group of Caymanian painters and sculptors which was formed to promote their work, with exhibitions held from time to time on Grand Cayman. More far reaching, the intuitive art of 'Miss Lassie' – Gladwyn K Bush – has captured the imagination of a wider audience, and is featured in a number of books. Examples of her work are exhibited at the art gallery in Maryland, Baltimore.

Architecture

While nobody would suggest visiting Cayman purely for its architecture, there are undoubtedly some gems of traditional buildings to be found tucked away from the eyes of most visitors. The traditional single-storey Cayman house with its corrugated iron roof and wooden porch is now the object of conservation programmes under the auspices of the National Trust, which sponsors an annual competition to reward the preservation of historic buildings.

Early houses were built of wattle and daub, based on a simple structure with wooden poles at each corner and a thatched roof. Later, wooden houses

DUPPIES

Don't never let nobody ever tell you there ain't no duppies! Duppies is!

from *Duppies Is* by Robert Fuller

Until the second half of the 20th century, it is said that a large number of Caymanians had personal experience of duppy visitations, supernatural phenomena that could not be explained away in practical terms. Certainly numerous islanders have told of their experiences, from appearances indicating impending death to apparently freeloading duppies hitching a ride on carts or horses. Duppies seem, too, to have pointed the way to buried treasure, while others, more greedy, have been attracted to people by the occasional drop of rum or apparent promise of 'heavy cake'.

Not surprisingly, reactions to these beings have varied. While some seem to have been in tune with their ways, and accepted them as an integral part of life, others have been far from philosophical. It was not unknown for those out alone to sprinkle a trail of rum or grains of corn behind them, a sort of offering to distract potentially marauding duppies from the bottle of liquor they were carrying.

So where have the duppies gone? Robert Fuller, in his book *Duppies Is*, contends that they are still there, but that their human counterparts today no longer have the time to be in tune with the real world. Who knows?

became the norm, sometimes raised off the ground both to allow air to circulate and to help keep out insects, and with a corrugated iron roof. The kitchen, or cookhouse, was located in a separate building.

Although some of the modern buildings that have sprung up in Cayman are innovative in design, particularly the Legislative Assembly, for example, quite a few are just plain boring, and look inappropriate in the setting of a Caribbean island. It's good to see that at least one of the newer shopping complexes, Grand Harbour to the east of George Town, has addressed this issue, the resultant buildings blending into the landscape far more effectively than some of the concrete blocks down West Bay Road.

Music

Many of the folk songs that have found their way into the hearts of Caymanians over the years have been lost with the passing of an oral tradition. Some, though, have been collected by the Cayman Islands National Archive in *Traditional Songs from the Cayman Islands* (see *Further Reading*, page 223). Many of these speak of a nostalgia for the ways of Cayman, often by sailors or those who found themselves living overseas and longed to return. Others record in song the everyday world of the early 20th century, when local musicians, typically playing a fiddle, guitar and 'grater', but sometimes including shakers or a home-made drum, would come together for celebrations and other local events.

A natural progression of these traditional songs, country music gained popularity among Caymanians, influenced by the southern US radio stations which were all that were available to the islanders until the 1960s.

Today, there is no clearly defined Caymanian musical tradition accessible to visitors, although Caribbean steel bands are popular throughout the islands. Sadly, the cost of large bands mean that most of the live music played today involves sequencing, with just one or two players and a range of high-tech equipment. Traditional calypso, with its offbeat rhythm and satirical lyrics, is complemented by *soca* – a modern variation that is faster, simpler and more dance-orientated. One international band based in the Cayman Islands is Tradewinds, who play throughout North America. Visitors to Grand Cayman will also hear about the Barefoot Man, who plays regularly at Rum Point (see page 164).

Sport

Not surprisingly for a Caribbean nation, cricket is popular here, as are rugby and football, but so too are more US-orientated sports such as basketball and baseball – the islands boast one of the largest baseball Little Leagues, with over 600 participants. Swimming is gaining in popularity among local youngsters, and athletes train and compete at the Truman Bodden Sports Complex in George Town. The islands had 15 participants in the 1998 Commonwealth Games.

Sport is the responsibility of the somewhat unwieldy Ministry of Community Affairs, Sports, Women, Youth and Culture, who may be contacted on tel: 914 3480.

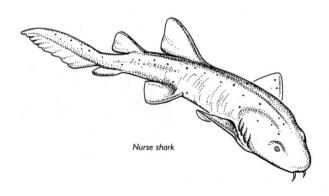

Nurse shark

Deeply Relaxing

In the Cayman Islands the beaches are powder white, the sea is turquoise and the average year round temperature 82°F. Snorkel with the stingrays. Visit charming Caymanian villages. Stroll through the Queen Elizabeth II Botanic Park. Play golf on a championship course. Rise to the challenge of exciting wall dives. Go island hopping from Grand Cayman to Cayman Brac and Little Cayman.

In a world where relaxation is hard to come by, it is good to know you will find it here in the Cayman Islands in the Caribbean, where the friendliness of the people is renowned.

There are regular direct British Airways flights from London Gatwick and frequent Cayman Airways flights from Miami and Orlando to Grand Cayman.

For your FREE Cayman Islands information pack, please call us on 020 7491 6951.

CAYMAN ISLANDS
Grand Cayman • Cayman Brac • Little Cayman

020 7491 6951
www.caymanislands.ky
www.divecayman.ky
e-mail: info-uk@caymanislands.ky

Planning and Preparation

WHEN TO VISIT

The most popular – and inevitably the most expensive – months in which to visit the Cayman Islands are from mid December to mid April, when the weather is usually dry and the temperature cooled by the northeast trade winds. Be aware, though, that the wind can occasionally veer round to the northwest, bringing short spells of quite windy and cloudy weather. Caymanians reckon that April is the ideal month – calm, settled and not too hot. June to November is the hurricane season in the Caribbean. Nevertheless, many visitors, particularly from Europe, go in the summer months, despite the heat.

In winter, average temperatures range from 75°F to 85°F (23–29°C), with a record high of 91°F (33°C) – and a record low of just 61°F (16°C)! The rainy season officially runs from late May to late November. Rain when it comes tends to be in short bursts, usually followed by clearing skies and sunshine, and giving rise to some spectacular sunsets. That said, there are occasionally times when it rains all day, so it's as well to be prepared. Humidity averages around 74.5% in February and March, rising to 81% in October, although actual humidity may vary from 68% to 92%.

Divers may choose to avoid August and September when tropical storms can stir the waters, although this is by no means the norm. The variety of dive locations means that it is almost always possible to dive somewhere around the islands.

Very occasionally, you may be lucky enough to glimpse the all-too-fleeting phenomenon known as a 'green flash', a trick of the light seen at

CLIMATE STATISTICS
Average temperature

	Jan	Feb	Mar	Apr	May	Jun	Jul	Aug	Sep	Oct	Nov	Dec
°F	78.3	78	79.3	82.4	83.8	84.5	85.3	84.5	85	83	81.6	79.3
°C	25.7	25.5	26.3	28	28.8	29.2	29.6	29.2	29.4	28.3	27.6	26.3

Average monthly rainfall

	Jan	Feb	Mar	Apr	May	Jun	Jul	Aug	Sep	Oct	Nov	Dec
in	2.2	1.2	1.9	0.4	5.4	12.4	6.5	6.1	6.8	13.2	12.2	3.4
mm	56	31	49	9	137	314	166	155	172	334	310	86

sunset just at the point when the sun dips below the horizon. Caused by a refraction of light through the Earth's atmosphere, it occurs in periods of exceptionally dry weather, and generally forecasts a clear spell during the next 24 hours.

See also *Climate*, page 14.

TOURIST INFORMATION

The head office of the Cayman Islands Department of Tourism is at Cricket Square, 1st Floor, George Town, Grand Cayman, Cayman Islands, British West Indies; tel: 949 0623; fax: 949 4053; web: www.caymanislands.ky.

The tourist office runs a privilege card programme valid on all three islands. Holders benefit from savings of up to 25% off goods supplied by participating restaurants, car hire companies, shops and attractions. The card is available from the tourist information office, or at their airport information booth, tel: 949 2635.

Overseas

The Cayman Islands Department of Tourism has offices in several countries, including five in the US. All share the website www.caymanislands.ky.

Argentina Esmeralda 847-15 1, 1007 Buenos Aires; tel: 5411 4314 2347; fax: 5411 4313 5647

Canada 234 Eglinton Av E, Suite 306, Toronto, Ontario M4P 1K5; tel: 416 485 1550; fax: 416 485 7578

France, Benelux, Scandinavia KPMG Axe Consultants, 12 rue de Madrid, 75005 Paris; tel: 1 53 42 41 36; fax: 1 43 87 32 85

Germany, Austria, Switzerland Marketing Services International, Walter Stohrer & Partner GmbH, Johanna-Melber-Weg 12, D60599 Frankfurt; tel: 069 60 320 94; fax: 069 62 92 64

Italy G & A Martinengo, Via Fratelli, Ruffini 9, 20123 Milano; tel: 02 4801 2068; fax: 02 4635 32

Spain Sergat España SL, Pau Casals 4, 08021 Barcelona; tel: 93 414 0210; fax: 93 201 8657

UK 6 Arlington St, London SW1A 1RE; tel: 020 7491 7771; fax: 020 7409 7773; email: info-uk@caymanislands.ky

US

Chicago 9525 W Bryn Mawr, Suite 160, Rosemont, IL 60018; tel: 847 678 6446; fax: 847 678 6675

Houston Two Memorial City Plaza, 820 Gessner, Suite 170, Houston, TX 77024; tel: 713 461 1317; fax: 713 461 7409

Los Angeles 3440 Wilshire Bd, Suite 1202, Los Angeles, CA 90010; tel: 213 738 1968; fax: 213 738 1829

Miami 6100 Blue Lagoon Drive, Suite 150, Miami, FL 33126-2085; tel: 305 266 2300; fax: 305 267 2932

New York 420 Lexington Av, Suite 2733, New York, NY 10170; tel: 212 682 5582; fax: 212 986 5123

HIGHLIGHTS

With 25 years of tourism based on diving, Cayman's **underwater world** is undoubtedly a 'must see' for visitors. Whether you are a diver or snorkeller, or are happier to keep marine life behind glass, there are ample means to explore this new world. It is the walls for which Cayman **diving** is renowned, with one of the greatest attractions being Little Cayman's spectacular Bloody Bay Wall. Don't overlook the very real attractions of Cayman's numerous other dive sites, though. From shallow reefs teeming with fish to complex tunnels, swim-throughs and caverns, no two dives are alike.

Among the highlights of the sea, do make time for **Stingray City**, whether as a snorkeller or a diver. Despite accusations of commercialism, entering the kingdom of these magical creatures feels like something out of a fairytale.

Above the waves, all manner of **watersports** are on offer, from windsurfing and kayaking to jetskis and parasailing, and much more besides. The opportunities are here to develop an existing interest, or to try something new, with scope for all ability levels.

Activities don't stop at the shoreline, of course: both **hikers** and **natural history** enthusiasts will find much of interest here. For the energetic, there are the hidden secrets of the Mastic Trail, an unexpectedly challenging hike that can be richly rewarding. Less demanding, but well worth a visit, is Queen Elizabeth II Botanic Park, a haven of tranquillity that offers a considerable insight into the islands' natural history and culture. And if you've ever dreamed of cantering along the beach on **horseback**, this is the place to try it.

There's also plenty to occupy the keen sports enthusiast. In particular, top-rank **golf** courses draw visitors back year on year, while many types of **fishing** are highly popular, with the annual sport-fishing tournament attracting large crowds and prize money to match.

With so many activities available, it's just as well that food plays a major part in the Cayman lifestyle, and a search for **restaurants** off the beaten track would be a pretty good basis for a tour of Grand Cayman. Become a beach bum and try the Saturday buffet at Rum Point, or spoil yourself rotten with Sunday brunch at the Westin. Take a picnic to East End and experience absolute peace less than an hour's drive from Seven Mile Beach. Or search out that perfect waterfront setting for a romantic night out.

It's easy to think that Grand Cayman has it all, but the quieter **sister islands** of Little Cayman and Cayman Brac are much more than just add-ons, as anyone who returns year after year will testify. Even if you can only squeeze in a day trip, do make time to visit one or – better still – both. And as an added bonus, the short flight from Grand Cayman affords some stunning aerial views.

CAYMAN FOR SPECIFIC GROUPS
Families

Grand Cayman is a superb place for families. Hotel rooms that routinely sleep four, plenty of friendly restaurants, long sandy beaches – what more could a family want? Many hotels will help with babysitting services, too. Some of the

WEDDINGS FOR OVERSEAS VISITORS

The romantic prospect of a beachside wedding in the Caribbean sun appeals to many a couple planning their big day. Here, Cayman comes into its own, offering not just the idyllic setting, but also top-class hotels, a wide selection of catering possibilities and a honeymoon in situ.

Special marriage licences for non-resident couples may be granted in advance or on the spot by the governor of the Cayman Islands. Marriages under the special licence provisions may be performed as soon as applications have been processed – usually the same day (although licences cannot be obtained at weekends or on public holidays).

Couples will need to present proof of identity in the form of a passport or birth certificate or similar, together with either an immigration card or landing card as proof of visitor status, and any relevant divorce or death certificates. Original documents are required; photocopies are not acceptable. The minimum age for marriage in Cayman is 16, although under 18s require parental consent (or that of a legal guardian).

Licensed marriage officers are either ministers of religion or civil registrars; a full list is available on request. In addition to the marriage officer, couples will require two witnesses – if required, these can be arranged by the marriage officer. Ceremonies may be conducted between 6.00am and 8.00pm.

resorts have kids' clubs, enabling parents to indulge their own interests while their children are having a whale of a time elsewhere. For older children and teenagers, the potential for watersports is almost limitless, from snorkelling and child-orientated diving courses to jetskis and parasailing. And if all this palls, there's always bowling or the cinema!

Disabled visitors

The fact that Grand Cayman and Little Cayman are predominantly flat makes them excellent venues for those with physical disabilities, though walks in the interior are not accessible with a wheelchair. Many of the larger hotels have wheelchair access. Cayman Brac, too, is fine in the southwest where the tourist hotels are situated, but elsewhere shingle or ironshore beaches and the uneven terrain of the bluff make the island less attractive for those with special needs.

Overseas workers

The number of expatriate workers on the Cayman Islands means that by joining their ranks you will regularly come into contact with people from all over the world. The islands are popular, safe and welcoming, with a high standard of living and plenty of activities. Numerous clubs and societies are run or heavily supported by overseas workers, from charitable foundations such as the Humane Society to amateur dramatics and sports.

Licence applications forms may be obtained from the Cayman Islands Government Information Services, or from the Deputy Chief Secretary, 3rd Floor, Government Administration Building, George Town; tel: 949 7900, ext 2222. Applicants must take or send the completed form, which should include the name of the marriage officer who will perform the ceremony, together with any relevant documentation and the fee of CI$160 (USS$200), to the Deputy Chief Secretary.

The following is a selection of companies that specialise in Cayman Island weddings, covering everything from the licence, marriage officer and witnesses to the venue, catering and the flowers:

Bevandale Island Weddings PO Box 458 WB; tel: 949 3435; fax: 949 7536
Cayman Weddings PO Box 678 GT; tel: 949 8677; fax: 949 8237; email: weddings@candw.ky; web: www.cayman.com.ky/com/weddings/. Wedding packages start at US$710.60.
Celebrations PO Box 1599 APO; tel: 949 2044; fax: 949 6947; email: unique@candw.ky; web: www.celebrationsltd.com

For further information, and a full list of both marriage officers and companies offering wedding services, write to the Cayman Islands Government Information Services (see page 65) for a copy of their leaflet, 'Getting Married in the Cayman Islands'.

Those used to a broader canvas may get the urge to escape from the confines of a small island occasionally, if only to Miami for the shopping. Cayman's location in the western Caribbean makes the islands of Jamaica and Cuba a popular getaway choice, along with Central American destinations such as Panama, Guatemala and Mexico.

If you are intending to take up residence on the islands, contact the Cayman Islands Government Information Services or the Cayman Islands Government Office in the UK (see page 65). Both can supply details of a practical nature, including apartment rental, local utilities and import restrictions. See also page 64, *Working in the Cayman Islands*.

TOUR OPERATORS

The rapid increase in direct booking through the internet continues apace. Nevertheless, many tour operators are in a position to negotiate favourable deals, and to offer advice on the best places for your particular circumstances. The following organisations cover several resorts on the Cayman Islands, and many will arrange tailormade trips:

UK

Classic Connection Concorde House, Canal St, Chester CH1 4EJ; tel: 01244 355500; fax: 0870 751 9309; email: cc@itc-uk.com; web: www.classicconnection.co.uk. Package tours for both general visitors and divers.

Caribbean Expression 104 Belsize Lane, London NW3 5BB; tel: 020 7431 2131; fax: 020 7431 4221; email: carib@expressionsholidays.co.uk; web: www.expressionsholidays.co.uk. Package tours only.

Delta Vacations Albert House, 17 Bloom St, Manchester M1 3HZ; tel: 0870 900 5001; fax: 0161 278 7755; web: www.deltavacations.co.uk. Covers Grand Cayman only.

Harlequin Worldwide Travel Harlequin House, 2 North Rd, South Ockendon, Essex RM15 6QJ; tel: 01708 850300; fax: 01708 854952; email: info@harlequin-holidays.co.uk; web: www.harlequin-holidays.co.uk. Upmarket hotel and dive holidays.

Hayes & Jarvis Hayes House, 152 King St, London W6 0QU; tel: 0870 898 9890; fax: 020 8741 0299 email: res@hayes-jarvis.com; web: www.hayesandjarvis.co.uk. Hotel and dive packages with a range of accommodation.

International Chapters 47–51 St Johns Wood, High St, London NW8 7NJ; tel: 020 7722 0722; fax: 020 7722 9140; email: info@villa-rentals.com web: www.villa-rentals.com. Luxury villas on Grand Cayman and Little Cayman.

Key to the Caribbean 23–47 High St, Feltham, Middx TW13 4UN; tel: 020 8890 8458; fax: 020 8844 2008; email: email@ktasales.fsnet.co.uk. Tailormade trips to all three islands.

Kuoni Travel Kuoni House, Deepdene Av, Dorking, Surrey RH5 4AZ; tel: 01306 747002; fax: 01306 744222; email: information@kuoni.co.uk; web: www.kuoni.co.uk. Tailormade and package holidays using three- to five-star hotels.

North America Travel Service The Kennedy Building, 48 Victoria Rd, Leeds LS11 5AF; tel: 0113 243 0000; fax: 0113 243 0919; web: www.northamericatravelservice.co.uk. Tailormade holidays to all three islands.

Thomas Cook Holidays PO Box 5, 12 Coningsby Rd, Peterborough PE3 8XP; tel: 01733 418450; fax: 01733 417784; email: tch@thomascook.com; web: www.tcholidays.com. Package or accommodation-only trips to Grand Cayman.

Diving and fishing specialists

Aquatours Shelletts House, Angel Rd, Thames Ditton, Surrey KT7 0AU; tel: 020 8398 0505; fax: 020 8398 0570; email: info@aquatours.com; web: www.aquatours.com. Cover just Cayman Brac.

Barefoot Traveller 204 King St, London W6 0RA; tel: 020 8741 4319; fax: 020 8742 8657; email: dive@barefoot-traveller.com; web: www.barefoot-traveller.com. Tailormade trips specialising in diving holidays.

Dive Worldwide 23 Burnham Av, Bognor Regis, W Sussex PO21 2LB; tel: 01243 870618; fax: 01243 870619; email: info@diveworldwide.com; web: www.diveworldwide.com. Tailormade and package dive holidays to all three islands.

Scuba Safaris PO Box 8, Edenbridge, Kent TN8 7ZS; tel: 01342 851196; fax: 01342 851197; email: info@scuba-safaris.com; web: www.scuba-safaris.com

Worldwide Fishing Safaris 21 Station Rd, Thorney, Peterborough, PE6 0QE tel: 01733 271123; fax: 01733 271125; email: peter@worldwidefishingsafaris.co.uk. Big-game fishing holidays to Grand Cayman and Little Cayman.

US

Of the numerous tour operators in the US that cover the Cayman Islands, this is just a small selection:

Cayman Airways Holidays 6100 Blue Lagoon Drive, Miami, FL 33126; tel: 800 422 9628; fax: 305 263 9039

Caradonna Caribbean Tours 435 Douglas Av, Suite 2205, Altamonte Springs, FL 32714; tel: 800 328 2288 or 407 774 9000; fax: 407 682 6000

Caribbean Concepts 99 Jericho Turnpike, Jericho, NY 11753; tel: 800 423 4433 or 516 876 0700; fax: 516 876 4770

Caribbean Connection Plus PO Box 261, Trumbull, CN 06611; tel: 800 893 1100 or 203 261 8603; fax: 203 261 8295

Caribbean Holidays 612 Bellevue Way NE, Bellevue, WA 98004; tel: 800 828 9204 or 425 413 8757; fax: 425 413 8907

The Cayman Connection 10200 Brogans Mill Rd, Suite 125, The Woodlands, TX 77380; tel: 800 468 6426 or 281 367 4023; fax: 281 292 0315

Cayman Express 692 W Brookhaven Circle, 2nd Floor, Memphis, TN 38117; tel: 800 247 9900 or 901 767 5046; fax: 901 682 0317

Go-go Tours 15902 A Halliburton Rd, PMB 284, Hacienda Heights, CA 91745; tel: 626 968 7686; fax: 626 934 7886; email: sales@GoGoTour.com; web: www.GoGoTour.com

Hurley Travel Services Thos Moser Bldg, 415 Cumberland Av, Portland, Maine 04101; tel: 207 874 7444; 800 874 1743; fax: 207 874 9007; email: lcaldwell@travelexperts.com; web: www.travelexperts.com

International Travel & Resorts 300 E 40th St, New York, NY 10016; tel: 800 223 9815 or 212 476 9444; fax: 212 476 9467; email: itrhotels@erols.com; web: www.itrhotels.com

Island Dreams Travel 8582 Katy Freeway, Suite 118, Houston, TX 77024; tel: 800 346 6116 or 713 973 9300; fax: 713 973 8585

Island Flight Vacations 6033 W Century Blvd, Suite 807, Los Angeles, CA 90045; tel: 800 426 4570 or 310 410 0909; fax: 310 410 0830

Island Resort Tours 300 E 40th St, New York, NY 10016-2154; tel: 800 251 1755 or 212 476 9400; fax: 212 476 9452

Liberty Travel Tel: 888 271 1584; web: www.libertytravel.com. 200 locations throughout the USA. A wide selection of hotels and condominiums on Grand Cayman and Cayman Brac.

New World Expeditions 1557 E St, Waynesville, OH 45068; tel: 513 897 7238; fax: 513 897 2902

Ocean Connection 211 E Parkwood Av, Suite 108, Friendswood, TX 77546-5153; tel: 800 365 6232 or 713 996 7800; fax: 713 996 1556

Premier Travel & Cruise Marketplace Shopping Center, 2901 Hamilton Blvd, PO Box 2120, Sioux City, IA 51104-2120; tel: 712 252 8008 or 800 759 0008; fax: 712 252 1412; email: travel@premiertravel.com; web: www.premiertravel.com

Starr Tours 1646 Nottingham Way, Trenton, NJ 08619; tel: 800 314 8411 or 609 586 6080; fax: 609 586 8558

Sunshine Tours 207 Grandview Drive, Fort Mitchell, KY 41017; tel: 800 879 5371 or 606 331 6818; fax: 606 578 1190

TNT Vacations 2 Charlesgate W, Boston, MA 02215; tel: 800 262 0123 or 617 641 9677; fax: 617 638 3310

Travel Impressions 465 Smith St, Farmingdale, NY 11735; tel: 800 284 0044 or 516 845 8000; fax: 516 845 8095

Tropical Adventures PO Box 4337, Seattle, WA 98104-0337; tel: 800 247 3483 or 206 441 3483; fax: 206 441 5431

Vacation Express 2987 Clairmont Rd, Suite 205, Atlanta, GA 30329; tel: 800 486 9777 or 404 321 7742; fax: 404 248 1237

Specialist tour operators

Caribbean Dive Tours 732 Johnson Ferry Rd, Marietta, GA 30068; tel: 800 786 3483 or 770 578 8028; fax: 770 565 0129

GolfTrips 893 Towne Center Drive, Kissimmee, FL 34759; tel: 800 428 1940 or 407 933 0032; fax: 407 933 8857

International Diving Expeditions 18380 Avenita Calera, Suite 201, Murrieta, CA 92562; tel: 800 544 3483 or 909 698 3189; fax: 909 698 3289

Oceans of Diving PO Box 350245, Fort Lauderdale, FL 33335; tel: 800 466 1400 or 305 489 7728; fax: 305 351 9740

Rothschild Dive Safaris 900 West End Av, Suite 1B, New York, NY 10025; tel: 800 359 0747 or 212 662 4858; fax: 212 749 6172

Underwater Adventure Tours 732 W Fullerton Pkwy, Chicago, IL 60614; tel: 800 858 8666 or 773 929 0717; fax: 773 929 2821

World Dive Adventures 10400 Griffin Rd, Suite 109, Fort Lauderdale, FL 33328; tel: 800 433 3483 or 954 434 8733; fax: 954 434 4282

RED TAPE
Paperwork

A valid passport is needed by all visitors, with the exception of nationals of the UK, Canada and the USA, who may provide alternative proof of nationality, such as a birth certificate. Visitors (as against expatriate workers) are also required to have a valid return ticket showing departure from the Cayman Islands within six months of arrival.

Visas are not required by nationals of the UK, Canada, USA, most Commonwealth countries and some European countries. Note that holders of passports from Australia, France, Germany, Ireland, the Netherlands, Spain and Italy *do* require visas. Visas are not required by cruise-ship passengers.

There are three types of visa: tourist, transit and business. Each is valid for a period of one to six months, and will normally cost £28 (US$37.50 or CI$30), although this may vary according to which British consulate you visit. Applicants should have two application forms, a valid passport, two photographs, and proof of funds available for the duration of their stay. Allow between three weeks and a month for visas to be processed. If you are planning to find a job in the islands, see *Working in the Cayman Islands*, page 64.

Applications to extend a visa should be made to the Department of Immigration in Grand Cayman (see page 64) or Cayman Brac (tel: 948 2651), and should be accompanied by proof of funds.

Pet owners will need a permit should they wish to take their animals to the islands. Pet owners need a permit or valid animal passport together with an official health certificate issued by the authorities in the country of origin.

Immigration and customs

Visitors are issued with a pink immigration slip on arrival. This should be kept with your passport or other travel document and given up on departure. The attractions of the Cayman Islands as a tax haven inevitably mean that the occasional person turns up in the hope of getting a job. Immigration laws are strict, and officials at the airport take a considerable amount of time going through the various formalities. As a rule, you should expect to be asked where you are staying and, if you don't know, then you may have to provide proof of sufficient funds for the duration of your stay – usually around US$500.

Customs officers are constantly on the alert for illegal drugs. The islands lie close to major drug-trafficking routes and, although drugs are not a major problem here, they are still an issue and there is constant surveillance.

Duty-free goods

Visitors over 18 are permitted to bring in one litre of spirits, one case of beer or four litres of wine duty free, plus up to 200 cigarettes (or 25 cigars or 250 grams of tobacco). If you are staying in self-catering accommodation, it's worth buying beer and/or liquor at the duty-free shop in the US or Grand Cayman on your way in, as the cost is about a third of what you will pay in ordinary shops on the islands themselves. Note that you are not allowed to get off the plane in Grand Cayman when you are on a flight that is booked through to Cayman Brac.

When returning home, visitors from the US are permitted to take goods up to a total value of US$400, while British citizens have an allowance of £136.

No visitor returning to the US, Canada or the UK may take with them products made from turtle, even at the Turtle Farm, as this contravenes the CITES agreement signed by these countries. Black coral goods (see page 21) must be accompanied by a certificate from the Department of Environment.

EMBASSIES

There are no embassies on the Cayman Islands, but there are representatives of the American and Jamaican consulates on Grand Cayman. Dates of consular visits are announced in the *Caymanian Compass*.

Consular representatives

Jamaica Tel: 949 9526. Robert Hamaty; assistants Elaine Harris and Gillian Harvey
US Tel: 945 1511. Gail Duquesnay (who works at Adventure Travel)

GETTING THERE
By air

The Cayman Islands have two international airports. On Grand Cayman, Owen Roberts Airport is situated 3.5km northeast of George Town (see page 69), while on Cayman Brac there is Gerrard Smith Airport on the western tip of the island (see page 194). There are over a hundred direct flights a week into Grand Cayman, from the US, UK, Canada, Jamaica, Cuba and Honduras, and to Cayman Brac from Miami. Flights from London may also conveniently be routed via Miami. The national airline is Cayman Airways.

There is an airport 'departure' tax of CI$10, or US$12.50, payable by all visitors over the age of 12. In practice, this tax is incorporated in ticket prices, rather than collected at the airport.

From the UK

British Airways (BA) has direct flights on Boeing 767s from Gatwick to Grand Cayman on Tuesday, Thursday and Saturday, returning on the same days. The plane touches down for about three-quarters of an hour en route at Nassau in the Bahamas or San Juan in Puerto Rico, but passengers routed to Grand Cayman stay on board. The total flight time is approximately ten hours. Prices in economy are from around £518 return (although a full-price economy fare is £1,859 plus tax). There is a weekend supplement of £19 each way, with no child reduction. Economy tickets may be upgraded to Club class for £1,299 return. Club-class fares are from £2,962 when booked at least seven days ahead, while a first-class round trip ticket will set you back a staggering £5,501. The first-class service on this route includes flat-bed seats.

Via Miami

British Airways flies twice a day, seven days a week from London Heathrow to Miami, from where there are three flights a day to Grand Cayman with Cayman Airways. The trip to Miami takes about eight and a half hours. Fares vary according to the time of year, day of travel and duration of stay, but for guidance a mid-week economy return fare based on a two-week trip in November 2000 was £244 plus £54 tax. If tickets are booked by email or on the internet, passengers may use the self-service check in at Heathrow. There are numerous other flights between the UK and Miami, including those via American Airlines and Virgin.

Remember to allow a reasonable period of time in Miami to change flights, particularly over public holiday periods. It's a busy – some say chaotic – airport at the best of times.

For details of connections between Miami and Cayman, see below.

From the US and Canada

Several airlines fly to Grand Cayman from **Miami**, between them operating some 70 flights each week, with the flight taking approximately an hour and a quarter. Other direct routes include Houston (2hr 40min), Tampa (1hr 40min) and Toronto (5 hours).

The national airline, Cayman Airways, has friendly and helpful staff both in the US and in Grand Cayman, a welcome change from the norm, and in stark contrast to the staff of some of the larger airlines in Miami. Once on board, the complimentary rum or fruit punch does wonders in expelling the hassle of hanging around at airports. There are regular flights to Grand Cayman from the US, as follows (though note that schedules change regularly):

Houston	four flights a week, Wed, Thu, Sat, Sun
Miami	three flights a day
Orlando	Mon, Tue, Fri
Tampa	daily

Cayman Airways also has five flights a week on Boeing 737s to Cayman Brac from Miami, with a short stop in Grand Cayman. For fares, see page 196.

American Airlines operates three flights a day between Miami and Grand Cayman. Continental Airlines has four non-stop flights a week, on Tuesday, Thursday, Saturday and Sunday, from **New York**'s Newark airport in Boeing 737s. Delta Airlines flies daily (December–April only) non-stop from **New York**'s JFK airport, in 737s, and twice a week from **Atlanta**, Georgia, throughout the year. Northwest Airlines has direct flights from **Detroit** during the winter season, from December to the end of March. Outside this period, connections from Detroit can be made via Minneapolis and Tampa or Miami. US Airways fly daily from **Philadelphia** and **Charlotte**, North Carolina, to Grand Cayman.

Air Canada will be introducing flights to Grand Cayman from **Toronto**, with effect from October 31 2001. Initially flights will be weekly, increasing to twice weekly in December.

From Jamaica
Cayman Airways has four flights a week to Grand Cayman from **Kingston**, on Monday, Wednesday, Friday and Sunday. Air Jamaica flies to Grand Cayman from Kingston on Thursday to Sunday, and from **Montego Bay** on Tuesday, Friday, Saturday and Sunday.

From Cuba
Cubana Airlines flies direct from **Havana** to Grand Cayman.

From Honduras
Both Cayman Airways and Islena have regular flights between Grand Cayman and **La Ceiba**, Honduras.

From Grand Cayman to Little Cayman and Cayman Brac
Local flight connections are run by Cayman Airways and Island Air. For details, see page 196.

Airlines
Air Canada (AC) Tel: US/Canada 888 247 2262; UK 08705 247 226; web: www.aircanada.ca
Air Jamaica (JM) Tel: US 305 670 3222; UK 020 8570 9171; Jamaica 876 922 3460–9; web: www.airjamaica.com
American Airlines (AA) Tel: US 800 433 7300; UK 08457 789 789; web: www.aa.com
British Airways (BA) Tel: US 800 AIRWAYS; UK 0845 7733377; web: britishairways.com

Cayman Airways (KX) US/Canada tel: 800 G CAYMAN or 800 422 9626;
UK/Europe tel: 020 7491 7771; Grand Cayman tel: 345 949 2311; Cayman Brac 948
2535/948 1221; web: www.caymanairways.com
Continental Airlines (CO) Reservations tel: US 800 231 0856; UK 0800 776464;
web: www.continental.com
Cubana Airlines (CUB) Reservations tel: UK 020 7734 1165; Cuba 537 33 4949;
web: www.cubana.cu
Delta Airlines (DL) Tel: US 800 241 4141; UK 0800 414767; web: www.delta-air.com
Island Air (G5) Tel: Grand Cayman 949 5252; web: www.IslandAirCayman.com.
Reservations may be made online.
Islena (WC) Tel: La Ceiba 504 443 0179; web: www.flyislena.com
Northwest Airlines (NWA) Reservations tel: US 800 225 2525; UK 0900 750900;
web: www.nwa.com
US Airways (US) Reservations and information tel: US 800 428 4322; UK 0845 600
3300; web: www.usair.com

Private aircraft
Private pilots should contact the Civil Aviation Authority of the Cayman
Islands (tel: 949 7811 or 949 8112) for information on landing on the
islands, including how to obtain an overflight permit from the Cuban
government. VOR/DME installed at Grand Cayman provides navigation
information over frequency 115.6. The ADF for Grand Cayman is 344 and
for Cayman Brac 415.

By sea
George Town is a port of registry for shipping, with a total of 729 vessels
registered in 1993, and the port is an important calling centre for cargo
carriers. Caymanian-owned ships, and those with Caymanian registration,
operate services between here and Florida, Jamaica and Costa Rica.

Cruise ships
Numerous passenger ships, sometimes as many as six a day, call in at George
Town as part of their Caribbean cruise itineraries. Most operators run their
own programmes, but visitors from cruise ships could easily organise a half
day or full day on Grand Cayman independently. Highlights might include
snorkelling at Stingray City, the Turtle Farm, the Atlantis submarine trip and
the museum in George Town. Cruise-ship operators include the following:

Carnival Tel: US 866 778 7447; web: www.carnival-cruises.com
Crystal Cruises Tel: US 310 785 9300; web: www.crystalcruises.com
Cunard Tel: US 800 7 CUNARD or 800 728 6273, UK 0800 052 3840;
www.cunard.co.uk
Holland America Tel: US 206-281-3535; web: www.hollandamerica.com
Peter Deilmann Tel: UK 020 7436 2931; web: www.peter-deilmann-cruises.co.uk
Princess Cruises Tel: US 800 774 6237; web: www.princess.com
Royal Caribbean Tel: US 888 313 8883; UK 01932 820381; web: www.royalcarib.com

Sun Line Cruises Tel: US 727 944 4468 or 978 741 1900; web:
www.sunlinecruises.com

Private yachts

The relative isolation of the Cayman Islands in the context of the Caribbean
as a whole means that very few yachts come into the islands. Those that do
should report to the port authority in George Town to clear customs and
immigration. For details, see *Chapter 3*, pages 71–3. Vessels entering Cayman
waters should display the red ensign version of the Cayman flag.

The Admiralty chart of the Cayman Islands is number 462. Weather
reports, including information about the tides and a five-day forecast, are
posted on the Department of Tourism website, www.caymanislands.ky.
Alternatively, contact the National Meteorological Service, PO Box 10277
APO, George Town; tel: 949 7811; fax: 941 0761; email: nwsgcm@candw.ky.

HEALTH
Preparations

There are no immunisation requirements for visitors to the Cayman Islands,
although it is suggested that visitors should be up to date on polio, diphtheria
and typhoid inoculations, as they would be at home. It is worth considering
routine vaccination against hepatitis A if you are a lover of seafood. This is a
general precaution with seafood anywhere in the world, since shellfish are
scavengers. Malaria is not a risk.

Pharmacies on the islands are comprehensively stocked, but do take
sufficient prescription medicines to last your trip. Insect repellent is an
essential, and plasters/Band-aids would be useful if walking in the interior
forms part of your plans.

Insurance

There is no free medical provision for visitors, nor any reciprocal agreement
with the UK National Health Service, so it is important to take out suitable
medical insurance, which should also cover the cost of emergency air transport
should a transfer from one of the sister islands be necessary. Health costs are
similar to those in the private sector in the UK, but lower than those in the US.

If you're planning to dive, do make certain that this option is covered by
your policy.

Local facilities

Both Grand Cayman and Cayman Brac have small government hospitals, with
128 beds and 18 beds respectively. For divers, there is a decompression
chamber at the hospital in George Town. There are also district clinics and a
dental clinic, staffed by both government medical officers and private doctors.
Little Cayman has only a small health clinic.

In addition to the pharmacy at the hospital in George Town, and others at
the two medical centres listed above, there are several **pharmacies** on Grand
Cayman (see page 135) and one at the hospital on Cayman Brac (see page 204),

LONG-HAUL FLIGHTS
Dr Felicity Nicholson
There is growing evidence, albeit circumstantial, that long-haul air travel increases the risk of developing deep vein thrombosis. This condition is potentially life threatening, but it should be stressed that the danger to the average traveller is slight.

Certain risk factors specific to air travel have been identified. These include immobility, compression of the veins at the back of the knee by the edge of the seat, the decreased air pressure and slightly reduced oxygen in the cabin, and dehydration. Consuming alcohol may exacerbate the situation by increasing fluid loss and encouraging immobility.

In theory everyone is at risk, but those at highest risk are shown below:

- Passengers on journeys of longer than eight hours duration
- People over 40
- People with heart disease
- People with cancer
- People with clotting disorders
- People who have had recent surgery, especially on the legs
- Women who are pregnant, or on the pill or other oestrogen therapy
- People who are very tall (over 6ft/1.8m) or short (under 5ft/1.5m)

A deep vein thrombosis (DVT) is a clot of blood that forms in the leg veins. Symptoms include swelling and pain in the calf or thigh. The skin may feel hot to touch and becomes discoloured (light blue-red). A DVT is not

but none on Little Cayman. Note that pharmacies may only fulfil prescriptions issued on the Cayman Islands.

Water

Water is safe to drink throughout Cayman. It is provided by desalination, either centrally or from individually run plants. Bottled water is also widely available from shops and supermarkets.

SAFETY

The islands, with their traditional emphasis on the family, are almost universally considered to be safe, friendly and welcoming, both in terms of property and of personal safety. That said, it's tempting providence to leave such things as cameras and wallets unattended on a beach or in an unlocked car. The sister islands have a laid-back attitude to security that is almost of a bygone era – on Little Cayman you're asked to leave the key in your hire car (after all, there's nowhere to take it), while on Cayman Brac the hire bikes simply don't have locks.

Women travellers need take no particular precautions, though do take care if hitchhiking, especially at night, as you would anywhere else.

dangerous in itself, but if a clot breaks down then it may travel to the lungs (pulmonary embolus). Symptoms of a pulmonary embolus (PE) include chest pain, shortness of breath and coughing up small amounts of blood.

Symptoms of a DVT rarely occur during the flight, and typically occur within three days of arrival, although symptoms of a DVT or PE have been reported up to two weeks later.

Anyone who suspects that they have these symptoms should see a doctor immediately as anticoagulation (blood thinning) treatment can be given.

Prevention of DVT

General measures to reduce the risk of thrombosis are shown below. This advice also applies to long train or bus journeys.

- Whilst waiting to board the plane, try to walk around rather than sit.
- During the flight drink plenty of water (at least two small glasses every hour).
- Avoid excessive tea, coffee and alcohol.
- Perform leg-stretching exercises, such as pointing the toes up and down.
- Move around the cabin when practicable.

If you fit into the high-risk category (see above) ask your doctor if it is safe to travel. Additional protective measures such as graded compression stockings, aspirin or low molecular weight heparin can be given. No matter how tall you are, where possible request a seat with extra legroom.

If you're out hiking, be aware that the ironshore beaches and inland rock base can be treacherous for walkers, so take particular care and wear strong shoes. And if you're heading off the beaten track, do be sure you can recognise poisonous plants such as the manchineel or maiden plum.

The location of Cayman on the international drug trafficking routes between North and South America makes the islands extremely vulnerable. Although constant vigilance is exercised by police and customs, drugs are still a problem, particularly ganja (marijuana) – some 80% of the prison population, or around 240 offenders, is in for drug-related offences. However, anti-drug laws are strict, and large fines and/or prison sentences may be imposed on anyone caught in possession of or importing any banned substance.

Marine safety

Safety on and around the sea is an important issue on islands renowned for their diving. In addition to the precautions you would always take when snorkelling or diving, watch out for currents when swimming near headlands, and for rocks just beneath the surface. Take care, too, where you put your feet – the sea urchins in these waters are huge, and poisonous stonefish can be difficult to see against the camouflage of the rocks. Underwater, divers and snorkellers should avoid cutting themselves on the coral, as such wounds tend to heal slowly. If you remember that you shouldn't touch the coral, then it can't harm you!

WHAT TO TAKE

Aside from the normal clothes that you would take on holiday to a warm climate, it's worth thinking about the following:

- Snorkel, mask and fins
- Dive equipment if you have it – renting is easy but expensive
- Dive certification
- Suncream
- Sunhat
- Insect repellent
- National or international driving licence
- Binoculars
- Camera equipment (remember that so-called 'underwater' disposable cameras cannot be used for diving)
- Light sweater or cardigan for air-conditioned restaurants and that odd breezy day – or for after diving
- Light waterproof jacket for that occasional shower
- Good walking shoes if you plan to walk in the interior

MONEY AND BANKING

The unit of currency is the Cayman Islands dollar (CI$), which is subdivided into 100 cents. There are four banknotes, in denominations of 5, 10, 25 and 100 CI dollars, and four coins, respectively for 1, 5, 10 and 25 cents. US dollars are accepted throughout the islands, although change is usually given in CI dollars. The British pound is not generally in circulation.

The rate of exchange against the US dollar is fixed at CI$1 = US$1.25 (US$1 = CI$0.80). Prices may be quoted in either CI or US dollars, or indeed both, which is confusing enough for Americans and even worse for visitors from the rest of the world. As a rule of thumb, the more local establishments and most restaurants and bars seem to work in CI dollars, while the majority of hotels and dive operators quote in US dollars. The currency quoted is usually marked on menus etc, but always check if in doubt.

Travellers' cheques

US$ travellers' cheques may be used like cash in shops etc, provided that you have some form of identification (eg: passport) with you. Alternatively, you can change them for cash at the bank – a good move since the exchange rate against US$ travellers' cheques is CI$0.82!

In the event of loss or theft of travellers' cheques, contact the issuer immediately. For Thomas Cook cheques, call 1 800 223 7373, and for those issued by American Express, call 1 800 828 0366.

Credit cards

As you would expect from a major offshore banking location, Amex, MasterCard, Visa and Diners' Club credit cards are widely accepted.

Note that payments made on credit cards are always converted to US dollars, and that conversion into a third currency is at the rate of exchange prevalent on the date of payment. So if the rate of exchange of your currency against the US dollar is falling rapidly, you would be well advised to invest in some US dollars at the beginning of your trip, rather than relying on credit cards. Cash withdrawals against Visa and MasterCard are sometimes afforded the slightly higher exchange rate for US$ travellers' cheques, ie: CI$0.82.

Credit card emergency numbers

Amex	UK: 01273 696933; US: 1 336 395 1111
Diners Club	www.dinersclub.com gives relevant numbers to report loss or theft
MasterCard	1 800 307 7309
Visa	1 800 847 2911

Banks

Banking hours are normally 9.00am–4.00pm, Monday to Thursday, and 9.00am–4.30pm on Friday.

There are ATMs at several banks and supermarkets, except on Little Cayman. Cash withdrawals are for a minimum of CI$25.

Money wiring services

Money wiring is available through MoneyGram or Western Union on both Grand Cayman and Cayman Brac.

Tipping

Tipping is expected in restaurants and other service-orientated establishments. The norm is 15%, which is frequently added to the bill in restaurants and elsewhere, so do check. Many hotels will add a gratuity of 10% to the room bill.

Budgeting

The cost of living on the Cayman Islands is high, and the tourist dollar doesn't go far, particularly as virtually all food and goods have to be imported. As an indication, postcards can be over US$1 each (though you'll find them if you look for US$0.30), and the going rate for a bottled beer is about US$4.40.

A two-course meal for two people in a mid-range restaurant with local specialities and a bottle of wine would be around US$95, including tax and gratuity. In a bar, a one-course meal for two, with beer, is more likely to be around US$45.00. And if you really can't survive without fast food, you're looking at US$5–6.25 a head.

It would be possible to spend a small fortune if money were no object, but by being reasonably sensible two people on a mid-range budget would be fine on US$369 per day, in low season (mid April to mid December), based on the following (all prices in US dollars):

Hotel (with kitchenette & breakfast)	$192.00 (inc 10% government tax and 10% gratuity)
Lunch (self catering)	$8.00
Water (large bottle)	$2.00
Dinner	$95.00 (inc 15% gratuity)
Beers x 2	$7.00
Transport (car hire + petrol)	$45.00
Sundries (museum, ice-cream, postcards)	$20.00

This, of course, does not include activities such as diving and other watersports. Allow about US$70 per person per day for a two-tank boat dive, exclusive of equipment.

Costs for accommodation, car hire and diving can be reduced significantly if booked in advance for a period of a week or so.

Cayman on the cheap

This is something of a contradiction in terms! Those on a tight budget could be in for a shock, but it's certainly possible to keep costs down, particularly if you're prepared to slow down to the Cayman pace of life. Discover Cayman out of season, from mid April to mid December, when it's quieter and prices are lower. Two can stay for the price of one in most places – four cost even less per person – so it's cheaper not to travel alone. Accommodation is available at the lower end of the range if you hunt around – try one of the guesthouses, or perhaps Harbour View or North Side Surf Inn – costs here are from US$70 per room. Transport using a combination of walking, local buses and maybe a hired bike for a day or two would be the most realistic budget option.

Obviously eating in is an option, but you're not going to experience much of Cayman that way. On the other hand, this offers the opportunity to try supermarket salad bars at CI$2.40–3 per pound (CI$5.30–6.60 per kilo), and hot buffets, too, are available for just a little more. Have a hunt round Farmer's Market (see page 132) for local produce, or try their lunchtime takeaway buffet. Prepare a picnic lunch instead of eating out, and buy drinks from one of the supermarkets too – or drink tap water; it's perfectly safe. In the evening, happy hours are a great source of budget succour: drinks on a two-for-one basis, and free buffets in many bars, can set you up for the evening. Alternatively, a bit of judicious research reveals gems such as all-you-can-eat barbecues, or you could head for smaller local restaurants and fill up on coconut rice and jerk chicken at a fraction of the price you'd pay on Seven Mile Beach. As for entertainment, bring your own mask, snorkel and fins and you'll be ready for endless hours of pleasure snorkelling on the reef at absolutely no cost.

GETTING AROUND
By air
Flights between the islands are covered on page 196.

By road

Grand Cayman and Cayman Brac have 436km of surfaced road in total. About a third of the road that encircles Little Cayman is surfaced, with the rest rough gravel.

Easily the best means of getting around Grand Cayman and Cayman Brac is by car. Vehicles are driven on the left, and seatbelts are compulsory. **Car hire** is available from several outlets on the islands (see pages 73–4, 176 and 197). You will need either an international driving permit, or your own driving licence. If you have only the latter, you will also need to purchase a visitor's driving permit (see pages 73 and 196 for prices). Visitor's driving permits are valid for six months or for the duration of your stay, whichever is the shorter. The minimum age to hire a car is 21, although some companies may stipulate 25. Note that the penalties for drink-driving are stiff – take a taxi.

In common with American practice, car-hire prices do not necessarily include full insurance (collision damage waiver) so do check this when comparing prices. (Note that insurance may be covered by your credit card company, so it's worth finding out about this before paying a supplement, though do check the level of cover provided.) As a point of interest, hire cars have white number plates, in contrast to the yellow of locally owned vehicles and blue of public transport vehicles.

Bikes are easily available on all three islands, often as part of an accommodation package, while **scooters** may be hired on both Grand Cayman and Cayman Brac. **Hitchhiking** is relatively easy, particularly on the sister islands, but is not a good idea on Grand Cayman for women on their own at night.

Fuel is unleaded, either standard or super, or diesel. It is sold in imperial gallons, which are slightly greater than the US gallon (five imperial gallons equal six US gallons). Average prices on Grand Cayman are as follows:

Petrol	US$2.69 a gallon (US$0.59 per litre)
Super	US$3.21 a gallon (US$0.70 per litre)
Diesel	US$3.33 a gallon (US$0.73 per litre)

Expect to pay a little more than this on the sister islands.

Taxis are freely available in George Town and elsewhere on Grand Cayman, but less so on Cayman Brac; there are no taxis on Little Cayman. A cheap **bus** service operates throughout Grand Cayman, with a regular timetable and frequent services along Seven Mile Beach. There are no buses on either of the sister islands.

Maps

Although there are a couple of maps available free to visitors, their accuracy is questionable if you plan to drive even slightly off the beaten track, and as for getting lost – don't! Probably the best map available for the visitor is the one published by International Map Services, available on the islands for CI$2.50. There are also detailed Ordnance Survey maps: a single sheet at a scale of 1:50,000, or four separate sheets at 1:25,000. The latter are available in the UK from Stanfords in Long Acre, London (tel: 020 7836 1321; web: www.stanfords.co.uk) at £9.95 each.

ACCOMMODATION

The range of accommodation in the Cayman Islands is pretty broad, from simple guesthouses to opulent hotels with everything the visitor could possibly wish for. There are no campsites, and camping is not permitted on any of the Cayman Islands. That said, you may well see Caymanians camping at Easter on Grand Cayman and, more specifically, on the tiny island of Sand Cay to the south of George Town.

Note that post office box addresses do not necessarily indicate the physical location of an establishment – where there's doubt, this has been made clear in the text.

Hotels and resorts

There is no shortage of luxury accommodation on Grand Cayman, with prices to match. There are plenty of medium-range hotels as well (many of them with self-catering facilities), but simpler establishments are thin on the ground unless you're after a dive lodge. Hotels are graded by a government board of control, with standards ranging from luxury to tourist. There is no star-rating system as such, although many of the hotels have in fact been graded by the AAA – the American Automobile Association.

Dive lodges

A number of smaller places cater specifically for the dive market, with facilities that may include on-site dive schools, rinse tanks, purpose-built swimming pools for dive training, and their own docks. Relaxed and informal, dive lodges tend to have a loyal following, with guests returning year after year to the same place.

Self-catering

There are plenty of opportunities for self-catering throughout the islands, from hotels with kitchen facilities, such as Sunshine Suites, to private condominiums and villas. Efficiencies, for the uninitiated, are effectively studio apartments, with a bedroom/living area and kitchenette. Virtually all self-catering units have a sofa bed in the living area, so that a one-bedroom suite can usually sleep four people, and a two-bedroom condominium will take six.

Guesthouses

Bed and breakfast and guesthouse accommodation is relatively scarce on Cayman. The few opportunities there are tend to be located inland and may be suitable for more mature visitors who are prepared to take the time to get to know their hosts.

Timeshare

There are currently three timeshare properties on Grand Cayman. Plantation Village is on Seven Mile Beach, while East End boasts both Morritt's Tortuga and Royal Reef, with Grand Morritt's under construction. Timeshare weeks can be exchanged through the International Vacation Exchange system, US tel: 1 800 826 7211.

Timeshare 'invitations' and promotional offers abound, with inducements ranging from free diving and other watersports to meals out. Be sure you know what you're taking on before you go along to one of these sessions; if in doubt – don't.

For further information, try one of the following:

Morritt's Tortuga Club and Resort, tel: 947 7449; web: www.morritt.com. Tours daily 10.00am–5.00pm. See also page 168.
Timeshare User's Group www.tug2.net/topten.htm. An independent website featuring surveys of over 1,400 resorts worldwide, including Royal Resorts (see page 168).

Prices

Rates quoted in this guide are walk-in rates, and should be seen as a sample of the options available. Clearly it is beyond the scope of this book to detail them all. Almost all establishments offer considerable discounts for advance booking and stays of several nights, with an almost infinite range of packages available. For the most part, rates have been split into high season, or winter (defined as mid December to mid April), and low season or summer (running from mid April to mid December). The precise timings may vary from one hotel or resort to another, so do be sure to check before booking. Where establishments have a more complex structure, this has been indicated; note that a swingeing supplement may be levied for the two-week Christmas period, particularly by the more upmarket establishments. Conversely, special deals abound in the low season, so it pays to shop around.

Several resort hotels and dive lodges offer all-inclusive packages for different groups, such as general holidaymakers, divers or fishing guests. Packages typically incorporate all meals and, in some cases, all drinks as well (particularly for divers, on the basis that few will drink heavily).

There is a 10% government accommodation tax – variously called a room tax or a tourist tax – payable on departure. Some hotels include this in their prices, but at many establishments it is an additional charge. Gratuities, too, are usually added to the bill, from 5% to 15% depending on the establishment.

Many resorts specify a minimum length of stay, varying from three to seven nights, particularly in high season. Cancellation charges can be hefty, so insurance is advised.

EATING AND DRINKING
Food

Fresh fish and seafood are the order of the day almost everywhere on the islands. You will frequently come across dolphin on the menu – this is a fish, not to be confused with the mammal of the same name; it is sometimes listed by its Hawaiian name of 'mahi-mahi', or as 'dorado'. Other popular local fish are yellow-fin tuna and wahoo (a bit like tuna but white), also known as kingfish. On the seafood front, almost everything is available, but one thing you may not have come across is conch (pronounced 'conk'), a chewy shellfish which appears on menus in various guises, from conch stew (delicious), to conch fritters (sometimes called 'flitters'), grilled conch and even conch burgers. A staple of Caymanian cuisine, it is reputed to be a natural aphrodisiac and has a high nutritional value. Other Cayman specialities include jerk chicken (or 'jerk' anything else, for that matter – effectively a spicy barbecue) and turtle stew. In local restaurants, meals are usually served with coconut rice and beans, and fried plantain.

Fruits such as watermelon, limes, bananas and pineapples are traditionally grown inland, despite the poverty of the island's soil. Look out for the knobbly soursop, which is in fact sweet. On the vegetable front, much of Cayman's staple diet is based on crops such as breadfruit, cassava, yams and beans. Most of the fruit and vegetables eaten on the islands today are imported, but there are moves in hand to redress the balance. Local-grown fruit may look less appetising than the immaculately shaped specimens found in supermarkets, but the flavour is infinitely superior. In particular, if you're in Grand Cayman in August, head for West Bay Road and treat yourself to some of the locally grown mangoes on sale just in front of the public beach.

Widely purported to be a typical Cayman treat, rum cake is available pretty well everywhere, with plenty of outlets having free tastings (you can get quite carried away at the airport waiting for a flight!). Variations on plain rum cake include banana and chocolate flavours. Caymanians will tell you that rum cake is actually an import from elsewhere in the Caribbean. Far more traditional is the 'heavy cake' which you may be able to sample on heritage days. Rather like a cross between a suet pudding and bread and butter pudding, it is, as its name suggests, heavy. Light cake, more sponge-like in consistency, is also popular. And for a true Cayman sweet treat, see if you can get hold of coconut ice.

Eating out

Any visitor to the Cayman Islands will be spoilt for choice when it comes to eating out. The high proportion of visitors, and the affluence of the islands as a whole, make for a competitive environment and restaurateurs have risen to the challenge with a startling array of choice and extremely high standards. Seafood lovers will be in their element, but there's plenty too for meat eaters, and most restaurants have at least one vegetarian option. For youngsters, children's menus are available in many restaurants.

While standards are high, so in general are prices. In a reasonable restaurant, lunchtime meals such as salads and sandwiches fall into the US$8.50–10 range. For dinner, expect to pay a minimum of US$5.50 for a starter, with main courses ranging from US$16 for a pasta or simple vegetarian dish to US$35 or more for seafood and steaks. Prices in restaurants specialising in local food tend to be considerably lower. It's quite possible to find a full-blown Cayman-style meal for around US$10–15, and you probably won't have room

Above left Horseriders discover the peaceful side of Grand Cayman. (TH)

Above right Climbing on Cayman Brac's Wave Wall presents some unusual challenges. (KS)

Left Sailing along the reef off Rum Point (TH)

Below Kayaking at Owen Island, Little Cayman (TH)

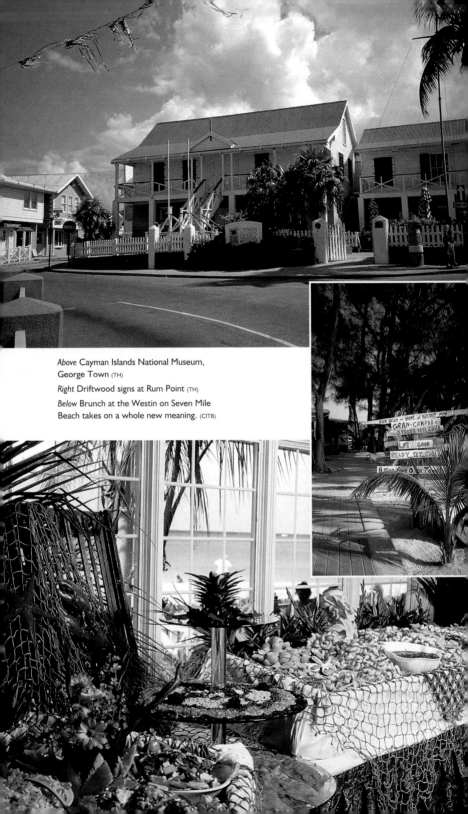

Above Cayman Islands National Museum, George Town (TH)

Right Driftwood signs at Rum Point (TH)

Below Brunch at the Westin on Seven Mile Beach takes on a whole new meaning. (CITB)

for anything else! Look out, too, for special lunchtime deals, particularly mid week, and for Sunday brunch menus that are usually of the 'all-you-can-eat' variety. Barbecues, too, tend to offer good value for money.

For the most part, prices for restaurants listed in this guide have not been given unless there are special deals or they fall outside the norms quoted above. Most menus are priced in CI$, but always check, or that extra 25% on your US$ credit card bill may come as a bit of a shock. A 15% gratuity is usually added to the bill.

Not surprisingly, for islands that have a large proportion of visitors from the US, there are a number of brand-name fast-food outlets, from Burger King to Domino's Pizza and Pizza Hut. Or you could try fast food, Cayman style. Patties, which are a spicy meat pastry not dissimilar to the British Cornish pasty, are available from cafés and shops for around US$1.50 each.

Street vendors are illegal throughout the islands, so there's no question of being pestered on the beach or in the street. During carnivals, though, look out for roadside stalls selling local specialities such as heavy cake or patties (see *Festivals*, pages 57–9). And in the evenings, particularly at weekends, local people may set up barbecues selling jerk chicken to take away.

Drinks

Stingray beer, brewed on Grand Cayman, is available throughout the islands. There are three types: Premium, Durty and the strongest, Dark. Visitors are welcome to visit the brewery (see page 155). Also popular is Jamaican Red Stripe. Several well-known international brand names are widely available, including Heineken and Michelob.

No visit to the Caribbean is complete without at least trying the rum punch, on offer almost everywhere. So, too, are various cocktails, including the mudslide – a Cayman institution based on a rather sweet but very popular mix of vodka, Kahlua (a coffee liqueur similar to Baileys) and Tia Maria on ice. For true decadence, try it with a combination of ice-cream, chocolate sauce and whipped cream.

If you care about your bank balance, keep wine for special occasions – with restaurant prices starting at US$20 a bottle for even the most ordinary wine, it's heading towards luxury status. Even in liquor stores, you're looking at US$12.50–18.

Soft drinks such as Coca-Cola and Seven-Up are to be found pretty well everywhere, as are canned fruit juices, with a variety of flavours from mango and apricot to pineapple and orange. Most readily available, though, is fruit punch, which ranges from a rather synthetic concoction to a very tasty mix of tropical fruit juices. Iced water is served automatically in most restaurants – a very welcome import from the US! More typically, you may come across coconut water, which is deliciously refreshing.

Under local licensing laws, all restaurants and bars must close by midnight on Saturdays and Sundays, and alcoholic drinks may not be served before 1.00pm on a Sunday. It is illegal to purchase alcohol under the age of 18 anywhere in Cayman.

PUBLIC HOLIDAYS

For the most part, shops and banks are closed on public holidays, particularly where they coincide with a religious festival.

January	New Year's Day
February/March	Ash Wednesday
March/April	Good Friday
	Easter Monday
May	Labour Day
	Discovery Day
	Whitsun (date may fall in June)
June	Queen's Birthday, a formal parade with marching bands in the grounds of the governor's residence.
July	Constitution Day
November	Remembrance Day. The Monday after Remembrance Day (November 11) is a public holiday.
December 25	Christmas Day
26	Boxing Day

SHOPPING

The Cayman Islands may be expensive, but George Town's status as a duty-free port makes shopping a highly attractive option for some visitors. Everything from classy boutiques to art galleries and duty-free emporia is there to attract the tourist, often in upmarket shops that would usually grace far more elegant surroundings. The majority of shops are located in George Town and along Grand Cayman's West Bay Road, where numerous small shopping plazas cater to the ever-growing demand. Shopaholics would do best to visit the sister islands after Grand Cayman; here a much greater degree of normality prevails and there is little to get those shopping glands salivating.

Duty-free goods such as jewellery, china, perfume and cigars may be most in evidence, as are designer clothes, but look further and you will find opportunities to purchase the work of local artists and craftspeople. Brightly painted wooden toys, natural woven baskets and quality T-shirts make good souvenirs, as do evocative paintings in all manner of styles. Don't buy products made from turtleshell (they shouldn't be on sale anyway) and think twice about black coral. The latter is protected around Cayman, so is imported from Honduras and Nicaragua, which seems pretty iniquitous (see box page 21). For the collector, a number of stores sell treasure coins, though few are from Cayman waters.

If local foods are your weakness, consider a bottle of jerk sauce to brighten up that barbecue at home. And then, of course, there's the ubiquitous rum cake (see *Food*, page 54). Unexpectedly, alcoholic drinks are subject to duty on the islands, so buy them tax-free at the airport.

ARTS AND ENTERTAINMENT

On Grand Cayman, several restaurants and bars have live entertainment throughout the week, offering anything from jazz to steel bands. There are also two theatres with a broad range of plays and concerts for every taste. The sister islands, however, have little to offer the night owl beyond open-air barbecues, so take a couple of good books and be prepared to relax! Gambling is prohibited everywhere.

Festivals

Various festivals held throughout the year appeal to the visitor as well as to Caymanians.

February/March

Little Cayman Mardi Gras Festival Shrove Tuesday each year sees this colourful parade around Little Cayman, organised by the local branch of the National Trust.

April/May

Cayfest The national cultural festival takes over the streets of Grand Cayman and Cayman Brac for a week at Easter each year. Based around open-air cafés, craft displays, and exhibitions of photography, food and art, it incorporates activities for children, special festival days, boat launches and parties. For further information, check the Cayfest website: www.artscayman.org.

Batabano This popular one-day carnival run by the Rotary Club centres on a colourful costume street parade, to the accompaniment of live calypso and soca bands, and with local food specialities available from roadside stalls. Visitors are welcome to join in, but only costumes made on the islands may be considered by the judges.

June

International Aviation Week is celebrated in the second week of June with aerial and marine displays and a family fun day.

July

Taste of Cayman This three-day event offers the opportunity to sample various Cayman specialities, from conch fritters to rum cake, with much more in between.

October/November

Pirates Week PO Box 51 GT; tel: 949 5859/5078; fax: 949 5449; email: pirates@candw.ky; web: www.piratesweekfestival.com. This well-established annual festival, the most important in the Cayman Islands and unique in the Caribbean, takes place in the last week of October. The fun gets off to a rattling good start on the first Saturday with a blood-curdling 'pirate invasion' of George Town harbour from two old-time sailing ships, followed by a themed parade through the streets, and music and dancing until midnight.

HINTS ON PHOTOGRAPHY
Nick Garbutt and John Jones

All sorts of photographic opportunities present themselves in the islands, from simple holiday snaps to that one-off encounter with a blue iguana. For the best results, give some thought to the following tips.

As a general rule, if it doesn't look good through the viewfinder, it will never look good as a picture. Don't take photographs for the sake of taking them; be patient and wait until the image looks right.

Photographing **people** is never easy and more often than not it requires a fair share of luck. If you want to take a portrait shot of a stranger, it is always best to ask first. Focus on the eyes of your subject since they are the most powerful ingredient of any portrait, and be prepared for the unexpected.

There is no mystique to good **wildlife** photography. The secret is getting into the right place at the right time and then knowing what to do when you are there. Look for striking poses, aspects of behaviour and distinctive features. Try not only to take pictures of the species itself, but also to illustrate it within the context of its environment. Alternatively, focus in close on a characteristic which can be emphasised.

Photographically, the eyes are the most important part of an animal – focus on these, make sure they are sharp and try to ensure they contain a highlight.

Look at the surroundings – there is nothing worse than a distracting twig or highlighted leaf lurking in the background. Getting this right is often the difference between a mediocre and a memorable image.

A powerful flashgun adds the option of punching in extra light to transform an otherwise dreary picture. Artificial light is no substitute for natural light, though, so use it judiciously.

During the days that follow, over 30 events ranging from district heritage days and sports competitions to music and fireworks displays are held throughout the islands, involving local communities every bit as much as visitors. Dates for 2001 are 26 October – 4 November.

November

Gimistory Festival Initiated in 1999 by the Cayman National Cultural Foundation, Gimistory brings traditional storytellers to selected outdoor venues in Grand Cayman and Cayman Brac for a week-long event at the end of November. Each evening, the audience gathers free of charge to listen to stories old and new told by narrators from both Cayman and other Caribbean islands. And after the final response of 'Jack Mandora, mi nuh choose none', signifying the end of the tale, there is the traditional Caymanian dish of fried fish and fritters, washed down by 'swankie', a local lemonade. Duppy (ghost) stories on the beach are unbeatable!

The strong American influence means that **Thanksgiving** dinners also abound in Cayman.

Getting close to the subject correspondingly reduces the depth of field. At camera-to-subject distances of less than a metre, apertures between f16 and f32 are necessary to ensure adequate depth of field. This means using flash to provide enough light. If possible, use one or two small flashguns to illuminate the subject from the side.

Landscapes are forever changing, even on a daily basis. Good landscape photography is all about good light and capturing mood. Generally the first and last two hours of daylight are best, or when peculiar climatic conditions add drama or emphasise distinctive features. Never place the horizon in the centre – in your mind's eye divide the frame into thirds and either exaggerate the land or the sky.

Film

If you're using conventional film (as against a digital camera), select the right film for your needs. Film speed (ISO number) indicates the sensitivity of the film to light. The lower the number, the less sensitive the film, but the better quality the final image. For general print film, ISO 100 or 200 fit the bill perfectly. If you are using transparencies for home use or for lectures, then again ISO 100 or 200 film is fine. However, if you want to get your work published, the superior quality of ISO 25 to 100 film is best.

* Try to keep your film cool. Never leave it in direct sunlight.
* Don't allow fast film (ISO 800 and above) to pass through X-ray machines.
* Under weak light conditions use a faster film (ISO 200 or 400).

For hints on underwater photography, see page 86.

December

Almost immediately after Thanksgiving, the islands start preparing for **Christmas**. A competition for the best Christmas lights results in some spectacular (some might say over-the-top) decorations of hotels, houses, shops and public buildings throughout the holiday period. Caymanians and visitors alike tour the streets to see the displays, many of which are open to the public in aid of local charities.

ACTIVITIES

Without a doubt, the Cayman Islands are a haven for the outdoor enthusiast. The islands maintain their reputation for some of the best diving in the world, with the Cayman walls the greatest draw. To this have been added over the years almost every watersport imaginable, from snorkelling and jet skiing to parasailing and windsurfing. Fishing, too, is deservedly popular, with operators offering a range of fishing for all enthusiasts.

Off the water, golf is a major attraction, with three golf courses on Grand Cayman. The relatively flat terrain means that cycling is well suited to softies

PHILATELY
John Moody of Stanley Gibbons

Visitors to the Cayman Islands are frequently surprised at the variety and colours of the country's stamps which they encounter at hotels and local post offices when they come to send postcards. In fact, the attractive designs of the stamps often match the pictures on the cards and act as miniature promotional posters for the islands' travel industry. The sale of postage stamps also contributes to the islands' economy as collectors from all over the world seek out their designs.

Although the first post office on the Cayman Islands was opened in April 1889, in the capital George Town, the islanders had to use Jamaican stamps until November 1900 when the first stamp to bear the Cayman Islands' name was issued. The stamp was a simple Victorian definitive, much beloved by collectors of early Empire stamps, although not half as interesting to visitors as the multi-coloured stamps available today. It was not until 1935, in the reign of King George V, that the islanders could display the wonders of their islands to the world through commemorative stamps. This first issue showed such images as the red-footed booby, the hawksbill turtle and conch shells, all of which can still be seen on and around Cayman shores today.

The Cayman Islands hold a strange philatelic record in so far as they are one of only two countries in the world that had postage stamps produced by the police. This happened in February 1908 when the islands ran short of 2½d stamps and local Police Inspector J H O'Sullivan took it upon himself to alter four sheets of 4d stamps by hand, to read 2½d.

(though avoid cycling up on to the bluff on Cayman Brac if you fit into this mould). For the more adventurous, horseriding is gaining in popularity, caving is easily accessible, and climbing in Cayman Brac has a steady but growing following.

Activities are not all about adventure pursuits and sport, however. The natural history enthusiast is well served by good birdwatching and hiking on all three islands, backed by the National Trust (see page 27), while photographers have plenty of scope for both land-based and underwater photography.

It is interesting to note that there are no totally private beaches in Cayman – land up to the high-water mark is Crown property, owned by the Queen, as are all the islands' lakes.

For details of all activities, see *Chapter 4*, and pages 183–7 and 205–13.

MEDIA AND COMMUNICATIONS

Telecommunications, as you would expect in one of the world's most important offshore banking locations, are excellent, with facilities available for every form of business link.

Although the current stamps portray exotic scenery, plants, flowers, fish and birds, they will also be vaguely familiar – at least in the eyes of British visitors – since the head of HM The Queen still appears on each stamp. As a member of the Commonwealth, the Cayman Islands has its stamps produced by the Crown Agents Stamp Bureau in Britain, on behalf of the Cayman Islands Postal Authority. Often these commemorate or celebrate British royal occasions or events from British/Cayman history. The islands also take part in what are known as omnibus editions, when each of a group of Commonwealth countries issues, in effect, the same stamps to commemorate a common theme. The celebration of HM The Queen Mother's 100th birthday in 2000 is a good example. Not all CI stamps are British orientated, however: a recent issue caused much delight amongst children with a set portraying the colourful characters from the popular US television series, *Sesame Street*.

Like the stamps, Cayman banknotes and coins also bear a picture of HM Queen Elizabeth II, although British visitors will be less familiar with the dollars and cents with which both money and stamps are denominated. The Cayman Island dollar replaced £sd (pounds, shillings and pence) in 1972, when Britain's money was decimalised.

It is well worthwhile popping into the Philatelic Bureau at the central post office in George Town, or at Seven Mile Beach Post Office in West Shore Centre on West Bay Road, to have a look both at current stamp issues and at earlier ones that are still held in stock. Alternatively, they can be contacted by post at Philatelic Bureau, Seven Mile Beach Post Office, Grand Cayman, Cayman Islands, British West Indies.

Telephone, fax and internet

Telephone, telex and fax are provided by Cable & Wireless (www.candw.ky). The telephone code for the Cayman Islands from overseas is + 345.

For **international calls** from Cayman, dial 011, followed by the national code, then the number required without the initial 0. The national code for the UK is 44. For calls to the US and Canada, dial 1 then the number required. A US$12.50 phonecard will pay for a five-minute call to the UK, or seven minutes to the US.

Local calls in Grand Cayman cost CI$0.09 for three minutes, and CI$0.03 for each additional three minutes. Calls from Grand Cayman to the sister islands cost CI$0.03 per 6.7 seconds, and from Cayman Brac to Little Cayman or vice versa, CI$0.09 for three minutes. Calls within Cayman Brac or Little Cayman cost a flat rate of CI$0.09. Calls from hotel rooms, here as anywhere else in the world, are exorbitant – witness a US$49 charge for a five-minute call to the UK! Use your credit card or a phonecard (see below).

Internet facilities are available at most of the larger hotels. In addition, there are a number of internet cafés in or around George Town (see page 137), and one on Little Cayman (see page 183).

Credit cards calls
Credit card calls can be made to any destination, from any phone in the Cayman Islands, by dialling 1 800 744 2000, followed by your card number. Instructions on how to proceed are given in English. Alternatively, for calls to the USA, dial 1 800 225 5872. You can also dial 110 for Visa and MasterCard calls.

Phonecards
There are two types of phonecard available. Prepaid phonecards are available from shops and petrol stations throughout the islands in various denominations, and can be used from private, public or hotel phones. Key in the number given on the card, then follow the instructions. You will be told how much money/time is left on the card. Phone-box calls cost very slightly more than when using coins.

Smart Phonecards may be bought in denominations of CI$10, $15 and $20 from most general shops. They can be used only in specially designated phones, which are clearly marked.

Payphones
There are over 200 payphones throughout the islands. Payphones may be used with either coins or phonecards; instructions are posted in telephone boxes. Only CI coins are accepted, in denominations of 10 and 25 cents. International calls may be made from a payphone only with a phonecard.

Mobile phones
Mobile phones that are compatible with 800MHz analogue or TDMA digital networks can roam in the islands, but those using credit card roaming services will not be able to receive calls. There's a pay-as-you-go service for hiring mobile phones through Cable & Wireless. Handsets are available from their shop on Andersen Square in George Town or Galleria Plaza on West Bay Road, with cards in denominations of CI$25, 40 and 100.

Important telephone numbers
Emergency (police, hospital, decompression, fire)	911
Non-emergency calls to the police	949 4222
Electricity	949 4743

Telephone services
Operator	0
International operator	010
Directory enquiries	411

Post
There is no door-to-door delivery service in the Cayman Islands, so all addresses feature a post office box number. Street names are a very recent introduction to the islands, and do not form part of the address. Letters to the Cayman Islands should be addressed as follows:

PO Box 000000 XX
Grand Cayman/Little Cayman/Cayman Brac
Cayman Islands
British West Indies

Most postboxes are painted blue and yellow. There are regular collections of mail from Monday to Friday, and on Saturday mornings, and letters normally take around five to seven working days to reach the UK or US.

Stamps for a postcard from the Cayman Islands to the US currently cost CI$0.20, and to the UK, CI$0.25. Stamps are available at post offices and some shops and hotels. See also *Philately*, page 60.

Newspapers and magazines

The *Caymanian Compass* is published daily at CI$0.25/US$0.31. The more expensive Friday edition (CI$0.50/US$0.62) features a supplement with listings of events across the islands over the weekend and through the next week. Other papers include the *New Caymanian*, published every Friday, and *Cayman Net News* (CI$0.25), published Tuesdays and Thursdays. For current and archive stories, check out www.caymannetnews.com, which is updated every Thursday.

What's Hot is a free monthly magazine geared towards tourists, and available at numerous outlets including hotels and the airport. Altogether more interesting is the monthly publication *Cayman Activity Guide* (www.CaymanActivityGuide.com). This, too, is free, but with intelligently written articles that are worth reading. The hardback *Key to Cayman* is a complimentary general guide to the islands, to be found in most hotel rooms. A highlight of this book is a series of recipes supplied by many of Grand Cayman's restaurants.

For the business community, there is *The Cayman Islands Yearbook and Business Directory*.

International newspapers on sale regularly on the islands include *The Miami Herald*, The *International Herald Tribune* and the *Financial Times*.

Television and radio

Cayman's four **television** stations are all privately run. The most popular, CITN, features 24-hour transmission of Caribbean, international and local news plus various entertainment programmes. Its sister company, CTS, is targeted at visitors – you'll soon tire of *Discover Cayman*, a relentless 45-minute newsreel of tourist-orientated promotional material backed up by countless adverts. The other two channels, CATN/TV-30 and CCT, broadcast religious programmes.

Most hotels on the islands have satellite or cable TV, making a broad range of programmes from the US available to guests.

There are effectively five **radio** stations operating on the islands. The government-owned Radio Cayman offers two separate stations, Radio Cayman I, on 89.9FM (93.9FM on the sister islands), and Radio Cayman II on 105.3FM (91.9FM on the sister islands). Both feature regular news bulletins and governmental broadcasts, together with educational, religious, cultural and entertainment programmes.

The privately run Radio Z99.9FM has round-the-clock music interspersed with news bulletins. Radio ICCI-FM is a non-commercial station for students at the international college, while the fifth channel, Heaven 97, features predominantly Christian music but also broadcasts dive reports every day at 8.00am and 5.00pm.

Other radio frequencies
BBC World Service: 17.84 kHz, 15.22 kHz, 9.740 kHz, 3.915 kHz
Voice of America: 15.21 kHz, 11.70 kHz, 6.130 kHz, 0.930 kHz

BUSINESS
The tax-free status of the Cayman Islands is central to the establishment of many businesses here. In addition, there are a number of other incentives designed to encourage the establishment of local industries, of which the most significant is the possibility of concessions on import duty, linked to investment, local employment and type of market. For further details, contact the Ministry of Tourism, Aviation and Commerce, Government Administration Building, Grand Cayman; tel: 949 7900.

Recent initiatives have also put Cayman Brac in a good position as a business location. With the same tax advantages as Grand Cayman, it also has lower licensing and work permit fees, and a considerably quieter pace of life. Details may be obtained from the Cayman Brac Customs Department, District Administration, Cayman Brac, tel: 948 2523; fax: 948 2546.

The Cayman Islands Government Information Services publish a series of booklets covering several aspects of business on the islands, including opening a business, licensing of captive insurance companies, real estate and development and company registration, as well as details of banking and trust company operators, and a list of professional, financial, governmental and retail services. For details of these, and other information, contact the government office (see opposite). It is also worth approaching the **Cayman Islands Chamber of Commerce**, MacDonald Square, George Town; tel: 949 8090; email: chamber@candw.ky.

Working in the Cayman Islands
A temporary work permit may be obtained before arrival in the islands, entitling the holder to carry out a specific job for a maximum of 30 days, with a maximum 30-day extension occasionally granted. Do note that permits are also required by anyone on a sales trip to the islands. Applications should be addressed to the Chief Immigration Officer, Department of Immigration, PO Box 1098 GT, Grand Cayman, tel: 949 8344. The office is open Monday to Friday, 9.00am–4.00pm.

Under the 1992 Immigration Law, employers may take on a non-Caymanian only if they are unable to find a qualified Caymanian to fill the post. Work permits are usually limited to two years, but may be renewed at the board's discretion. Open work permits are rarely granted.

Those planning to work in the Cayman Islands need to provide the following information to their prospective employer, who will then apply for the relevant work permit:

- completed application form for work permit
- evidence of professional qualifications and experience
- 4 passport-size photographs (3 full face; 1 profile)
- police clearance certificate or similar
- medical certificate
- character references

Self-employed people need to supply the above details, together with details of the business or profession and evidence of financial status. For further information, and details of fees, contact the Chief Immigration Officer at the above address, or one of the following:

Cayman Islands Government Information Services George Town, Grand Cayman; tel: 949 8092; fax: 949 5936
Cayman Islands Government Office in the United Kingdom 6 Arlington St, London SW1A 1RE; tel: 020 7491 7772; fax: 020 8491 7944

Normal office hours are 8.30am–5.00pm, Monday to Friday.

OTHER PRACTICALITIES
Electricity
Electricity is 110 volts, 60 Hz. Flat, two-pin US-style plugs are standard, so take an adaptor if you are visiting from the UK or elsewhere.

CULTURAL DOS AND DON'TS
The traditional pace of life in the Cayman Islands is slow and relaxed. Don't try to rush things if you're talking to Caymanians – it's not worth it, and you'll lose the opportunity to get to know what makes this country tick. Remember, too, that Cayman society is very much of the old school, with a high standard of manners born of natural courtesy and an in-bred respect for the older generation in particular. Older women are generally addressed as ma'am, or the more familiar Miss Emily, or Miss Jenny; older men as 'sir'.

For the visitor, the lifestyle in Grand Cayman is comparatively smart, and visitors are requested to cover swimwear when leaving their resort. Certainly in the smarter restaurants, men should expect to wear trousers, not shorts, when dining out in the evening. On the sister islands, swimwear and shorts are the order of the day – and evenings are generally pretty casual too. Sunbathing nude or even topless is strictly forbidden everywhere.

On the business front, the norm is to wear suits for meetings and formal occasions, with a handshake the usual greeting.

There has until recently been a ban on gay relationships, with financial penalties incurred on the rare instances that prosecutions have been made. However, in a highly controversial move during 2000, the British government stated that this ban will have to be lifted in line with the European Convention on Human Rights, which came into effect in the UK during that year. The implications of this move could well be far more reaching than the edict itself, with questions being raised about the right of Britain to impose European law on the islands, and renewed calls in some quarters for self-determination.

GIVING SOMETHING BACK

The standard of living in the Cayman is so high compared with other Caribbean islands that it is easy to forget that even here there are groups that would benefit from the support of visitors. Those listed below are just three that seem particularly apt:

Humane Society PO Box 1167 GT, 153 North Sound Rd; tel: 949 1461; web: www.humane.ky. A voluntary organisation primarily run by expatriate workers in Cayman, the Humane Society looks after lost or unwanted animals.

Lighthouse School Bosun Bay, Grand Cayman; web: www.lhs.edu.ky. The school specialises in the care and education of children with special needs.

National Trust for the Cayman Islands PO Box 31116 SMB, Courts Rd, Eastern Av, George Town; tel: 949 0121; fax: 949 7494; email: ntrust@candw.ky; web: www.caymannationaltrust.org. An institution so well known that it hardly needs any introduction, the National Trust for the Cayman Islands has a far higher profile here than its counterpart in Britain. On such small islands, the potential for upsetting the balance of nature in the interests of development is huge; the National Trust works tirelessly to protect and promote the Cayman environment, both natural and cultural.

Part Two

Grand Cayman

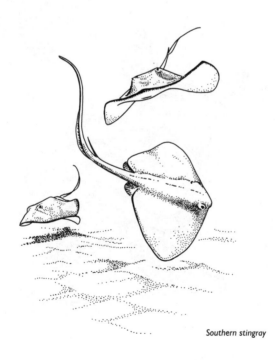

Southern stingray

Green sea turtles

The Basics

> Low and full of trees ... it is very
> dangerous in the night, being almost
> surrounded by a reef of rocks.
>
> George Gauld,
> *The Island of Grand Cayman*, 1773

Grand Cayman is the largest and most popular of the three Cayman islands, lying northwest of Jamaica at 19°2' north and 81° west. Fringing coral reefs hug the ragged L-shaped coast on three sides. On the lee side, to the west, spur-and-groove coral leads out to the wall that reaches down into the abyss of the Cayman Trench. Where mangroves once covered this western shore, lines of buildings now grow, icons to the god of tourism that has brought prosperity but could so easily have swamped such a tiny island. Yet natural beauty still prevails, in the gentle sway of the trees above powdery white-sand beaches, in the rocky shores to the east, in the sunsets that bring depth to the colours of a sun-bleached landscape.

With a total land area of 76 square miles (197km^2), the island is just 22 miles (35km) long, by nine miles (14.5km) wide at its widest point in the west, and narrowing to less than a mile (1.25km) near the airport. The main settlements are the capital, George Town, with a population in 1999 of 20,626, followed by West Bay (8,243) and Bodden Town (5,764).

ARRIVAL
Airport

Owen Roberts Airport is located just east of George Town, a short taxi ride from Seven Mile Beach. The small airport concourse has just one gift shop, but upstairs is a fairly substantial restaurant, the Hungry Horse (tel: 949 8056), open from 7.00am till late, and serving everything from soft drinks and snacks and burgers to cocktails and full meals. Money can be changed at the restaurant.

Through the barrier, there is a bar that also sells snacks of the hot dog and burger variety, and several small duty-free shops which, aside from the inevitable rum and rum cake, also stock a selection of jewellery and souvenirs. Alcohol is pretty good value at the airport shops, with a litre of spirits around US$7–12. No newspapers or books are on sale, though, so go prepared. Note that shops here will not accept credit cards for transactions of less than US$20.

Getting into town

Taxis can be hired just outside the airport building: queue at the small wooden booth to be allocated the next available taxi. Fares from the airport are set by the government, based on one to three people sharing a taxi. Sample prices (end 2000) are as follows:

Seven Mile Beach (southern end)	US$10.00
Seven Mile Beach (northern end)	US$20.00
East End (Morritts Tortuga/Royal)	US$57.50
Cayman Kai	US$63.00

Additional passengers are charged at one third of these rates.

Alternatively, all the major car hire companies have offices at the airport – simply turn left out of the airport building and cross the road. (See *Car hire*, pages 73–4.) There is no bus service from the airport, and hotels are not permitted to collect guests on arrival.

Aside from the taxi rank at Grand Cayman airport, there are usually taxis outside North Terminal at the port in George Town.

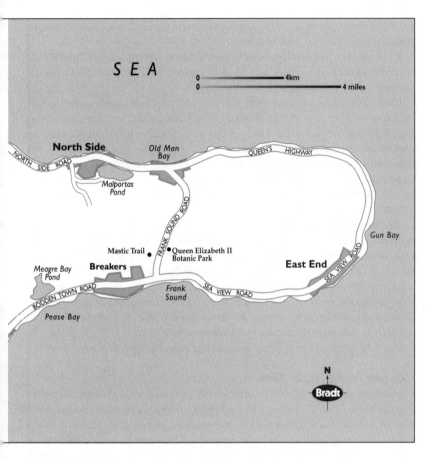

Cruise ship

Numerous cruise-ship operators include the Cayman Islands on their itineraries – several ships anchor off George Town each day. The size of Grand Cayman makes its attractions very accessible even for just a short stop, with possibilities ranging from diving and snorkelling to sightseeing and duty-free shopping.

Cruise passengers come ashore at one of the terminals in the centre of George Town, close to the museum and the shopping area. For a suggested walking tour of George Town, see pages 141–5.

Yacht

Very few yachts find their way to the Cayman Islands, since their relative isolation in terms of the rest of the Caribbean means that they are rarely on a natural sea route. In addition, the fringing reef makes access to the islands something of a challenge. Except in bad weather, yachts should first clear customs and immigration at the Port Authority in George Town. Customs may be contacted on channel 16 Marine VHF, or tel: 949 2055. Opening hours are Mon–Fri 8.30am–4.30pm; Sat 8.30am–midday. There is also a 24-hour manned VHF radio at port security.

There are no port fees for visiting yachts during opening times, but outside these hours there is a charge of CI$56, rising to CI$72 on public holidays, so it makes sense to plan arrival times carefully.

Once formalities are complete, it is essential that you check with the Port Authority where you should anchor. Those anchoring without permission may find themselves faced with a stiff fine for inadvertently stopping in an environmental zone – easily done as the zones are not marked on the Admiralty chart. There are hundreds of permanent government moorings that can be used by the public. A full list may be obtained from either the Cayman Islands Sailing Club (see page 103) or the Department of Environment (tel: 949 8469; fax: 949 4020).

Smaller yachts may head for one of the two marinas, both located in North Sound – Cayman Islands Yacht Club, to the west, or Kaibo Yacht Club, to the east. In theory, the marinas are accessible by craft with a draught of up to 7ft (2.1m); in practice – and without local knowledge – the likelihood of running a boat of this draught aground in North Sound is pretty high, although you may just scrape into Cayman Islands Yacht Club. There are conflicting reports of the depth of the main channel in North Sound, ranging from 6ft (1.8m) to 9ft (2.7m), but even these may be an overestimate.

For tide times around Cayman, check the daily *Caymanian Compass.*

Cayman Islands Yacht Club

Located on the west side of North Sound, in Governor's Harbour, Cayman Islands Yacht Club (PO Box 30985 SMB; tel: 945 4322; fax: 945 4432; email: ciyc@candw.ky) is the larger of the two marinas on the island. In spite of the name, there is no actual club building, with all port transactions conducted at the shop by the fuel station. The club has 138 slips, with a maximum length overall of 150ft (45.7m).

Fees are CI$8 per foot per month, or for short stays CI$0.80 per foot per day. Fuel, water and electricity are available, as well as toilet facilities, public telephones and a shop selling basic commodities. Opening hours are Mon–Fri 7.00am–6.00pm; Sat 7.00am–5.00pm; Sun and public holidays 7.00am–4.00pm.

Vehicular access to the marina is from West Bay Road, opposite the Anchorage Condominiums. The nearest bus stop is number 16. The flat and relatively traffic-free roads in the vicinity are often used by people out running, roller blading or just walking with their children.

Kaibo Yacht Club

Across the bay at Cayman Kai, just south of Rum Point, Kaibo Yacht Club is also something of a misnomer. There are both permanent and tie-up docks, with no fee payable if the crew is eating at the restaurant. Otherwise fees are similar to Cayman Islands Yacht Club (above). Facilities include a fuel dock and gift shop (run by Red Sail Sports). The bar, and upstairs Cecil's Restaurant, are open to all (see page 166).

Morgan's Harbour

This little harbour north of Cayman Islands Yacht Club is really not suitable for any but the smallest vessels, such as fishing boats.

GETTING AROUND
By road

The island is relatively traffic free with the exception of roads around George Town, particularly along West Bay Road, which runs parallel to Seven Mile Beach. These are best avoided Monday to Friday during the rush hours (7.15–8.45am and 4.45–6.00pm).

In spite of a very limited road network, it is surprisingly easy to get lost in the residential streets that lead off the main roads. The signposting isn't great, either, so stick to the main roads or buy a good map.

Car hire

Without doubt, the simplest means of getting around Grand Cayman is by car. Traffic is minimal outside George Town (though do avoid West Bay Road at peak hours) and parking is rarely a problem except in the centre of George Town.

Drivers must be over 21 to hire a car (some companies stipulate over 25), and in possession of either an international driving licence or a current national driving licence. If you have only the latter, you will need to purchase a visitor's driving permit from the car hire company at a cost of US$7.50 – some companies charge slightly more. Vehicle insurance is run on American lines, and is fairly complex, so do check that the car you hire is comprehensively insured (including collision damage waiver, or CDW) rather than just third party.

Remember that driving in the Cayman Islands is on the left, as it is in the UK. The speed limit in Grand Cayman is 30mph (48km/h) in urban areas, and 40mph (64km/h) on most other roads, with the exception of a small stretch of road between the blowholes and the village of East End, which is 50mph (80km/h).

Rental rates vary according to season. Winter (mid December to mid April) is high season, with prices some 35% greater than the rest of the year. Rates quoted below are for the most part summer rates for the cheapest vehicle, and are exclusive of insurance. Basic insurance starts at around US$3.75 per day for third party, up to approximately US$7.50 with CDW (but with an excess or deductible), or as much as US$18 or so for a fully-insured, top-of-the-range model with no excess. Check the current rates before you sign! Almost all companies offer a reduced rate for rentals of a week or more. You can also expect to have unlimited mileage, with free pick up and drop off, although many companies limit the area in which this applies, so do check first.

Ace Rent-a-Car PO Box 53 GT; tel: 949 2280/0572, US 800 654 3131; fax: 949 0572; email: acehertz@candw.ky; web: www.imexpages.com/ace. A Hertz licensee, with locations at the airport and at the Beach Club.
Andy's Rent-a-Car PO Box 127Hl; tel: 949 8111; fax: 949 8385; email: info@andys.ky; web: www.andys.ky. Located both at the airport (open

6.00am–10.00pm) and opposite the Marriott on Seven Mile Beach (open 6.00am–8.00pm). Helpful and friendly staff, and a full range of cars and jeeps. Rates from US$32 per day (US$44 in high season) for an economy two-door automatic with AC. Additional driver US$2 per day. Baby seats available.

Budget Rent-a-Car PO Box 10681 APO; tel: 949 5605; fax: 949 8223; email: budget@candw.ky. Locations at the airport and Treasure Island Resort. Free delivery and pick-up.

Cayman Auto Rental PO Box 103 GT; North Church St, George Town; tel: 949 1013/6954; fax; 945 7081; email: cayauto@candw.ky; web: www.cayman.com.ky/com/cayauto/rates.htm. In the centre of George Town, close to the harbour. Chevrolets, Jeeps and Nissans. Rates from US$33 per day (US$40 in high season).

Cico Avis Rent-a-Car Airport office: tel: 949 2468/9. Open 7.00am– midnight. Offices also at the Hyatt Regency, Westin Casuarina and Marriott hotels.

Coconut Car Rentals PO Box 1991 GT; tel: 949 4377/4037/7703, US: 800 941 4562; fax: 949 7786; email: coconut@candw.ky; web: www.coconutcarrentals.com. Offices in George Town, Seven Mile Beach, Crewe Rd and the airport. Daily rates from US$39 per day (high season US$45) for Suzuki Alto with AC.

Economy Car Rental PO Box 1570 GT, Airport Rd; tel: 949 9550; fax: 949 1003; email: economy@candw.ky; web: www.economycarrental@com.ky. Also at The Falls, West Bay Rd, tel: 949 8992. Hyundai cars from US$32 per day.

Just Jeep Rentals PO Box 30497 SMB; tel: 949 7263, US 800 625 6174; fax: 949 0216; email: justjeep@candw.ky. Offices at the airport and on Seven Mile Beach.

Marshall's Rent-a-Car PO Box 1754 GT, 201 Owen Roberts Dr; tel: 949 7821; fax: 949 6435; email: mar_rac@candw.ky; web: www.imexpages.com/marshalls/. Also next to the Radisson Hotel, tel: 949 2127. Cars, jeeps and vans. Rates from US$35 per day (US$50 high season).

Soto's 4 x 4 PO Box 2176 GT, West Bay Rd; tel: 945 2424, US ; fax: 949 2425; email: sotos4x4@candw.ky; web: www.sotos4x4.ky. Open-top Jeep Wranglers from US$65 per day. Free pick up and drop off to George Town and Seven Mile Beach only, not the airport.

Sunshine Car Rentals Seven Mile Shops; tel: 949 3858; fax: 949 3636. Open Sun–Thu 8.00am–8.00pm, Fri 8.00am–6.00pm, Sat 7.00am–9.00pm. Rates from US$45 for economy car. Bicycles US$15 per day.

Bicycles/scooters

Grand Cayman is pretty flat, and the roads relatively quiet except for Seven Mile Beach and other access roads to George Town during the morning and evening rush hours. Bicycles are favoured by locals as a cheap and efficient way to get around, and many hotels have bikes available for rent to visitors. Although the island is generally considered safe, bike theft is common so do use a suitable lock.

While bikes are great for local excursions, touring the whole island on cheap hotel bikes is not an easy option. An alternative is to rent from a specialist company (where you may have the choice of mountain bikes with variable speeds) or to hire a scooter, giving a little more freedom at around US$25 a day, which includes hire of a helmet and the cost of a permit. All scooter riders must wear a helmet, by law, and should have previous experience.

Bikes and scooters may be hired from the following:

Bicycle Cayman Eastern Av, on the right just after Texaco; tel: 949 0608/945 4865. Delivery and pick-up service available.
Cayman Cycle Rentals Coconut Place, West Bay Rd, PO Box 31219 SMB; tel: 945 4021. Office also at Treasure Island (tel: 949 8711). Mountain bikes US$15 for 24 hours; scooters US$30 for 24 hours (comprehensive insurance an additional US$6.25).

In addition, Sunshire Car Rentals (see above) also rents out bicycles.

Taxis

There are taxi ranks at the airport, and taxis may be hired in front of the cruise-ship terminals in George Town. They are also stationed at all the major hotels on Seven Mile Beach and on Edward Street, near the post office.

Taxis at the terminals are allocated by a despatcher, who will also tell you the fare payable. There is a fixed rate for one-way transfers to local beaches:

US$3   Beach Club colony; Royal Palms Beach Club
US$4   Public beach, West Bay Rd; Westin Casuarina
US$5   Cemetery Reef beach
US$6   Morgan's Harbour

To call a taxi, try one of the following:

AA Chauffeur Service Tel: 949 7222; fax: 947 6222; email: aatours@candw.ky
Ace Tel: 949 3676
Cayman Cab Team Tel: 947 1173. 24-hour service.
Holiday Taxi Tel: 945 4491; 949 4811; 947 1066
Rivers Tours & Taxi Tel: 916 1855/2798; email: riverfam@candw.ky
Websters Tel: 947 1718

Taxis based either at the airport or at the port terminals in George Town operate tours of the island – see *Island tours,* pages 77–9, for ideas.

Buses

There is an island-wide bus service from the bus depot in George Town's Edward Street, close to the Peace Memorial and the public library. The singular exception to this service is the airport, which remains accessible only by taxi or by private car.

The services uses 15- or 29-seater minibuses, each with the route number posted on the back of the bus in a colour appropriate to that route. All public transport vehicles have blue number plates – helpful to prevent you hailing a private minibus by mistake! Bus drivers blow the horn on approach; to stop the bus, hold out your hand. Although there are numbered bus stops on Seven Mile Beach and at West Bay, these are relatively new; buses will often stop on request. The 'timetable' is equally flexible – you're talking 'Cayman time' here; don't expect total reliability.

Fares are payable at the destination, in either US or CI dollars, and must be posted on the buses, which are privately run. Services start at 6.00am every day. If you have any comments about the service, you are invited to call 945 5100.

Routes

Seven Mile Beach and West Bay Route 1/yellow (Eastern Av/Turtle Farm) and Route 2/bright green (West Bay: Water Coast Rd and Spanish Bay Reef). Buses run approximately every 15 minutes, with the last bus at 11.00pm, or midnight on Friday and Saturday. US$2 one way; US$3.75 round trip.

Bodden Town Route 3/blue. Buses run every half-hour until 11.00pm, or midnight on Friday and Saturday. Routes 4 and 5 also go through Bodden Town. US$2 one way.

North Side and East End Route 4/purple (East End direct); Route 5 (North Side via East End); Route 8/orange (North Side). There are two buses per hour on island-wide routes, running until 9.00pm, or midnight on Friday. North Side and East End US$3.50 one way; US$6 round trip.

George Town Routes 6 and 7/dark green. Buses ply between South Church Street and South Sound throughout the day, but there is no timetable.

By sea
Ferries

The **Rum Pointer** ferry runs across North Sound between the Hyatt Regency dock on the east side of Seven Mile Beach and Rum Point. The trip, in a large two-deck open-sided boat with a capacity of 150 people, takes around 45 minutes. Note that there are no toilets on board, and no drinks either, though there is shade. Take a bottle of water if it's hot (note that drinks are not sold at the shop

FERRY TIMETABLE TO RUM POINT
Winter service

Depart Hyatt	Depart Rum Point
9.30am	11.00am
12.00 midday	1.00pm
2.30pm	4.00pm
5.30pm	6.30pm
7.30pm	8.30pm
9.30pm	10.30pm

Summer service

Depart Hyatt	Depart Rum Point
8.00am	9.15am
10.00am	12.00 midday
1.00pm	4.00pm
5.30pm	6.30pm
7.30pm	8.30pm
9.30pm	10.30pm

at the Hyatt dock). Tickets are available at the dock and from the gift shop at Rum
Point itself. For ferry times and reservations, tel: 947 9203.

Fares are US$10 single or US$15 round trip; children 6–11 half price;
under 5s free. There is a discount for Cayman residents. On Saturdays, all
children travel free of charge.

In high season, from Tuesday to Sunday, Kaibo Yacht Club runs a ferry
service across North Sound from Safehaven to Cayman Kai, just south of
Rum Point. The *Kaibo Express* departs at 6.30pm and 8.00pm, returning by
10.30pm. The journey takes less than 20 minutes and the CI$10 fare is
refundable against dinner at the yacht club's restaurant, Cecil's. Call 947 9975
for ferry times and reservations.

TOURIST INFORMATION
Cayman Islands Department of Tourism Cricket Square, 1st Floor, George
Town; tel: (354) 949 0623; fax: (345) 949 4053; web: www.caymanislands.ky

A newly introduced Heritage One Passport offers savings of 25% off
admission fees for four separate attractions on Grand Cayman: the National
Museum, the Turtle Farm, Pedro St James and Queen Elizabeth II Botanic
Park. Passports cost US$19.95 for adults or US$10.95 for children aged 6–12,
and are available from hotels, car rental offices and post offices, or from the
attractions themselves. There is no limit on their validity, making them
particularly useful for those who visit the islands regularly. The passport
cannot be bought overseas.

ISLAND TOURS
Taxis based either at the airport or at the port terminals in George Town
operate tours of the island. A 1½–2-hour tour taking in Turtle Farm, Hell,
the conch shell house, the government administration building, Britannia
Golf Course, the public beach and the governor's residence will cost US$45
per four people sharing a taxi. Alternatively, create your own tour at
US$37.50 per hour for up to three people. For contact telephone numbers,
see *Taxis* page 75. For details of areas beyond George Town, see *Chapter 6*.

Majestic Tours Tel: 949 7773
Island-wide tours with Mrs Annie Smith or Mrs Susy Smith.
Reality Tours PO Box 439 SAV; tel: 947 7200/916 2517; fax: 947 7222.
Half- and full-day tours collect visitors from West Bay between 9.00am and 9.30am
every day. The full-day trip takes in the Turtle Farm, Hell, Rum Cake Centre, Pure
Art gallery, Stingray Brewery, Pedro St James and the blowholes, followed by either
the botanic park or Rum Point, and including a stop for lunch at the Lighthouse. The
day may be rounded off with an add-on excursion to the sandbar at Stingray City,
with equipment included in the price. The half-day trip, in either the morning or the
afternoon, takes guests as far as the Pure Art gallery, then back to George Town for a
tour of its major attractions. A third option takes in Pedro St James, the Rum Cake
Centre, Pure Art, the Lighthouse club, the blowholes, the botanic park and Stingray

Brewery, finishing at around 2.30pm. In addition, the company runs day trips to Little Cayman and Cayman Brac (see below), provides airport transfers, and will customise trips to suit.

Prices Full-day trip CI$60 per adult, CI$35 for children under 12; Stingray City extension CI$20 per person; lunch not included. For the half-day trip, adults are CI$35, children under 12 CI$20. The third option costs CI$54 per adult, CI$25 for children under 12. Up to two children under six go free on any tour, and discounts are available for two or more people travelling together on the same trip.

Silver Thatch Excursions PO Box 344 WB; tel/fax: 945 6588, 949 3342; email: silvert@hotmail.com; web: www.silverthatch.ky

Geddes Hislop and his wife Janet set up Silver Thatch to promote ecotourism on Cayman, bringing their knowledge of natural history and Caymanian culture to a wider audience. Formerly employed by the National Trust, and involved in the development of both the botanic park and the Mastic Trail, Geddes' enthusiasm for natural history is infectious, and his guided trips extremely rewarding. In addition to leading walks along the Mastic Trail, Geddes takes guided trips to East End, West Bay and the botanic park, with the emphasis on history or the environment. Participants are collected from Seven Mile Beach and George Town Mondays to Saturdays between 7.30 and 8.30am, returning between 12.30 and 1.30pm, while early morning birdwatching trips run from 6.00am to 11.00am.

Prices On request, but expect to pay around US$30 per head for the Mastic Trail. No credit cards.

Tours of Cayman Tel: 949 8534

Morning tours in air-conditioned buses start with a pick up between 8.00 and 8.30am, and take in half the island at a time. Tours, with full commentary, are run on alternate days, with the west of the island on Monday, Wednesday and Friday, and the eastern end on Tuesday, Thursday and Saturday. Tours of the west include the Turtle Farm, Hell, Cardinal Ds and the Rum Cake Centre, followed by a choice from the National Museum, shopping or a trip on the *Seaworld Explorer* for the last hour. The eastern tour incorporates Pedro St James, Bodden Town, the botanic park and Stingray Brewery. Tours finish between 12.30 and 1.00pm.

Prices Western tour, adults US$33; children US$23 (museum additional US$5, or US$2.50 for senior citizens, Seaworld Explorer additional US$33 per adult, US$19 per child). Eastern tour, adults US$40, children US$30.

Tropicana Tours PO Box 2071; tel: 949 0944; fax: 949 4507

The original tour operator on Grand Cayman, Tropicana has three separate tours running every day except Sunday, as well as handling airport transfers, snorkel and fishing trips and more besides. At 9.00am and 3.00pm, there is a half-day trip (tour C) that concentrates on the highlights of the western end of the island. Tour A extends this to a full day, encompassing the whole island, while tour B combines tour C with a visit to the National Museum followed by free time to explore George Town's shops.

Prices, including entrance fees as appropriate: tour C CI$25; tour A CI$60, including lunch; tour B CI$30 (return transportation not included).

Tropics Island Tours Cayman Falls Plaza, West Bay Rd; tel: 946 5232

Five different tours cover the whole island in one way or the other. Their recommended trip is the Natural Heritage Tour, 9.00am–1.00pm, which features the

East End, including the botanic park and Pedro St James, as well as Hut Land Farm to see the whistling ducks. A second tour of similar duration operates on Mondays and Thursdays, taking in Hell and the Turtle Farm, followed by places of interest on Seven Mile Beach, and ending in George Town with Cardinal D's park and plenty of shopping time. A two-hour trip on Monday, Wednesday and Thursday mornings covers the same route, but finishes after Seven Mile Beach, and a second short trip, Town and Around, covers the George Town element. Finally, Wednesday's all-day trip covers highlights of the whole island, including lunch. Reservations may also be made here for a variety of visitor attractions and activities.

Prices, including entrance fees and lunch where relevant: Two-hour trip CI$20; Town and Around CI$25; four-hour trip CI$40; full-day trip CI$65.

Effectively a sort of 'one-stop shop' for tours and charters, **Charter House** (tel: 916 0113), near the Lobster Pot in George Town, operates a booking service for island tours, as well as for fishing, snorkelling, diving, submarine and parasailing. Open daily 9.00am–7.00pm. A similar service, which extends to restaurants, car rental and shopping, is operated by **Cayman Concierge Service**, tel: 946 0142, from their three offices on West Bay Road at The Strand, Galleria Plaza and West Shore Centre.

Trips to Little Cayman and Cayman Brac

Regular daily flights are operated by **Island Air** (tel: 949 0241/949 5252; fax: 949 7044; email: iair@candw.ky; web: islandaircayman.com) to both of the sister islands, making a day trip perfectly feasible. Departure is at 7.45am, returning to Grand Cayman after 5.00pm. Fares for non-residents for a day trip are US$105 per adult, US$84 per child.

If you're not sure what to do when you get there, two resorts on Little Cayman offer day-trip packages. **McCoy's Lodge** (tel: 948 0026, see page 177) has day tours of the island at US$50 per person, including airport transfer, lunch, Little Cayman Museum, the National Trust Visitors' Centre, Booby Pond Nature Reserve and Point of Sand beach, together with snorkelling or a boat trip to Owen Island, and swimming at the lodge's pool. **Little Cayman Beach Resort** (tel: 948 1033, see page 176) has an island and snorkel tour with buffet lunch, followed by an afternoon relaxing by the pool or on the beach. US$110 per person.

Alternatively, join **Reality Tours** (see above) for one of their guided day trips to either of the sister islands. Each tour departs from Grand Cayman at 8.00am, returning between 5.00 and 6.00pm. On the Brac, the trip includes the museum, a drive across the bluff, three of the caves, lunch at Captain's Table and time to spend on one of the beaches in the southwest. The trip to Little Cayman takes visitors to Owen Island, Point of Sand and Bloody Bay Wall, with plenty of opportunity for snorkelling at each, plus a traditional lunch. Prices for each trip, including lunch and flights, are US$250 for adults, with children under 12 US$190.

For more information on the sister islands, see *Chapters* 7 and 8.

Diving and Other Activities

DIVING

Diving in the Cayman Islands has come a long way since Bob Soto set up in business in the 1950s with a wooden boat and tanks filled at the local gas station. Today, there are over 30  dive operators and 159 designated dive sites on Grand Cayman alone, and the islands are consistently rated among the best in the world for all-year-round diving.

Grand Cayman, like the sister islands, is effectively the tip of a submarine coral mountain surrounded by small fringing reefs which fall sharply off into the abyss, creating the walls for which the islands are famed. With visibility between 100ft and 200ft (30–60m), and the water temperature ranging from 78°F (26°C) in winter to around 84°F (29°C) in the height of summer, opportunities to explore the underwater world are almost unlimited. The lack of industry on the islands also means that the waters are relatively unpolluted and wildlife is flourishing. Inevitably, though, the relentless to and fro of cruise ships in George Town harbour is having an effect on the environment in the immediate vicinity, and of course the sheer number of divers on the reefs is bound to take its toll.

Since the fringing reefs are for the most part very shallow – some just 16ft (5m) or so – divers can combine spectacular wall dives with plenty of time along the reef, exploring in and around the rocks for the myriad creatures that inhabit this colourful world. Second and third dives offer the opportunity to navigate among the unique spur-and-groove formations – coral fingers interspersed by rivers of sand that flow towards the wall – or to weave through tunnels and runs, perhaps spotting a nurse shark lurking in the shadows or coming upon a shimmering silver tarpon suspended in the blue. Add to this a number of wrecks and it's not difficult to understand the appeal.

Many of Grand Cayman's dive sites are less than half a mile from the shore, making diving extremely accessible. Indeed, the proximity of the reef means that plenty of dives are accessible from the shore, while boat dives rarely require a journey of more than 20–30 minutes. The prevailing winds are from the east, making West Bay the most sheltered area for diving.

Conservation and safety

Almost all dive operators on the islands are members of the Cayman Tourism Alliance Watersports Committee (tel: 949 8522), which is concerned both with the safety of recreational divers and the preservation of the marine environment. The maximum depth limit permitted for recreational divers is 100ft (30m). Children under ten (recently lowered from 12) may not dive with any of the commercial organisations in the open sea. Divers should find out about the area in which they plan to dive before setting off. Briefings on dive boats are the norm, with a maximum bottom time given based on computer or dive-table calculations, as appropriate. As a rule, you should always dive with a buddy.

When diving, swimming or snorkelling from the shore, make sure that you can be seen by any boat that may be in the vicinity by clearly displaying a light or 'diver down' flag. The 'diver down' flag may be either the blue-and-white international code 'A' flag, or the American white diagonal stripe on a red background. Lights used to indicate diving at night feature a series of three vertical lights in the sequence red, white, red, and should be visible all round.

Conservation policies, monitored by Marine Parks Officers, mean that the marine environment is strictly protected. All designated dive sites on the reef have permanent moorings to avoid anchor damage. Boats may anchor in sand away from the reef, provided that there is absolutely no contact with the coral. Moorings should never be left unattended.

Guidelines issued by the Department of Environment remind divers that it is a serious criminal offence to:

- take any marine life anywhere while scuba diving
- take corals, sponges etc from any Cayman waters
- possess a speargun without a licence from the Cayman Marine Conservation Board
- export live fish or any other marine life
- take or molest a turtle.

It's a sobering thought that poor diving practice is one of the causes of reef destruction. Before you set off, ensure that you can establish and maintain neutral buoyancy and check that trailing consoles are properly secured. Don't wear gloves – you shouldn't be touching anything underwater, so they're unnecessary, and you could inadvertently spread disease too. And watch where you put those fins. Not only can the sediment stirred up choke the surrounding life, but a quick flip against the coral or a sponge can destroy years of fragile growth.

Suggestions that you feed the fish and other aquatic life around you are fairly common, but it's not a good idea. Feeding them, even with specialist food, may give you pleasure, but it could lead to a dependence on humans that may endanger the fish and other marine life, and eventually upset the delicate balance of nature upon which the whole underwater ecosystem depends.

Equipment

Diving fees usually include the use of tanks and weights/weight belts, but that is all. European divers in particular should note that, unlike in Europe and much of the rest of the world, all other diving equipment is charged extra,

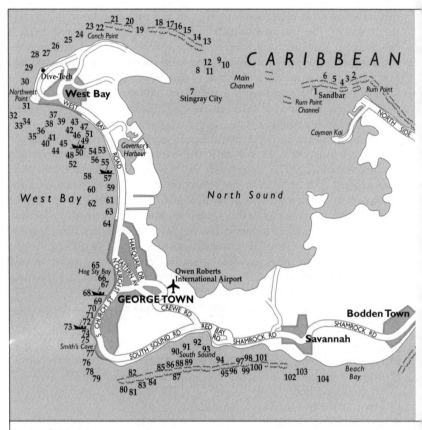

KEY TO DIVE SITES
Note that location of dive sites is approximate

1 Sandbar at Stingray City	28 Hepps Pipeline	54 Sand Chute
2 No-name Drop-off	29 Turtle Farm Mini Wall	55 Paradise Reef
3 Grand Canyon	30 Hepps Wall	56 Marty's Wall
4 Gail's Mountain	31 Bonnie's Arch	57 Wreck of *Oro Verde*
5 Chinese Wall	32 Northwest Point Drop-off	58 Eagle's Nest
6 Hammerhead Hill	33 Orange Canyon	59 Hammerhead Hole
7 Stingray City	34 Sentinel Rock	60 Rhapsody
8 Channel's End Reef	35 Big Tunnel	61 Wildlife Reef
9 Eagle Ray Pass	36 Little Tunnel	62 Caribbean Club Sand Chute
10 Westgate	37 Cemetery Reef	63 Lone Star
11 Lemon Drop-off	38 Slaughterhouse Reef	64 Royal Palms Ledge
12 Valley of the Rays	39 Mitch Miller Reef	65 Pageant Beach Reef
13 Josh's Canyon	40 Dragon's Hole	66 Soto's Reef
14 Tarpon Alley	41 Big Dipper	67 Lobster Pot Reef
15 Main Street	42 Spanish Anchor	68 Wreck of *Balboa*
16 Hole in the Wall	43 Razorback Reef	69 Eden Rock
17 Cliff Hanger	44 Little Dipper	70 Devil's Grotto
18 Blue Pinnacles	45 Round Rock Cave	71 Parrot's Reef
19 Martin's Wall	46 Aquarium	72 Seaview/Sunset Reef
20 Pete's Ravine	47 Angel Reef	73 Wreck of *David Nicholson*
21 Bears Claw	48 Trinity Caves	74 Waldo's Reef
22 Ghost Mountain	49 Three Trees	75 Armchair Reef
23 Sponge Point	50 Wreck of *Doc Polson*	76 Eagle Ray Rock
24 Spanish Bay Reef	51 Peter's Reef	77 Frank's Reef
25 Little Tunnels	52 Neptune's Wall	78 Black Forest
26 Schoolhouse Reef	53 Jax Dax	79 Blackie's Hole
27 Cemetery Reef	54 Sand Chute	80 South Tarpon Alley

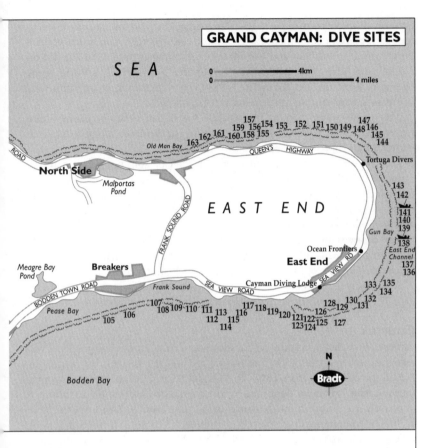

GRAND CAYMAN: DIVE SITES

81 Big Table Rock	109 Frank Sound Caves	137 Shark Alley
82 Three Sisters	110 White House	138 Old Wreck Head
83 Kent's Caves	111 Fantasy Land	139 Lost Valley
84 Palace Wreck Reef	112 Tarpon Taproom	140 Snapper Hole
85 Palace Pinnacle	113 Little House	141 Wreck of *Methuselam*
86 Little Pinnacle	114 Ironshore Drop-off	142 Cinderella's Castle
87 Big Pinnacle	115 Kelly's Caverns	143 Chub Hole
88 Hole in the Wall	116 Maggie's Maze	144 Cabafia Wall
89 Gary's Wall	117 Ironshore Caves	145 Turtle Pass
90 Gary's Reef	118 River of Sand	146 Barrel Sponge Wall
91 Pirates' Cove	119 Tunnel of Love	147 Valley of the Dolls
92 Christina's Reef	120 Chimney/High Rock Caves	148 Black Rock
93 Red Caves	121 Cebert's Sand Chute	149 Black Rock Drop-off
94 Crossroads	122 No-name Corner	150 Split Rock
95 Phantom's Ledge	123 Seven Buck Reef	151 Photographic Reef
96 Bull Winkle's Reef	124 Kangaroo Gulch	152 Omega Reef
97 Japanese Gardens	125 Last Wally	153 Lost Lens
98 Oriental Gardens	126 Three Sisters	154 Old No 12
99 Chinese Gardens	127 Lighthouse Wall	155 Anchor Point Drop-off
100 Tin City	128 The Arch	156 Little Bluff Reef
101 Spotts Caves	129 Lodge Anchor	157 Skinny Palm Tree Drop-off
102 Pedro Castle	130 Catacombs	158 Skinny Palm Tree Reef
103 Teachers' Caverns	131 Playing Field	159 McCurly's Drop-off
104 Paul's Wall	132 The Maze	160 Babylon
105 Lighthouse Wall	133 Jack McKennedy's Canyon	161 Julie's Wall
106 Rutty's Caves	134 Pat's Wall	162 Mermaid's Point Drop-off
107 Wahoo Wall	135 Grouper Grotto	163 Mermaid's Point Reef
108 Frank Sound Gardens	136 Parrotfish Caverns	

even on all-inclusive dive packages. The average (but not top) rate is US$10 to rent each piece of equipment for 24 hours, so if you need a buoyancy control device (BCD), regulator and wetsuit you're looking at some US$30 a day on top of your dive costs, with a dive computer a further US$10–15. Some operators limit the rental cost to US$30, but others will charge more for compasses, snorkels, fins and masks, etc. Be warned!

The warm waters around the islands mean that a full wet suit is not necessary. A skin is useful for protection in the summer months, while in winter a thin shorty suit (approx 3mm) is usually all that is required. Most of the dive operators insist on a dive computer per person, not per pair. If you cannot fulfil this requirement, and don't want to hire a computer, you'll be restricted to diving within the limits of recreational dive tables, rather than those of a computer. The only other essential is your certification – without which you'll be back to square one.

For those with their own equipment, shore dives offer an extremely economical means of exploring many of Grand Cayman's underwater treasures. The cost of hiring a tank for a day is from US$10.

A number of shops on Grand Cayman specialise in diving equipment (see page 131), and several of the dive operators also have their own shops.

Courses

Almost all the dive specialists on the island are PADI affiliated, although all will recognise other qualifications, and some are also licensed to run courses by NAUI, NASDS, SSI, HSA, IANTD, TDI and BSAC. The most popular course on the island is without doubt the Resort course, or Discover Scuba, which is effectively an introduction to scuba diving. For around US$80 per person, including equipment, divers have a two-hour theory session based in a pool, followed by a boat dive to around 40ft (12m). The course may be completed in half a day, but is more usually spread out over a day with a break for lunch.

Costs for the PADI Open Water course are from US$360, with Open Water referral (where the classroom element has been completed in advance) around US$250. As a rule, both these and other 'entry' courses include equipment; for more advanced courses, equipment is extra. Many of the operators start courses on specified days, so do be sure to check this out in advance.

DIVE ORGANISATIONS

BSAC	British Sub Aqua Club
HSA	Handicapped Scuba Association
IANTD	International Association of Nitrox and Technical Divers
NASDS	National Association of Scuba Diving Schools
NAUI	National Association of Underwater Instructors
PADI	Professional Association of Dive Instructors
SSI	Scuba Schools International
TDI	Technical Diving International

Diving for children

Two new initiatives in the diving world make diving accessible even for fairly young children. With SASY (Scuba Assisted Snorkelling for Youth), children over the age of eight can try out the fun of scuba diving in open water. Equipped with a regulator and buoyancy aid, they nevertheless remain at the surface, breathing from a continuous air supply and thus with none of the risks associated with water pressure at depth. Alternatively, the Bubblemaker course is designed to introduce children aged 8–12 to scuba diving through various activities carried out in the confines of a swimming pool. Both are available through Red Sail Sports and Don Foster's, among others. Courses cost around US$30.

Diving for the less confident

SASA (Scuba Assisted Snorkelling for Adults) is the adult equivalent of SASY, above, and is ideal if you want the experience of breathing from a scuba regulator and tank without going beneath the surface.

The technique of 'SNUBA' diving is slowly gaining popularity among snorkellers who want to venture further but aren't ready for scuba diving. Rather than wearing heavy dive gear, participants are effectively 'moored' to an inflatable raft, and breathe from a regulator attached to a surface tank. This allows for shallow dives to a depth of around 20 inches (0.5m) without wearing a BCD. After just 15–20 minutes' orientation, you can follow your guide, either towing the raft behind you, or with a long hose from the raft allowing you the freedom to explore.

Night diving

The opportunities for night diving are as varied as in the day time, but after dark there's a whole new world to explore. As darkness falls, the seas are the realm of creatures such as the octopus and squid, the lobster and the eel. Most dive operators run night dives, but many keep these to a specific day of the week, so it's worth checking well in advance. Of course, diving from the shore can be done on the night of your choice. Just remember to give advance notification of any equipment needs, including an underwater torch per diver, to the relevant organisation, and to get an orientation briefing, as most dive shops close around 5.30pm.

Technical and speciality dives

Nitrox diving is gaining popularity for the extended bottom time it can give at shallow depths. By adjusting the mix of air in a tank to 32/68 oxygen/nitrogen (the norm is 21/79), divers can dive to a maximum of 100ft (30m) but can stay at that depth for up to 30 minutes on a first dive. On 50/50 oxygen/nitrogen, divers are limited to 30–40 ft (9–12m) but bottom time is increased by up to 50%. Nitrox certification is offered by most dive schools. It takes from two days for an initial course, up to four days for an advanced course (upwards of US$500). Nitrox tanks are usually charged at an additional cost to the dive, from around US$5 per tank. Most dive companies can supply nitrox tanks, with tuition available from a large number of them on request.

TIPS FOR UNDERWATER PHOTOGRAPHY
with Karen Stewart

Many are the snorkellers and divers who have set off with a cheap throwaway camera only to find that the long-awaited results when they get home vary from bad to awful. The most important thing to remember here is that these so-called 'underwater' cameras are not intended for divers. Waterproof they may be, but you need to remain on or close to the surface. As with any other camera, you also need to compose your picture carefully, taking care to prevent movement and poor light – both of which are difficult to avoid in the water. If you are stationary, so much the better. As for light, try to keep the sun behind you and avoid reflection on the water. As the contrast right on the surface can confuse the camera (and splashing is a potential problem here too), photographs taken just below may actually be clearer.

For true underwater photography, you'll need to hire or buy a suitable camera – several shops in Grand Cayman stock these, while rentals are available both in shops and from dive operators. Take time to familiarise yourself with the equipment – most shops will help here.

One of the most important things to remember is to get close to your subject, then look up to take your shot. Water acts like fog – the farther you are from your subject, the more blurred it will be, so get as close as you can for the lens that you are using. Many underwater cameras that you rent will be fitted with a 35mm lens. That means you need to be about three feet (1m) from the subject (underwater this is about two arm-lengths). By staying at this distance you will have sharper and more colourful images. You will also want to try to make that intriguing fish, or sponge or piece of coral, stand out. This can easily be accomplished by shooting upwards, effectively using the deep blue water as background. Underwater shots that are taken shooting down into the sand or coral tend to lose their three-dimensionality and everything blends together.

To really bring out the beauty of the underwater world, your camera should be fitted with some sort of strobe. Remember that as we descend in water, we quickly lose colour and light. By the time you are at 50 feet (15m), everything appears monochromatic blue or green. If you take pictures at this depth without a strobe, your picture will also appear blue or green. Strobes bring back the vibrant colours and make your subject stand out from its background.

Before you try underwater photography, make sure that you are comfortable in the water with your scuba equipment and also with your buoyancy. Adding a camera when you are uncomfortable will increase stress. Having good buoyancy and keeping gauges and hoses tucked away means that you can get closer to subjects without injuring the reef. Watch that your feet don't kick the coral or stir up the sand as you are taking the picture, and never grab on to a live reef to steady yourself.

Rebreather diving means effectively that you can dive without the sound of bubbles released from your regulator. The silence can be awesome. A one-day introduction to rebreather techniques, comprising a half-day theory and two afternoon dives, costs around US$199. Other possibilities include **scooter dives**, with a DPV scooter (minimum four passengers), and a **shark-awareness** dive.

Free diving
The skill of diving without scuba equipment offers a whole new dimension. For tuition, contact Dive-Tech, who operate out of West Bay.

Underwater photography
Several dive operators have their own photographic division, enabling divers to rent equipment or have instruction in underwater photography. It is possible to hire a basic 35mm underwater camera from about US$10, or a video camera for around US$75. Most outfits will also produce a video of your dive, so do ask (and check the price, too – the range is approximately US$100–150!). For in-depth photography course, contact Cathy Church (see page 135).

Dive operators
Among the 40 or so dive operators on Grand Cayman, costs are very similar and safety standards are exceptionally high. The things that do vary, however, are the size of the operator, from one-man bands to larger operators with a fleet of boats, the location, and the style in which the dives are run. From the super efficient to the totally laid-back, the choice is yours.

Most hotels and resorts have affiliated dive schools, but there is plenty of choice so do shop around for the one that suits you rather than your resort. The bigger operators may be more efficient, but sometimes the squash on board boats with large numbers of divers can justify the analogy with cattle trucks. Ask, too, about special deals. With so many dive operators, competition is fierce and almost all outfits offer discounts or extra dives for those booked for a couple of days or more.

The majority of operators listed below will have an instructor on board, and dives are usually accompanied by at least one experienced guide. That said, the short site briefing, with relevant safety instructions, means that divers may usually explore at their own pace – in pairs, of course. For dive courses, expect a ratio of one instructor to between four and six divers. The accessibility of dive sites means that the west, north and south walls are visited by pretty well all dive operators, though the east is the general preserve of just three: Cayman Diving Lodge, Ocean Frontiers and Tortuga Divers. If you have a request for a particular site, do ask – with so many options, boat captains usually welcome suggestions.

Boats usually have drinking water on board for their guests, and some offer soft drinks and snacks or fruit as well. Almost all companies are also able to arrange videos of your dive on request, with costs from around US$50 for a tape of about 15–20 minutes' duration.

Costs

A typical two-tank boat dive will consist of a 20-minute dive to 100ft (30m) in the morning, followed by a 40–50-minute dive 50ft (16m). The average cost is US$60–85, excluding equipment. A further afternoon dive would cost an additional US$45–55. Dives to Stingray City average US$55, while snorkel trips are from US$30.

Most of the operators listed below offer a variety of dive packages, ranging from a couple of days' diving to a full week. Alternatively you can book an all-inclusive dive/accommodation package with one of the resorts or dive lodges – for details, see the accommodation index, pages 221–2. Prices range from approximately US$330 to US$475 for six days' diving, based on a two-tank boat dive per day. Many operators will also allow unlimited shore diving for those who take out a package. It's worth noting that packages booked in advance may work out considerably cheaper than those booked once on the island. In the event of cancellation, there is unlikely to be any refund where packages have been booked on the island, while pre-booked packages are normally subject to a minimum cancellation period.

For ease of comparison, prices are given below for a two-tank boat dive, the Resort course, the full Open Water course, and daily hire of BCD and regulator, with a selection of other prices given where a particular deal is on offer. These figures are walk-in prices; various discounts are available for pre-booking, package deals and all-inclusive deals.

Abanks PO Box 31206 SMB; 96 South Church St, George Town; tel: 945 1444; fax: 945 3319; email: abanksx@aol.com; web: www.abanks.com.ky
Based at Club Paradise just a few minutes' walk from the centre of George Town, Abanks shot into the limelight as the dive company featured in *The Firm*. With diving close to the shore in the harbour marine park, and snorkelling just off the wall, this is

CAYMAN MADNESS

Once a year, Bob Soto's Diving sponsors a six-week diving event in September/October known as Cayman Madness. Up to a hundred divers from all over the world get together each week of the promotion to take part in a week of diving and social activities at 1970s' prices – an all-inclusive US$999! The cost includes Cayman Airways flight from Miami, Tampa or Houston, transfers, accommodation, six days' unlimited diving, taxes and services. And it doesn't stop there. Several organisations come together to lay on parties and celebration dinners, plus free use of diving and photography equipment. Competitions throughout the week, including an underwater treasure hunt, complete the picture, with plenty of prizes such as gift vouchers for local restaurants. You even get the T-shirt! For further information, contact Bob Soto's, or check out the dedicated website, www.caymanmadness.ky.

an all-round location, popular with cruise-ship passengers. A single accompanied dive to Eden Rock and Paradise Reef, suitable for beginners, costs US$75, inclusive of all equipment.

Rates Two-tank boat dive US$70; Resort course US$75; Open Water US$350.

Ambassador Divers Tel: 916 1064; email: ambadive@candw.ky; web: www.ambassadordivers.com

Jason Washington runs a small dive operation offering a very personal service with a maximum of 12 divers on board. His small, fast boat cuts down on travelling time to divesites, meaning he can sometimes go further afield than most. He offers all PADI courses up to Divemaster, as well as semi-closed circuit rebreather certification.

Rates Two-tank boat dive US$70; Resort course US$80; Open Water US$350. BCD/regulator US$10 each.

Aqua Adventures PO Box 30379 SMB; tel/fax: 949 1616, 916 1616; email: aqua@candw.ky

This small, flexible company takes a maximum of eight divers on any trip.

Rates Two-tank boat dive US$70; Resort course US$80; Open Water US$360.

Aquanauts PO Box 30147, Morgan's Harbour, West Bay; tel: 945 1953; US: 800 SUN NUTS; email: aquanaut@candw.ky; web: www.aquanautsdiving.com

This West Bay company aims to offer 'big boats with small groups'. Dive and gift shop.

Rates Two-tank boat dive US$75; Resort course US$100; Open Water US$325. BCD/regulator US$10 each.

Bob Soto's Diving PO Box 1801 GT, Seven Mile Shops, West Bay Rd; tel: 949 2871/2606, US 770 497 8311, 800 262 7686; fax: 949 8731; email: bobsotos@candw.ky; web: www.bobsotosdiving.com.ky.

The first dive operator in the Caribbean, Bob Soto's was established in the Cayman Islands in 1957, and to this day retains its ethos of teamwork and fun. The company has eight boats, each taking a maximum of 20 people at any one time. It is a PADI five-star resort, one of only two operators on the island to offer PADI instructor qualifications. Affiliated to Treasure Island (where they have a shop) and Seaview Hotel, the company also has shops at Coconut Place, the Strand and by the Lobster Pot in George Town. One of the more expensive operations on the island, it maintains a high reputation.

Rates Two-tank boat dive US$85; Open Water US$395; Resort course US$99. BCD/regulator US$15 each. Pre-paid dive packages available, with savings up to 25% after six days. Night dives Tue, Thu, Sat. Camera and video rental available.

Cayman Diving School PO Box 1308 GT, Coconut Place; tel: 949 4729; fax: 946 4729; email: caydive@candw.ky; web: www.caymandivingschool.com

A new US-owned dive operator reputed to offer excellent personal service. A recent introduction is their multi-language facility, whereby all PADI courses and other dive services are offered in German, French, Italian and Spanish, as well as English.

Rates On application.

C&G Watersports Tel: 949 3742

A one-man operation based on 16 years of diving in the Cayman Islands, Jeff Kingstad offers individual scuba instruction and private guided dives, from beginners to experienced divers and night dives. Dive videos on request.

Rates On application.

Divers Down PO Box 1706 GT; tel/fax: 945 1611; mobile: 916 3751; email: andyp@candw.ky; web: www.divers-down.com. With no more than eight divers per trip, the emphasis here is on the personal, with private charters also available from US$325 for one-tank dives.

Rates Two-tank boat dive US$70; Resort course US$100; Open Water US$425. BCD/regulator US$10 each.

Dive-Tech PO Box 31435 SMB; tel: 949 1700/1701; email: divetech@candw.ky; web: www.divetech.com

Located next to the Turtle Farm in West Bay (and with a second office at Cobalt Coast), Dive-Tech is responsible for the farm's personal turtle release programme. The shore diving here is considered to be among the best on the island, with very little marine disturbance and just a three-minute swim at a depth of 25ft (7.6m) before a 60ft (18m) mini wall. In addition to all the standard diving courses (the company is affiliated to and runs courses certified by PADI, NAUI, SSI, NASDS, IANTD, TDI and BSAC), plus scooters, rebreathers and the like, Dive-Tech offers a range of technical and free-diving courses, from a half-day introduction to professional and competition level. Indeed, one of their staff, a member of the Canadian free-diving team, came third in the World Championships in France.

Rates Two-tank boat dive US$65; Resort course US$100; Open Water US$375. BCD/regulator US$10 each. Guided shore dives US$30 (night US$40); free-diving courses from US$10 for ½ day.

Don Foster's Dive Cayman PO Box 31486 SMB, North Church St, George Town; tel: 945 5132; fax: 945 5133; email: dfd@candw.ky; US: 800 83 DIVER/972 907 9821; fax: 903 560 1654; email: dfosters@swbell.net; web: www.donfosters.com

Established in the 1980s, Don Foster's prides itself on the continuity of its staff and the local knowledge they have built up over the years. Indeed, even their Texas office is manned by their own staff. With four flat-top boats, plus a comprehensive range of courses, including the Bubblemaker course for children, theirs is one of the larger operations on Grand Cayman. As well as the main office just in front of the wreck of the *Cali*, there is a second office and shop at Comfort Suites, and a photo centre offers underwater photo instruction and camera rentals.

Rates Two-tank boat dive US$75; Resort course US$100; Open Water US$450. BCD/regulator US$10 each.

Cayman Diving Lodge PO Box 11 EE; tel: 947 7555, US 800 TLC DIVE; fax: 947 7560; email: divelodge@aol.com; web: www.divelodge.com

Located in the East End, and also known as East End Dive Lodge, this is one of just three dive operations that covers this part of the island. As an all-inclusive resort, it caters for its own guests, who have unrivalled access to diving and snorkelling on site. For full details, see page 166.

Eden Rock Dive Centre PO Box 1907 GT, South Church St, George Town; tel: 949 7243; email: edenrock@candw.ky; web: www.edenrockdive.com

This company is ideally situated for shore dives of Eden Rock and Devil's Grotto, which lie just opposite to the south of Hog Sty Bay. Guided tours are available, as are underwater maps of both areas. Affiliated to PADI, NAUI, SSI and BSAC, Eden Rock runs courses for each organisation, and is one of only two dive operators on the islands to offer BSAC courses. Resort courses take place daily.

Rates Two-tank boat dive US$65; Resort course US$75; Open Water US$400.

Neptune's Divers PO Box 30520 SMB; tel: 945 3990, 916 0088; email: neptune@candw.ky

Neptune specialise in small groups, with a maximum of eight divers per trip, and diving to the west, south and north walls. PADI, NASDS and SSI courses.

Rates Two-tank boat dive US$70; Resort course US$90; Open Water US$400. BCD/regulator US$15 each. Night dives Mon, Wed.

Ocean Frontiers PO Box 30433 SMB; tel: 947 7500; fax: 947 7600; email: oceanf@candw.ky; US tel: 561 477 6941; toll free: 800 544 6576; fax: 800 886 1509; email: oceanf@adelphia.net; web: www.oceanfrontiers.com

Established early in the 1990s, this is a PADI five-star operator that specialises in diving off the East End, one of only three dive operators that cover this area. The 48ft (14.6m) Nauti-Cat can reach most sites within ten to 20 minutes. Referring to their style as 'gourmet diving', they limit divers to 12 per boat and boast personal touches that include towels and illustrated dive briefings. Their 11ft-deep pool, designed specifically for dive tuition, is the deepest on the island. They are also the dive specialists for Royal Reef Resort, and act as a full travel agent for divers islandwide.

Ocean Frontiers is one of only two outfits on the island to offer PADI instructor qualifications, the other being Bob Soto. A wide range of other courses includes Bubblemaker, Gold Advanced Certification and rebreather, while a recent introduction is their unique programme that involves research into the behaviour of the Caribbean reef shark. For this and other 'X-dives' (scooter and technical), participants must have logged 20 previous dives, at least one of which was with Ocean Frontiers. The company's courtesy bus collects divers from anywhere on the island free of charge. For details of guided nature and historical snorkelling trips, see page 102. Private charters and camera rental available.

Rates Two-tank boat dive US$85; Resort course US$100; Open Water US$350 (private instruction US$600). BCD/regulator US$10 each.

Off the Wall Divers PO Box 30176 SMB; tel/fax: 945 7525, mobile: 916 0303; email: fish@candw.ky; web: www.otwdivers.com

This small group operation takes between two and ten divers per trip, with courses up to advanced, and nitrox available on request.

Rates Two-tank boat dive US$65; Resort course US$95; Open Water US$375. BCD/regulator US$10 each.

Quabo Dives PO Box 157, Coconut Place, West Bay Rd; tel: 947 4769; fax: 947 4978; email: quabo@candw.ky

A relative newcomer to the diving scene in Grand Cayman, Quabo is run by Arthle Evans, a Caymanian instructor who has been diving here since 1972. The emphasis is on small groups, with dives to the north and west walls. Camera and video rental available.

Rates Two-tank boat dives US$60–70; Resort course US$90; Open Water US$400. BCD/regulator US$10 each. Night dives Wed.

Red Baron Dive Charters PO Box 11369 APO; tel/fax: 949 9116; cell: 916 1293; email: baronred@candw.ky.

Half- and full-day private charters take a maximum of six people for a variety of dive

opportunities, as well as PADI and NAUI courses. Underwater photography and video services include the opportunity to work alongside a professional photographer. *Rates* Two-tank boat dive US$75; Resort course US$90. BCD/regulator US$10 each.
Red Sail Sports Coconut Place, West Bay Rd, PO Box 31473; tel: 945 5965; US: 877 733 7245; fax: 945 5808; email: redsail@candw.ky; web: www.redsail.com
One of the biggest operators on Grand Cayman, and one of the most organised, Red Sail Sports operates throughout the western side of the island, including the north wall. It also runs community programmes in schools on Cayman. The company is affiliated to four hotels on Seven Mile Beach – the Westin (tel: 949 8732), Marriott (tel: 949 6343), Hyatt (tel: 949 8745) and Holiday Inn (tel: 946 4433) and has dive shops in these as well as at Rum Point (tel: 947 9203). With seven boats, each working in different locations and with space for between 12 and 24 people, Red Sail offers PADI, NAUI, NASDS, SSI and HSA courses up to Divemaster, and including Bubblemaker and SASY, under the guidance of experienced and friendly staff. Camera and video rental. Private charters available.
Rates Two-tank dive US$75; Resort course US$120; Open Water US$440. BCD/regulator US$15 each. Night dives Mon, Wed.
Seaview Dive Center PO Box 31900 SMB, South Church St, George Town; tel: 945 0577; email: seadive@candw.ky
The dive operation that forms an integral part of the Seaview Hotel ensures that everything is available to guests on site, with good shore diving to boot.
Rates Two-tank boat dive US$60; Resort course US$82; Open water US$350 (private lessons US$438). BCD/regulator US$10 each.
Sunset Divers PO Box 479 GT, South Church St, George Town; tel: 888 281 3826, US 800 854 4767; fax: 949 7101; email: sunsethouse@sunsethouse.com web: www.sunsethouse.com
The dive set up at Sunset House is geared to the resort's clientele, with a range of courses available up to Divemaster, including nitrox and rebreather programmes. Affiliated to PADI, NAUI, SSI, NASDS and IANTD, the company has a fleet of boats visiting sites to the west, north and south, while their super-fast catamaran, *Manta*, can go further afield, including to locations off East End. The reef just off the resort is excellent for shore diving, with a couple of wrecks as well, not to mention the area's newest attraction, the Mermaid of Sunset House (see page 91).
Rates Two-tank dive US$75; Resort course US$95; Open Water US$350. BCD US$10, regulator US$15.
Seven Mile Watersports PO Box 30742 SMB, West Bay Rd; tel: 949 0332; fax: 949 0331; email: smbrsort@candw.ky; web: www.7mile.ky
This well-priced dive operation located at Seven Mile Beach Resort is affiliated to PADI and offers diving mostly to the north wall, with free pick up from Seven Mile Beach. Their two dive boats, one of 40ft (12m) and the other 23ft (7m), operate from Cayman Islands Yacht Club. Trips are for a maximum of 15 divers, including staff.
Rates Two-tank boat dive US$60; Resort course US$110; Open Water US$400. BCD/regulator US$10 each.
Tortuga Diving PO Box 496 GT, Morritt's Tortuga Club, East End; tel: 947 2097; fax: 947 9486; email: tortugad@candw.ky

This friendly outfit has been operating for ten years, taking divers off the reef at East End and to Stingray City. Courses include PADI Open Water and Advanced, and free snorkelling lessons are offered at weekends. Boat charters available. Night dives Wed.
Rates Two-tank boat dive US$85; Resort course US$120; Open Water US$425. BCD/regulator US$12.50 each. Discount of 20% for owners at Morritt's Tortuga Club. Prepaid packages range from three days at US$224.40 to six days at US$448.80. Packages bought on the island are marginally more expensive (US$237.15 and US$474.30 respectively).

Treasure Island Divers PO Box 30975 SMB; tel: 949 4456, US 800 872 7552; fax: 949 7125; email: tidivers@diveres.com; web: www.tidivers.com
The dive operation based at Coconut Harbour is not to be confused with Treasure Island Resort, where Bob Soto is now the 'official' operator. A PADI five-star dive centre, established in the late 1980s, Treasure Island Divers' fleet of boats leave from Coconut Harbour itself at 8.00am for the morning dives, which means that divers usually have first choice of the island's sites. On board, the atmosphere is relaxed, with stereo player and an upper sun deck. Nitrox diving available.
Rates Two-tank boat dive US$75; Resort course US$100; Open Water US$395. BCD/regulator US$12 each.

Live-aboard boats

Cayman Aggressor IV PO Box 10028 APO; tel: 949 5551; fax: 949 8729; email: cayman@aggressor.com; web: www.aggressor.com. US reservations: PO Box 1470, Morgan City, LA 70381-1470, USA; tel: 800 348 2628; fax: 504 384 0817
An 18-passenger live-aboard, *Cayman Aggressor IV* covers each of the three islands during its week-long cruise, weather permitting, with up to five dives per day for passengers. Operating out of George Town, the 110ft (33.5m) purpose-built boat is designed for luxury. Carpeted staterooms off the main salon have en-suite facilities, AC and TV/VCR, while up above are the dive deck and sun deck, complete with loungers, hot tub and beer on tap.
Rates US$1,995 per person.

For details of *Little Cayman Diver II*, based at Cayman Brac, see page 206.

Dive sites

The sheltered western side of Grand Cayman is the most popular area for diving. Ideal for beginners, it also boasts a wide variety of diving to challenge even the most experienced. When the wind is coming from the west, dive operators tend to make for the south, so it is very rare for dives to be cancelled.

The numerous tunnels to the northwest make this a fascinating place to dive, although currents on the point can cause occasional problems for divers. The shallow reefs to the north itself make for excellent diving. Finally, there are the less explored waters of the East End, where few boats venture and crowds are unknown.

There are over 200 buoyed areas around the three islands, plus infinite possibilities for sand anchorages. It is beyond the scope of this book to give an in-depth assessment of all the recognised dive sites around the Cayman

Islands. The following is therefore just an overview. For more details, check out the Department of Tourism's dive website – www.divecayman.ky – or whet your appetite with their short *Dive Guide*, available free from the tourist office. For a selection of books on diving in Cayman waters, see *Further Reading*, page 224.

Shore dives

It's no accident that many of Grand Cayman's dive lodges are located to the southwest, near George Town. Grand Cayman has numerous good shore-dive sites in this vicinity; those that follow are just a selection.

Although the water in the harbour itself is not as clear as it once was, a result of so much cruise-ship traffic, this is only relative to the absolute clarity of waters around the islands generally. Rest assured, visibility in these waters is still pretty good. If diving in the harbour, be particularly careful to take advice in advance, leave a 'diver down' flag on the surface before you dive (see page 81) and watch out for marine traffic.

A short surface swim of some 200yds (182m) from the Lobster Pot is **Soto's Reef**, while nearby is the wreck of the *Cali* (see page 96), easily accessible from Don Foster's on North Church Street.

To the south of the harbour, well away from the disturbance caused by shipping, **Eden Rock** and **Devil's Grotto** lie some 100ft (30m) or so offshore from Eden Rock Dive Centre, which offers guided dives of the two sites, and also has underwater maps. Both sites feature a maze of tunnels and caverns, frequently visited by tarpon, at depths of 35–45ft (10.6–13.7m). Straight out from Seaview Resort is the eponymous **Seaview**, where there is an inner reef within 30ft (10m) of the shore, separated by sand from a second reef at 68ft (22m), and then a third which takes you on to the wall. And if you're looking for something a bit different, check out Cayman's latest dive attraction, the sunken **mermaid**, or siren, in 40ft (12m) of water just off Sunset House (see page 97). Other possibilities for shore diving here lie out from Coconut Harbour, including **Parrot's Landing** and **Waldo's Reef**.

North of George Town, just beyond the Turtle Farm in West Bay, is an ideal location for shore dives, with excellent visibility and little disturbance. A three-minute swim in 25ft (8m) of water brings the diver to a 60ft (18m) mini wall, and you could well have the place to yourselves. Night diving here is popular, too.

Boat dives

No matter where you are diving, rest assured that it will be amazing! Go with an open mind, too – even if you've set your heart on a particular dive, you're pretty well guaranteed to enjoy any alternative that may be offered. With over 50 anchored sites on the west wall alone, there's no shortage of choice.

Stingray City

Justifiably popular among visitors, Stingray City is actually two separate locations, both in North Sound, where snorkellers and divers may experience the almost balletic grace of these extraordinary creatures as they glide among us comparatively awkward mortals. Almost all the boat trips on Grand Cayman will take you either to the sandbar, which is so shallow that you can stand, or to the nearby shallow dive spot, where divers kneel and wait just 12ft (4m) below the surface. Either way, expect a full briefing before your encounter, so you know exactly how to behave.

Stingrays were originally drawn to the site by leftover bait thrown overboard by local fishermen, and they soon became accustomed to being fed. Before long, the potential for bringing divers here was realised, and the concept of Stingray City was born. The attraction of handfuls of squid is almost instantaneous, as female southern stingrays, with their wingspan of around 4ft (1.2m), appear silently from all sides. Stingrays effectively feed like underwater vacuum cleaners, sucking up their food from the sea bed. They have plates, not teeth, and although they can clamp these shut quite tight, they don't do any harm if they accidentally catch a finger – even if it does hurt momentarily. Rumour has it that the stingrays also have a penchant for certain hair conditioners, but this is probably hearsay! For what it's worth, the sting is set well back on the tail and, since the animals are attracted by food, they do not feel threatened; there is no record of anyone having been stung since Stingray City was established.

Of course, female stingrays are not the only animals to be attracted by squid. The smaller and far more aggressive male is likely to want to get in on the act, as is the occasional pufferfish, not to mention a host of colourful reef fish into the bargain. Even the menacing moray eel can be tempted from his lair beneath the rocks by a tasty morsel.

Walls and reefs

Stingray City aside, it is Cayman's walls that are its greatest underwater attraction, offering some of the best wall diving in the world. To be surrounded one moment by the sunlit world of the reef, then suddenly to find yourself staring over the edge into nothingness is truly extraordinary. Corals of every shape and pattern decorate the wall as far as the eye can see, their bright colours fading to deep blue as the abyss beckons. Here you may see the spotted eagle ray, or perhaps a hawksbill turtle, while out to sea keep an eye open for the occasional patrolling shark.

With the first dive of the day likely to be a wall dive to around 100ft (30m), the second is usually over the reef, which is for the most part shallow enough to allow periods of up to 45 minutes underwater. Here, nature's playground is in full swing. Colourful fish of all hues dart in and out of the coral; great purple sea fans wave in the currents; lobsters peer out from under rocks, often visible only by their fragile antennae. Resist any temptation to climb into those huge barrels that perch atop the coral – they've grown to that size over hundreds of years and even a slight knock can cause untold damage. Do, though, take the time to peer inside both these and the narrower tube sponges. For an extraordinary array of tiny creatures, this is a hiding place of relative safety.

The **west** wall is the most sheltered bay on the island, ideal for beginners and in windy conditions, and useful for acclimatisation as well. Don't be put off by this, though; the west offers some superb diving at all levels, with 50 or so anchored sites. With a less dramatic drop-off than the south and north walls, the west features intriguing sand-and-groove coral formations, with long fingers of coral interspersed with narrow ribbons of sand, making navigation relatively straightforward. There is no shortage of marine life here. Gaudy parrotfish, French and queen angelfish and smiling tangs are just a few of the numerous species that weave through the coral, with the almost transparent trumpetfish like a silent ghost and the odd algae-encrusted grouper lurking in the depths.

The names of many of the dive sites give you a flavour of what is to come. Aquarium acquired its name from the huge plastic sheets that were used during a study of the reef structure, then left behind by the scientists because it was too windy to move them. Although most of them have since been removed, one or two are said to remain, so the occasional diver may just find out what it's like to be on the inside of a fish tank! Orange Canyon, at the northernmost tip of West Bay, is prone to strong currents, but is well recommended, as is Texas Wall, a shallow, shelving wall with wonderful sponges and coral formations, and black durgon very much in evidence.

For most dive operators, the **north** wall involves a 20–25-minute boat ride which can occasionally be choppy. That said, the diving here is spectacular, with sharp drop offs from 40–45ft (12–13.7m) on to the wall and sites such as Eagle Ray Pass and Tarpon Alley indicating some of the highlights of the area.

The deeper reef of the **south**, at 60–70ft (18–20m), features plenty of crevices and channels to explore. Caves are very much in evidence here, with Pirate's Cove, Hole-in-the-Wall and Spotts Caves setting the scene.

Only three companies regularly run dives to the **east**: Ocean Frontiers, Tortuga Diving and Cayman Diving Lodge. Here, where the pace of life is slower and the island uncrowded, the occasional diver is something of a rarity among the marine life, and you'll be very much the stranger in their underwater world. As the walls plunge vertically from around 45ft (15.6m), the scenery is one of mazes and caverns, overhangs and chutes. In parts of the East End shark sightings are almost to be guaranteed, while very occasionally a manta ray may come into view. On a practical note, the prevailing onshore wind tends to whip up the sea a little, with waves of 3–5ft (0.9–1.5m) not uncommon.

Wrecks and other attractions

It's not surprising that Cayman waters have their fair share of wrecks, given the number of ships that plied these seas in the days of sail. In fact, the current inventory of shipwrecks stands at 111 sites off Cayman shores. Such wrecks are the property of the Crown, so treasure hunters should keep away, but divers and snorkellers are free to explore at their leisure.

Two that are easily visited lie to the west of George Town. The closest to shore, only 50yds (45m) out from Don Foster's in North Church Street, is the **Cali**, a 220ft (67m) Colombian freighter that went down in the 1940s. Lying in 24ft (7m) of water, the *Cali* is now home to a wide variety of marine life, and popular with shore divers and snorkellers alike. Further out, but still in comparatively shallow water at 35ft (10.6m), is the **Balboa**, a 375ft (114m) steam-driven cargo ship which sank during the 1932 hurricane. Its proximity to the port and heavy shipping means that it is not always accessible to divers.

The **Oro Verde**, a Jamaican cargo vessel, went aground in West Bay in 1980 when its crew mutinied on discovering that the cargo of 'bananas' was in fact *ganja*. The boat, left untended, ran aground, and its cargo was washed ashore. The ship was sunk by dive operators in 1983 in 60ft (18m) of water, some 500yds (45m) off the centre of Seven Mile Beach. Now covered in coral, it makes a popular dive both in the daytime and at night.

Although East End has been the site of many a shipwreck over the years, there is only one designated wreck dive in this area, that of the **Methuselam**. Most of the wrecks in this vicinity are either on the reef, so not suitable for diving, or very old and scattered, so not really classified as wreck dives. However, Ocean Frontiers runs a historical maritime snorkel trail which gives the opportunity to take a look at what is left of some of these old ships, including the *Methuselam*, the *Marybelle* and the *Geneva Kathleen*.

A recent addition to the underwater world is the Siren of Sunset Reef (see below).

SNORKELLING, FISHING AND BOAT CHARTERS
Snorkelling
Even the most nervous swimmer can have a go at snorkelling: it's inexpensive, simple – and addictive! An ordinary mask and snorkel are all that is needed to open up a world that can otherwise be scarcely imagined; fins just mean you can go that much faster. If you don't have your own kit, you can always hire it

THE SINKING OF A SIREN
It was on a hot morning in November 2000 that 'Amphitrite, Siren of Sunset Reef' was last seen on land. A 9ft (2.7m) bronze mermaid, the creation of Canadian sculptor Simon Morris, she was brought to Grand Cayman with a view to creating an artificial reef off Sunset House.

In a glare of publicity, the statue was unveiled to the watching crowd. Her simple lines were rapidly marred as she was trussed up in some bizarre form of bondage and hoisted by a crane into the clear waters to the southwest. From this vantage point, poised above the sea, she was slowly lowered until she seemed to be swimming, then escorted by a team from Sunset Divers to her final resting place. Here, in 50ft (15m) of warm, clear water off the southwest coast, she was set free into the underwater world, eventually to form a home for all manner of aquatic creatures. With her bronze sister already attracting divers in the cold waters off British Columbia, it looks as though Amphitrite has drawn the best card.

for around US$10 per day from one of the many dive operators on the island. Do try the equipment on first – it's important that the mask should fit snugly and the fins shouldn't rub or you'll have blisters in next to no time.

Rules and regulations
As with diving, please remember the following:
* If you are diving or snorkelling outside a buoyed swim area or more than 200yds (180m) offshore, display a 'diver down' flag (see page 81), or a white float, light or other marker which is visible from this distance.
* Watch out for boats in the area, particularly in areas of heavy boat traffic.
* Do not touch the coral. Each time you do it affects or damages living creatures.
* Remove nothing from the water. Everything has a purpose and use; every empty shell will become a home for another creature.

Snorkelling sites
You don't have to go far to find good snorkelling on Grand Cayman. In fact, with such good visibility almost throughout the year, many of the dive sites, including some of the wrecks, are also popular with snorkellers. And although you'll always hear of an enticing spot just that bit further on, almost every stretch of beach has its attractions.

On **Seven Mile Beach**, there may be no sand in front of the Marriott, but beach sand is superfluous when just offshore the shallow reef is a haven for countless colourful fish, while delicately waving antennae alert you to the presence of spiny lobsters, presumably as intrigued by us as we are by them. There's good snorkelling in front of the Westin and Indies Suites, too, while further north both Cemetery Reef (see page 139) and the public beach are good spots from which to set off. In West Bay itself, up by the Turtle Farm, the quieter waters mean that you may well have **Turtle Reef** (just offshore from Dive-Tech) to yourself.

At the other end of the bay, in **George Town**, Eden Rock and Devil's Grotto both offer excellent snorkelling, while the wreck of the *Cali* (see page 96) is easily visible from above. To the south the rockier environment of Smith's Cove harbours its own secrets, watched over by the occasional barracuda, though be careful not to accidentally tread on a sea urchin.

To the **north** of the island, at Rum Point, snorkelling is popular. But walk just a little way east on the beach and you'll find yourself nearer to the reef, where squirrelfish move in and out among deep purple sea fans and you may even spot a flat fish or two. And to the **east** of the island, there are any number of secluded spots, each offering almost limitless scope for anyone with a mask and snorkel and time on their hands.

If you're hankering after sites further afield, there are numerous operators who run half- and full-day snorkel trips out to Stingray City and almost anywhere on the reef. Many of these outfits also offer seafood lunch on a full-day trip as part of the deal. Half-day snorkel trips will cost upwards from US$30. In addition, Ocean Frontiers runs guided nature and historical snorkel trips from US$29.

Sandbar at Stingray City

Trips to the sandbar in North Sound, where the water is only 3ft (1m) deep in places, can be arranged through most operators on Grand Cayman for around US$30 per person. Many of the visitors here are passengers on the cruise ships that anchor off George Town, so it can get very busy when the ships are in. That said, practicalities pale into insignificance beside the beauty of the southern stingrays that give this location its name. To share just a few moments with these magical creatures is like dancing in a dream – ignore the crowd and savour it!

Coral Gardens

Full-day snorkel trips make one of their stops at the Coral Gardens in North Sound, where sea fans beckon you to an abundance of coral formations, and multi-coloured fish dart in and out in the shallows. You may even be lucky enough to spot one of the island's turtles, either underwater or as they surface for air.

Further information

The Cayman Island Tourist Board in London (see page 34) issues a *Snorkelling Guide*, which features information on 39 snorkelling sites: 18 on Grand Cayman, 12 on Cayman Brac and 9 on Little Cayman. Of these, all but 15 sites are directly accessible from the beach. For further information, see their website: www.divecayman.ky.

Fishing

The waters off the Cayman Islands offer a tremendous variety of fishing for both experienced anglers and complete novices. Whether your interest is in fly, bone, tarpon, reef, night or big-game fishing, there's likely to be something here that will test your skill. Fully equipped boats can be chartered for almost every type of fishing. Charters are usually for a half or full day, with prices starting from US$300 and rising to a staggering US$1,500, depending on the type of fishing and the specification of the boat. Night fishing is also available through some operators.

No licence is required to fish Cayman waters, but there are stringent conservation laws that restrict fishing in protected areas. It is illegal to take any lobster except the spiny lobster, for which there is a minimum size allowable. No more than 15 conch molluscs may be taken per person per day, or 20 per boat, whichever is the smaller. Turtling is strictly controlled by licence, which may be granted only to Caymanians working in accordance with traditional practices, with further restrictions imposed regarding numbers and season. The use of spearguns by visitors is not permitted.

Fishing from the shore is not permitted in protected areas. Elsewhere, likely catches include small barracuda and bonefish, as well as tarpon and permit.

Deep-sea or sport fishing for blue marlin, yellowfin tuna, wahoo, dolphin and barracuda goes on throughout the year, with fish to be found relatively close to the shore, and almost always within a 20-minute boat ride. That said, certain times of the year are better than others. The best season for wahoo, for example, is said to be November to March, and fish are generally considered to be bigger during the winter and spring.

Reef fishing is best scheduled on a high incoming tide. This is light-tackle angling for fish with an average weight of 1–20lb (0.45–9kg), including snapper, grouper and jack. Conversely, **bonefishing** and **tarpon fishing** are best on a low outgoing tide, particularly in shallow waters of around 6ft (1.8m) such as Grand Cayman's North, South and Frank sounds. Bonefish averaging 3–8lb (1.4–3.6kg) are to be found on the flats of all three islands, while smaller tarpon around 4–5lb (1.8–2.3kg) may also be found in canals or dykes and brackish ponds.

Bottom fishing is popular with novices, including children, who quite often enjoy baiting their own hooks. Use natural baits wherever possible, such as squid or conch, available from Melody Marine in Spinnaker Square, Red Bay, tel: 947 1093, or at any of the supermarkets.

Fly fishing for bonefish, tarpon and permit is another possibility, again in the flats, with guides available, though you would be advised to bring your own tackle.

The highlight of the Cayman sport-fishing year is the annual week-long **International Fishing Tournament**, a sport-fishing jamboree that takes place at the end of April/early May. Organised by the Cayman Islands Angling Club, it's a high-value affair, with significant cash prizes. Registration is open to all comers, who compete, among other accolades, for the heaviest fish caught by a visiting angler. For details of this, or just to check out the local angling scene, contact the Cayman Islands Angling Club at PO Box 30280 SMB, Grand Cayman; tel: 945 6300/949 7099; email: fishing@candw.ky. It's also worth having a look at the fishing page on the Department of Tourism website, www.caymanislands.ky.

Boat operators

Many of the companies that offer boat trips cover both fishing and snorkelling. In addition to those listed below, most of the dive operators (see pages 87–93 also run snorkel trips, as do Cayman Windsurf (see page 104) and Nautilus (see page 146). Neptune's Divers also run fishing trips. Most operators running snorkel trips include use of snorkel, mask and fins as part of the package, and most will arrange collection from your hotel.

Several companies who run snorkel and fishing trips also charter their boats out on a private basis, allowing you to make up your own group for fishing or snorkelling, with the freedom to choose where and when you go, and perhaps the opportunity to sail the boat as well. Many of the larger companies also act as agents for some of the individual boats listed.

Bayside Watersports Morgan's Harbour, West Bay, PO Box 30570 SMB; tel: 949 3200/1750; fax: 949 3700; email: bayside@candw.ky; web: www.cayman.com.ky/com/bayside

Established in 1983, Bayside reckons it is the largest charter-boat booking agent on Grand Cayman, with boats ranging from 25ft (7.6m) to 60ft (18m), and is the only operator to have a truly complete fly-fishing set up. Half- and full-day trips for deep-sea, inside reef, bone, fly, flat and boat fishing. Sunset cruises and sailing charters also available.

Rates Bone, tarpon and fly fishing from US$300 per half-day (up to four anglers, US$50 for each additional person). Deep-sea fishing US$450–800 half day, US$650–1,500 full day, depending on boat. Night shark fishing US$450–1,000 per charter. Half and full-day snorkel trips at US$30/50 may include the chance to watch moray eels and nurse sharks being fed.

Capt Bryan's North Church St, PO Box 31058 SMB, George Town; tel: 945 7197/0038, mobile: 916 2093; fax: 949 2087

Sailing, snorkelling and fishing trips in 50ft (15m) boats. Sunset charters and private snorkel charters also available. Open 7.30am–4.00pm.

Rates Three hours US$30 per person; six hours with lunch US$55 per person.

Capt Crosby's Watersports Coconut Place, West Bay Rd, PO Box 30084 SMB; tel: 945 4049; fax: 945 5994; email: crosby@cayman.org

One of the founders of Stingray City, Captain Crosby takes half- and full-day snorkel trips both here and elsewhere on the island on a 40ft (12m) sailing trimaran, with freshly prepared seafood lunch on offer as well. Bone and reef fishing also offered.

Rates per hour US$12 per person in high season; US$10 in low season. Lunch extra.

Capt Marvin's Water Sports Cayman Falls Shopping Centre and Coconut Place, PO Box 413 WB; tel: 945 4590; UK: 0800 96 9459 ext 3451; US: 800 550 6288 ext 3451; fax: 945 5673; email: captmvn@candw.ky

Another of the original founders of Stingray City, Captain Marvin takes snorkel trips both here and to various wrecks and reefs around the coast, regaling passengers with old seafaring stories. Trips are Mon–Sat. A variety of fishing charters are also available.

Rates per person Snorkel trips half-day US$35, full day with beach lunch US$50. Half-day (3–4 hour) fishing charters: reef/fly US$300–400; tarpon US$350; bottom US$600. Also deep-sea fishing.

Captain Ron Ebanks Coconut Place, West Bay Rd; tel: 945 4340; fax: 945 5531; web: cayman.com.ky/com/fishing

One of the largest fleets of fishing vessels on the island, offering bone, tarpon, reef, night, big-game and deep-sea fishing. Half and full-day snorkel trips on 36ft (12m) trimaran *Mi Boat*, with seafood lunch. Dinner and sunset cruises. Private charters by arrangement. Fishing tackle for rent.

Cayman Delight Cruises Tel: 949 6738/8111/1617

Half-day snorkel trips US$35 per person; children 5–10 half price; under fives free. Book through Andy's Rent-A-Car (see page 73); packages available.

Cayman Holiday Charters Tel: 949 6772

Six-hour snorkel trips with lunch on board their 50ft (15m) sailing trimaran (CI$31 per person), or three-hour trips on this or a 40ft (12m) fishing boat (CI$51 per person). Snorkel gear included. Fishing charters available for deep-sea and bottom fishing.

D&S Charters PO Box 286 SAV; tel: 947 6814, mobile 916 8508

Half- and full-day fishing trips from East End aboard the *Fantasy*, with a maximum of eight people. Also three-hour snorkel trips exploring wrecks or on the reef, and sunset cruises. Private charters available. Pick up and drop off at Morritt's Tortuga.

Rates per person Deep-sea US$150/200; reef US$125/200; snorkelling US$35 (US$40 for wrecks); sunset cruise US$35.

Fantasea Tours PO Box 30654 SMB; tel: 949 2182; fax: 949 5459; email: fantasea@candw.ky

Half-day trips from Cayman Islands Yacht Club to Stingray City and the reef in 38ft (11.6m) sailing catamaran, captained by its Caymanian owner. Complimentary rum punch and snacks.

Rates Adults CI$24; children 6–12 CI$12; children under six free.

Frank's Watersports Coconut Place, West Bay Rd; tel: 945 5491/949 3134; fax: 945 1992. Half- or full-day trips with Capt Frank Ebanks in large motorboats, with complimentary rum punch. Snorkelling to Stingray City, including fresh seafood lunch. Deep-sea, reef, bone and night fishing. Private charters available.

Giga Bite Slip A26, Cayman Islands Yacht Club; tel: 945 4769

Half- or full-day fishing charters.

Rates Deep-sea (US$400/550), bone and reef fishing (US$400/500). Night fishing US$100 per hour.

Gizmo Charters PO Box 131, Hell, West Bay; tel: 916 3799/9024; fax: 949 1146. Big-game fishing aboard the *Gizmo*, with video presentations on board. Maximum four anglers.

Rates Full day (seven hours) US$675; half day (4½ hours) US$550. Night drift fishing (four hours) US$70 per person (maximum six people). Private snorkelling charters US$450 half day (five hours).

Just Fish'n tel: 949 8745, mobile 916 0113; email: justfish@candw.ky. Private charter boat based at the Hyatt Regency dock off West Bay Road, available for full- and half-day charters for reef, deep-sea and bottom fishing.

Ocean Frontiers PO Box 30433 SMB; tel: 947 7500; fax: 947 7600; email: oceanf@candw.ky; web: www.oceanfrontiers.com

In addition to the standard trips to Stingray City and the reef, Ocean Frontiers offers two excursions, each lasting two hours, which appeal to snorkellers, photographers, naturalists and historians. The Eco-Adventure trip features a snorkel and tour through the mangrove forests, with opportunities to see seahorses, queen conch and much else besides, as well as birdwatching for such rarities as whistling ducks and the Cayman parrot. Trips leave from Kaibo Yacht Club; US$39 per person. The Historical Maritime Snorkel Trail visits numerous shipwreck sites around the island, including *HMS Convert* and the *Marybelle*. Trips leave from the Ocean Frontiers dock at East End; US$29 per person. Private charters available.

Oh Boy Charters Cayman Falls Shopping Centre; tel: 949 6341

Half- and full-day trips by motorboat, offering snorkelling or fishing trips (deep-sea, reef, bone and tarpon). Private charters available to Little Cayman, Cayman Brac and Cuba.

Red Baron Charters PO Box 673 GT; tel/fax: 945 4744; mobile: 916 4333; email: redbaron@.cayman.org; web: www.cayman.org/redbaron/

Small-group (2–8 people) charters in the 39ft (11.9m) *Red Baron* allow for passengers to help with the crewing – if they want to. Half- and full-day private charters with snorkelling, and sunset sailing cruises.

Rates Half day US$350; full day US$600; sunset sail US$200. Charters to sister islands and Cuba from US$750 per day, with up to four passengers.

Red Sail Sports Coconut Place, West Bay Rd, PO Box 31473; tel: 945 5965; US: 877 733 7245; fax: 945 5808; email: redsail@candw.ky; web: www.redsail.com

Red Sail's two luxury catamarans – the 65ft (19.8m) *Spirit of Ppalu* and the 62ft (18.9m) *Spirit of Cayman* – sail from the Hyatt dock for two-hour sunset cruises or 3½-hour dinner cruises, and snorkel trips to Stingray City. In the summer season, between April and December, trips may also be taken along Seven Mile Beach. Glass-bottomed boat cruises on the *Coral Queen* run Mon–Sat from Rum Point to Stingray City and the reef.

Rates Sunset cruise US$27.50; dinner cruise US$62; snorkel trip US$65 (catamaran). Children under 12 half price. Glass-bottomed boat snorkel trip US$30 (snorkel equipment additional US$10 per person). Full- and half-day fishing charters for 4–6 people from US$300 for half-day reef fishing to US$700 for full-day deep-sea fishing.

Soto's Cruises PO Box 30192 SMB; tel: 945 4576; fax: 945 3439

Daily half-day trips in 40ft (12.2m) motorboat to Stingray City Sandbar, Coral Gardens and the reef.

Rates Adults CI$30, children under 12 CI$15.

Xanax Sailing Cruises PO Box 1010 GT; tel: 949 1186

Half- and full-day sailing and snorkel cruises, plus sunset dinner cruises with dinner, on a 32ft (9.8m) Erikson yacht. Private charters available on request.

OTHER WATERSPORTS

In addition to diving and snorkelling, the range of other watersports available on the islands is vast.

The usually calm waters inside the reef make **kayaking** a real pleasure, whether you're paddling up and down Seven Mile Beach or exploring the coves of South Sound. Kayaks are available for hire at the public beach on Seven Mile Beach, at South Sound, at Rum Point, and at East End from Cayman Windsurf at Morritt's Tortuga. Expect to pay around US$20 per hour for a single kayak, US$25 per hour for a double.

Sailing dinghies, particularly Waveriders – small plastic-hulled trimarans that demand almost no previous knowledge of sailing – can be launched in minutes and are great fun, though be prepared to get wet! Waveriders are available for hire in a number of locations, both on Seven Mile Beach and in the East End, and will take up to three adults. Just 15 minutes' tuition and you're off.

The Cayman Islands Sailing Club at the bottom of North Sound (not far from Red Bay) offers lessons to visitors and has Lasers and Laser Picos available for hire to recreational sailors at CI$20 per hour. At weekends, the club hosts both sailing races and social events, while during April they organise the annual round-the-island regatta, a three-day event in which boats of all sizes compete to be the fastest to circumnavigate the island. For further information, contact David Carmichael on tel: 947 7913; email: sailing@candw.ky.

At the other end of the spectrum are **sailing charters**, offered by several of the boat operators, some of whom will allow you to help crew the boat. See *Snorkelling, fishing and boat charters*, page 100.

Windsurfing comes into its own off the eastern shores of the island, opposite Morritt's Tortuga. On quiet days, in the shallow waters inside the reef, beginners can learn in calm, confined conditions with a steady wind, but when the wind is up, they would do better to head for the more sheltered waters to the west. That, however, is when experienced windsurfers come into their own, taking advantage of a narrow gap in the reef to surf the waves beyond. No guarantees, but if you're looking for the stronger winds then November to March is the time to be here. *The* place to go for windsurfing in the East End is Cayman Windsurf, while Sailboard Caribbean handle windsurfing off Seven Mile Beach.

The sight of colourful parachutes skudding along 400ft (122m) up just off the beach is pretty tantalising. Three or four different companies offer **parasailing** along Seven Mile Beach. Participants may go up singly or in pairs, weight permitting. Just walk along the beach until you find one of the booths where parasailing is on offer, or contact an operator from the list below. Rates are around US$60 per person single, or US$100 double.

Jetbikes or **jet skis,** also known as **waverunners**, can be hired both on Seven Mile Beach and at Rum Point for around US$50 per half hour. Capable of speeds up to 15mph (24km/h), they can cause considerable damage in the wrong hands, so do read the rules before you set off. Penalties for infringement are strict, including fines or even imprisonment.

Waterskiing is available both on Seven Mile Beach and at Rum Point, through Red Sail Sports. A 15-minute session costs US$40. Waterskiing is permitted only within specifically designated watersports areas, as shown on pages 106–7. Boats must always have two crew members, in addition to the skier. Further options include **tubing**, **paddleboats** and **banana boat** rides.

Operators

Cayman Windsurf PO Box 866 GT, East End; tel: 947 7492; fax: 947 6763; email: cawin@candw.ky

The original windsurfing operator on Grand Cayman, Bruno Schermuly's company is based at Morritt's Tortuga on the eastern end of the island, and is open to all visitors. A full windsurfing service is offered here, including tuition at all levels, plus rentals – on or off site – of the latest BiC performance boards and a range of sails. For sailors – or indeed would-be sailors – there is a fleet of bright yellow Waveriders, while other rentals include ocean kayaks, snorkel gear and bicycles. The operation has recently expanded to include snorkel trips. Open daily 9.00am–5.00pm.

Rates per hour Windsurfer US$35, sailboat US$40, single kayak US$15, double kayak US$25; waverunner US$50 (¹/₂ hour). Snorkel equipment US$10 per day, float (raft) US$10 per day. Windsurfing tuition from US$45 for an introductory lesson; sailboat tuition US$35. Three-day packages at US$150 give unlimited access to kayaks, floats (rafts) and either sailboats or windsurfers. Other prices on request.

D&S Charters PO Box 286 SAV; tel: 947 6814, mobile 916 8508

Waterskiing and tubing off East End, with pick up and drop off at Morritt's Tortuga. *Rates per half hour* Waterskiing US$50; tubing US$30.

Parasailing Professionals Tel: 949 8100, mobile: 916 2953

Operates anywhere on Seven Mile Beach.

Rates US$60 per person or US$100 per pair.

Red Sail Sports Seven Mile Beach tel: 947 8745/8732; Rum Point tel: 947 9203/949 9098

A broad range of watersports is offered by Red Sail, with equipment for hire, including snorkelling gear.

Rates Sailboat US$25 per hour; kayak US$20–25 per hour; paddleboat US$20 per hour. Waterskiing US$40 per 15-minute session (tuition available at US$65 for 25 minutes); tubing US$15 for ten minutes; waverunner US$50 single, US$65 double. Parasailing on Seven Mile Beach costs US$60 single, US$100 double. Snorkel gear US$15 per day.

Sailboard Caribbean PO Box 30246; tel/fax: 949 1068, mobile: 916 0903; email: windsurf@candw.ky

Based at the public beach on Seven Mile Beach, Sailboard Caribbean is a bit of a misnomer, since the company rents out all sorts of beach toys, with tuition available. Owner Jay also has plans to offer kayaking trips in the mangrove swamps, so do ask him about this.

Rates per hour Windsurfer US$25–30; Waverider sailboat US$30; ocean kayak US$15 (single), US$20 (tandem). Jetski per half hour: single US$50, double US$65. Parasailing per half hour: single US$60; tandem US$50 per person.

HORSERIDING

Unlikely though it may sound, horseriding up in West Bay is well worth fitting in, even if it's not something you'd normally consider. Cantering along a deserted beach where stingrays swim among the turtle grass has to be one of the highlights of a trip here, while walking back past mangrove swamps alive with carpet sea anemones offers an opportunity to see a side to the island that one might otherwise fear had long since fallen to the hands of the developers.

On the practical side, wear long trousers and shoes, not sandals, and bring sunscreen and a camera. Hard hats are not provided by any of the outfits below. On average, a ride lasts around an hour and a half. Experience is not necessary – these horses are pretty forgiving, and the ability of each rider, including children, is assessed in advance. All three companies will collect riders from the vicinity of Seven Mile Beach.

Honeysuckle Trail Rides Tel: 947 7976, mobile: 916 3363; fax: 947 1051

Guided rides, including sunset tours, cost from US$60 per person for a non-private ride, walking only, to US$80 per person for a private ride, where riders may choose from walking through to galloping. Weight limit approximately 275lb (123kg). Both English and Western tack are available. Disabled riders can be accommodated by appointment, as can large groups.

Nicki's Beach Rides PO Box 10749 APO; tel: 947 5839, mobile: 916 3530

Groups of up to four people are escorted on early morning or afternoon rides, both along the beach and inland. Nicki was brought up in Grand Cayman and her enthusiasm for the island is infectious. With her raft of anecdotes about life here, and her in-depth knowledge of the local flora and fauna, this is an outing that far outlasts your hour and a half in the saddle. Weight limit approximately 200lb (90kg). US$75 per person.

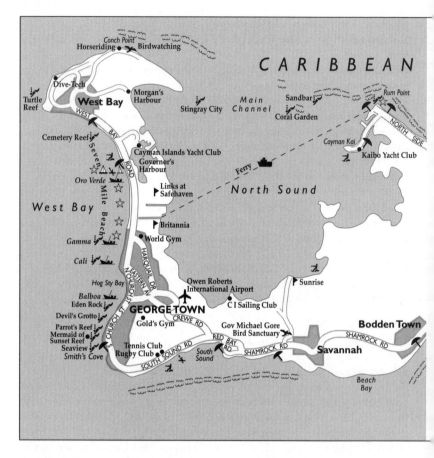

Pampered Ponies PO Box 455, West Bay; tel: 945 2262; web: www.ponies.ky
In addition to daily beach and trail rides, Pampered Ponies, who work closely with
Nicki's, above, offer early morning and sunset rides, and escorted beach rides at full
moon each month for up to four people. Spanish spoken. US$100 per rider.

OTHER SPORTS
Golf
Grand Cayman has two world-class golf courses, both just opposite Seven Mile
Beach, and both offering a challenge to amateur and professional golfers alike.
There is also a family golf centre beyond George Town towards North Sound.

Britannia Golf Club PO Box 1588; tel: 949 8020
The only Jack Nicklaus designed course in the Caribbean, the links-style Britannia is
set back from West Bay Road behind the Hyatt, overlooking North Sound to the east.
With palm trees set atop the bunkers and tropical birds for background noise, it's
something of a golfer's paradise. The course is effectively two courses in one: the 9-
hole regulation course is 3,202yds (par 35) and the 18-hole executive course, or short

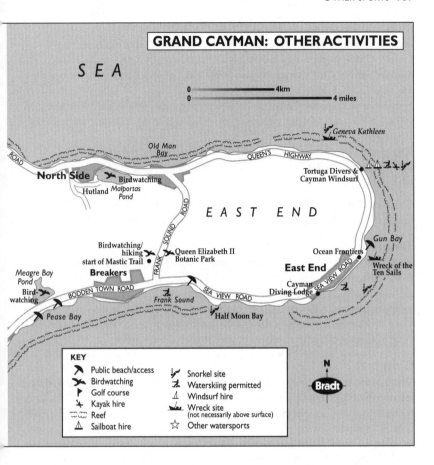

GRAND CAYMAN: OTHER ACTIVITIES

SEA

0 ———————— 4km
0 ———————— 4 miles

Geneva Kathleen

Old Man Bay

QUEEN'S HIGHWAY

North Side Birdwatching

Hutland *Malportas Pond*

Tortuga Divers & Cayman Windsurf

EAST END

Birdwatching/ hiking start of Mastic Trail ● Queen Elizabeth II Botanic Park

Gun Bay

Ocean Frontiers

Breakers

East End

Meagre Bay Pond

Wreck of the Ten Sails

Bird-watching

BODDEN TOWN ROAD

Cayman Diving Lodge

SEA VIEW ROAD

Frank Sound

Pease Bay

Half Moon Bay

KEY

➤	Public beach/access	ʅ	Snorkel site
⤡	Birdwatching	⟲	Waterskiing permitted
▶	Golf course	△	Windsurf hire
⚓	Kayak hire	⟱	Wreck site (not necessarily above surface)
∿	Reef	☆	Other watersports
△	Sailboat hire		

N

Bradt

course, is 2,847yds (par 57). The 18-hole regulation (championship) course is 6,206yds (par 70). For the 18-hole courses, allow 3 hours and 4½ hours respectively. Electric golf carts are compulsory, and a strict dress code is enforced, although tailored short trousers are permitted. Resident professional, with lessons available on request. Tee off from 8.00am. Guests at the Hyatt may reserve tee times up to 48 hours in advance; other players may make reservations up to 24 hours in advance. Golf shop open 7.30am–6.00pm.

Rates Green fees per person, low/high season US$30–50/$40–60 (November to May) for Hyatt guests, US$40–65/$50–80 for other players. Note that high season here is defined as November 1 to May 31.

The Links at Safehaven PO Box 1311GT; tel: 949 5988; fax: 949 5457

This 18-hole championship golf course off West Bay Road on the edge of North Sound is par 71, 6,605yds. Built to USGA standards (rating 75.1), it offers a challenge to both amateur and professional golfers. Electric golf carts are compulsory, and a strict dress code is enforced. Aqua driving range. Resident professional. Tee off from 7.30am. Members may book up to 48 hours in advance; other players 24 hours in advance (four players maximum). Patio bar and restaurant. Golf shop open 7.00am–6.00pm.

Rates Green fees per person: 9 holes US$65; 18 holes US$100. Package rates also available. Aquarange US$6 (50 balls), US$12 (110 balls). Club rental from US$15. Lessons US$36.50 per half hour.

Sunrise Family Golf Centre PO Box 10940 APO, Sunrise Landing, Savannah; tel: 947 4653; email: Sunrise1@candw.ky

Located some 15 minutes' drive east of George Town, this 9-hole, par 3 (per hole) golf course also has a full-length driving range and clubhouse. Pull carts are available. Golf shop open 7.30am–6.30pm.

Rates Green fees adults CI$17, juniors CI$8. Driving range CI$5 (small bucket), or CI$7 (large bucket). Golf lessons US$25 per half hour, US$45 per hour. Club rental adults CI$8, Junior CI$4.

There is a **mini-golf** centre just beyond the entrance to the Hyatt Regency, heading north along West Bay Road. Open 4.00–11.00pm daily.

Tennis

Many hotels have their own tennis courts. In addition, there is the Cayman Islands Tennis Club, located just behind the rugby club on South Sound Road, tel: 949 9464. This is an active club, with resident professionals, regular tournaments, and the occasional masterclass run by celebrities such as Jim Courier. Visitors may play at the club up to 5.00pm at a cost of CI$5 per person. Annual membership for residents costs CI$200, plus a joining fee of CI$200.

Gym

Many of the top hotels have their own gyms open to residents. In addition, there are two gyms open to visitors. **World Gym** on Harquail Drive, tel: 949 5132, is set back from the road opposite the cinema and next to Bed restaurant. The gym is well equipped, with personal trainers on hand, daily aerobic classes and massage as well. Daily and weekly passes are available, as well as long-term membership. Open Mon–Fri, 5.30am–10.00pm; Sat/Sun 9.00am–6.00pm. Prices are CI$12 for a day pass, CI$25 for a three-day pass, and CI$35 for a week.

The recently opened **Gold's Gym** is located at Pasadora Place on Smith Road, George Town, tel: 949 7016. As well as the full range of exercise equipment, the gym has a nutrition store where you can find various vitamins and supplements, plus clothing and accessories. Open Mon–Thu 5.00am–10.00pm; Fri 5.00am–9.00pm; Sat 8.00am–6.00pm; Sun 8.00am–4.00pm. Prices are CI$12 for a day pass, or CI$35 for a week.

Rugby

The popular Cayman Islands Rugby Club is located at South Sound, just east of George Town, tel: 949 7960. Matches are played most weekends, and spectators are welcome.

HIKING AND BIRDWATCHING

The major hiking trail on Grand Cayman is the Mastic Trail (see page 161). There are numerous other possibilities for hikers, however, particularly towards the eastern end of the island where tracts of woodland and open countryside remain undisturbed, and little-known caves are rarely visited other than by the resident bats. Don't expect marked paths, though – this is relatively uncharted and challenging terrain.

It's a good idea to take a guided walk first, if only so that you can identify Cayman's poisonous trees and take evasive action. A visit to the botanic park is also highly recommended – it's a lovely place to spend a morning, and the self-guided woodland trail offers another opportunity to recognise various native trees. For guided walks, including the Mastic Trail, contact Silver Thatch Excursions, tel: 945 6588, fax: 949 3342, email: silvert@hotmail.com, web: www.silverthatch.ky.

Before you set off on your own, get hold of a copy of the relevant 1:25,000 Ordnance Survey map and plan your route, preferably telling someone where you're going. You'll need strong shoes as the terrain can be very unforgiving. Take plenty of water and some good insect repellent, particularly in the rainy season – Cayman mosquitoes can be voracious.

The best times to see birds are in the early hours of the morning or a couple of hours before sunset. A good place to start is the botanic park, where all the island's landbirds have been spotted, and a good proportion of the aquatics as well. Similarly, the Mastic Trail is an excellent place for birdwatching, with some unexpected sightings at any time of the year. For aquatic birds, Meagre Bay Pond just to the east of Bodden Town is a good venue, as are Governor Michael Gore Bird Sanctuary and the bird sanctuary in West Bay by Pappagallo's restaurant. To see the West Indian whistling-duck, head for Willie Ebanks' farm in North Side. Malportas Pond at the edge of the farm is a haven for this species, Cayman's only native duck.

Keen birdwatchers are welcome to join the Cayman Islands Bird Club on one of their regular outings, usually on Saturday mornings. Contact John Benbow 945 5348 or 949 7554, or approach the National Trust, tel: 949 0121. Alternatively, call Silver Thatch (see above) and get the first-hand benefit of Geddes Hislop's years of experience on a guided birdwatching trip, perhaps on the Mastic Trail. Pick up is at 6.00am, returning at around 11.00am.

Patricia E Bradley's *Birds of the Cayman Islands* (see *Further Reading*, page 224) not only covers around 200 species to be seen on the islands, but also gives details of the best locations for birdwatching as well. A handy checklist derived from the book is also available from bookshops and gift shops for CI$3.

George Town and Seven Mile Beach

Mention Grand Cayman to almost anyone who has been there, and it is usually Seven Mile Beach that springs first to mind. This seemingly endless stretch of white-sand beach effectively forms the centre of Grand Cayman's highly sophisticated tourist industry. George Town, by contrast, could pass for a small seaside resort town, the clapboard houses that line the small harbour hardly being the stuff of which financial capitals are made. Yet here, too, there is much to attract the visitor. While Seven Mile Beach has the hotels and upmarket shops, George Town has the history and the sense of place that, taken together, serve to make Cayman unique. A duty-free shopping emporium par excellence, yes, but somehow George Town seems to have taken this on board and still retained a character of its own.

WHERE TO STAY

The whole range of accommodation is available on Grand Cayman, with the most expensive and luxurious hotels situated on Seven Mile Beach. Pressure on building land here is huge, with land prices, at over US$50,000 per foot, some of the highest in the world. The most beautiful area of Seven Mile Beach is to the north, but hotels to the south have the added advantage of easy proximity to George Town. Places on the southern side of George Town tend to be smaller and more secluded, though the occasional aircraft coming in to land may disturb your afternoon siesta. For accommodation in West Bay, including the northern end of Seven Mile Beach, see page 148. For elsewhere on the island, see pages 158, 163, 165 and 166. For an alphabetical list of all accommodation, see *Appendix 1*, page 221. All prices quoted are subject to 10% government accommodation tax unless otherwise stated.

Hotels

Almost all hotels, villas and guesthouses have en-suite bathrooms, and most offer a wide range of facilities for the tourist. The larger hotels are also geared to the business traveller, with well-equipped business centres and conference suites. Note that, in common with most hotels throughout the world, telephone calls made from your room and use of internet services at your hotel will cost significantly more than from payphones or external internet cafés. Given the ease with which you can pay by phonecard or credit card (see

Telephones, fax and internet, pages 61–2), it is simple to avoid these charges without the hassle of finding a public telephone. Note, too, that room safes may be subject to an additional daily charge of around US$2.50 – an iniquitous practice that really ought to be challenged.

Luxury

Holiday Inn PO Box 30620 SMB, 1590 West Bay Rd; tel: 946 4433, US toll free 800 HOLIDAY; fax: 946 4434; email: hicayman@candw.ky; web: www.holiday-inn.com (231 rooms)
Opened at the end of 2000, the Holiday Inn is located on the opposite side of the road to Seven Mile Beach, close to the public beach, and makes little concession to the Caribbean environment. The predominantly Jamaican staff are friendly and helpful, though, and facilities for the disabled are excellent. Rooms each have one king-size or two double beds, and include AC, minibar, TV and telephone. Mangrove Grill, bar, business centre, car rental, lobby shop, laundry. Swimming pool, beach bar, massage centre, snack bar and dive shop on beach, fitness centre. Diving/watersports through Red Sail Sports.
Rates For one or two people per night, low/high season: island view US$99/250; ocean view US$129/280; one-bedroom suite US$360/560; two-bedroom suite US$459/800. Additional adult US$20 per night. All rates subject to 10% service charge.
Hyatt Beach Club (50 suites)
The Hyatt Beach Club has none of the elegance of the Regency, but makes up for this with a superb location right on Seven Mile Beach. On-site watersports through Red Sail Sports. For all other details, see Hyatt Regency below.
Hyatt Regency PO Box 1588 GT; West Bay Rd; tel: 949 1234, US toll free 800 55 HYATT; fax: 949 8528; web: www.hyatt.com (289 rooms, including 50 villas and beachfront suites at Hyatt Beach Club)
Set back from West Bay Road amid palm-lined lawns and cooling fountains, the colonial style of the Hyatt Regency oozes calm and luxury as you pass through its gates. Located in the grounds of the Britannia Golf Club, just three miles north of George Town and 20 minutes from the airport, it is just a short walk across the integral bridge to Seven Mile Beach and the Hyatt Beach Club. All rooms have one king or two double beds, AC, bath and shower, TV, minibar and safe. Island or golf/courtyard views available. Four restaurants, including Garden Loggia, Hemingways and Bamboo, plus several bars. Six swimming pools, whirlpools and swim-up bar; floodlit tennis courts, Jack Nicklaus-designed golf course, fitness centre and beauty spa, variety of shops. Diving and other watersports, including own marina, through Red Sail Sports. Supervised activities for children 3–12 years. Car and moped rental. Business, conference and banqueting facilities.
Rates per room per night: low season US$210–1,350; high season US$375–1,990. All rates subject to 10% gratuity.
Marriott Beach Resort PO Box 30371, West Bay Rd; tel: 949 0088, US toll free 800 228 9290; fax: 949 0288; email: marriott@candw.ky; web: www.marriott.com (309 rooms, 4 suites)
The Marriott's beachfront location on Seven Mile Beach has been somewhat marred by erosion of the beach at this point. Visitors are currently being bussed further north to the beach adjacent to one of its sister hotels, the Westin Casuarina or the Holiday

Inn. Negotiations are underway with the environment agency on the best way to restore the beach. The hotel remains elegant, however, from palm-edged fountains to wrought-iron bar stools. Each room has AC, telephone, TV and minibar. Swimming pool and whirlpool, exercise room and jogging trail. Diving and watersports through Red Sail Sports. Restaurants and bars, including The Grille, which is open for breakfast 7.00–11.00am, and Peninsula. Gift shop and boutiques.

Rates per room per night, low/high season: standard US$175/254; partial ocean view US$200/303; oceanfront US$240/375, one-bedroom suite US$600/750, two-bedroom suite US$900/1100. Additional person US$15 per night, up to maximum of four (six in deluxe studio). For single occupancy deduct US$10 per night. Two-bedroom and master suites, sleeping six and four people respectively, are US$260/365 per suite per night. A hefty surcharge is payable for the two-week Christmas period. All rates subject to 10% service charge.

Ritz Carlton When it opens in mid 2002, after considerable controversy, the Ritz Carlton on West Bay Rd will be the first five-star hotel on the island, with a projected 366 rooms, incorporating 71 condominiums, and a nine-hole golf course.

Westin Casuarina PO Box 30620 SMB, West Bay Rd; tel: 945 3800, US toll free 800 228 3000; fax: 945 3804; email: salesing@candw.ky; web: www.westincasuarina.com (343 rooms, 4 suites)

This elegant if somewhat labyrinthine hotel is set right on Seven Mile Beach, its old-world décor masking thoroughly modern facilities. Each room has TV, minibar, ceiling fan, safe and marble bathroom, and most have French doors with balconies. Two restaurants, La Casa Havana and Ferdinand's. Two swimming pools, swim-up bar, tennis, fitness centre. Diving and other watersports through Red Sail Sports. Hair and beauty salons; jewellery and gift shops. Two boardrooms and meeting facilities.

Rates per room per night, low/high season, based on single or double occupancy: island view US$195/390; ocean view US$225/440; oceanfront US$278/500, deluxe oceanfront US$332/550, one-bedroom suite US$700/1,000, two-bedroom suite US$900/1,500. Deluxe suite US$1,325/1,950. Additional person US$25 per night. Prices during the two-week Christmas period are heavily inflated. All rates subject to 10% service charge.

Medium class

Comfort Suites and Resort PO Box 30238 SMB, West Bay Rd; tel: 945 7300, US toll free 800 517 4000; fax: 945 7400; email: comfort@candw.ky; web: www.caymancomfort.com (110 suites)

This newly opened hotel with a rather drab exterior offers studio and deluxe studio rooms, plus apartments, each with kitchen, living area, TV and safe. Rooms are also available for the disabled. Gift/dive shop, fitness centre, business centre, conference rooms, laundry, swimming pool; games room, scuba centre, poolside restaurant (Stingers) and bar. There's direct access to the beach from the pool via a narrow path, but note that shifting sands mean that the water now comes right up to the wall – fine for swimmers but not much good for lazing on the beach. Just to the right there's good snorkelling – be careful not to disturb the reef. Prices include continental breakfast – of the buffet, throwaway style. Diving (Don Foster's). Other watersports by arrangement.

Rates (including complimentary breakfast) for two people per night, low/high season: studio US$160/240; deluxe studio US$175/255; one-bedroom suite US$190/275. Additional person US$15 per night, up to maximum of four (six in deluxe studio). For single occupancy deduct US$10 per night. Two-bedroom and master suites, sleeping six and four people respectively, are US$260/365 per suite per night. A surcharge of US$15 per room is payable at Christmas. All rates subject to 10% service charge. Dive packages available.

Grand Caymanian Golf Resort PO Box 30610 SMB, Crystal Harbour at SafeHaven; tel: 949 3100, US toll free 1 888 452 4545; fax: 949 3161; email: info@grandcaymanian.ky; web: www.grandcaymanian.ky (132 suites/villas)
Located on North Sound with direct access to the neighbouring Links at Safehaven golf course, the resort has a sandy area for beach games etc, but the coast here is ironshore so a shuttle bus ferries guests to a private stretch of Seven Mile Beach a couple of miles away. One-bedroom suites and two-bedroom villas have king-size beds, kitchen, bathroom, AC, private balconies and computer data ports. Daily maid service.
Rates per unit per night, low/high season: standard room US$120/145 (two people); suite US$175/215 (four people); villa US$265–330/330–410 (six people). Hefty increase over the two-week Christmas period.

Indies Suites PO Box 2070 GT, Foster Drive, West Bay Rd; tel: 945 5025, US toll free 800 654 3130; fax: 945 5024; email: indiessuites@worldnet.att.net (40 suites)
Situated opposite Seven Mile Beach, the family-owned Indies Suites with its distinctive blue roof is five miles from George Town. Each suite has one king size or two double beds, AC, kitchen, bathroom, living room with sofa bed, TV, balcony or patio. Facilities include swimming pool and jacuzzi, with poolside bar and parties. Dive courses with Red Sail Sports. Beach access across the road.
Rates (including complimentary breakfast): low season US$180–215; high season US$299–360. Packages available for divers and non-divers alike.

Sammy's Airport Inn PO Box 10646 APO, Owen Roberts Drive, George Town; tel: 945 2100 fax: 945 2330 (60 rooms)
Located very close to the airport, Sammy's is a modern hotel owned by Best Western, and is ideal for business travellers on a short visit. Simple rooms have TV and AC. Shirley's restaurant (see below), bar, swimming pool. Free shuttle bus to the airport.
Rates per room: low season US$120; high season US$125 plus 20%.

Sleep Inn PO Box 30111 SMB, West Bay Rd; tel: 949 9111, US toll free 800 SLEEP INN; fax: 949 6699; email: sleepinn@candw.ky; web: www.sleepinn.com/hotel (115 rooms suites)
This modern, rather dull hotel at the southern end of Seven Mile Beach is very close to George Town and minutes away from Seven Mile Beach. Rooms, including those for the disabled, have queen-size bed, AC, shower, fridge/microwave, TV, safe and telephone. Superior rooms and junior suites also have a sofa bed and a view of the pool or garden. Laundry available. Swimming pool, pool bar, grill and dive shop/boutique, with watersports and deep-sea fishing available through Treasure Island Divers.
Rates (including complimentary breakfast) for two people per night, low/high season: standard US$109/130; superior US$120/145; junior suite US$145/175. Additional person US$15 per night, up to maximum of four (two in standard rooms). For single

occupancy deduct US$10 per night. A surcharge is payable at Christmas. All rates subject to 10% service charge.

Sunshine Suites PO Box 30095 SMB; 1112 West Bay Rd; tel: 949 3000, US toll free 877 786 1110; fax: 949 1200; email: mail@sunshinesuites.com; web: www.sunshinesuites.com (132 suites)

Opposite the Westin on West Bay Rd, behind Cayman Falls Plaza, this three-storey yellow-painted complex is in a peaceful location well back from the road, but within easy reach of Seven Mile Beach. Wooden outside steps lead to light, airy rooms with a personal touch. Studios, deluxe suites and one-bedroom suites all have living/dining area, kitchenette (no oven), TV and telephone. Swimming pool, picnic areas with barbecues, laundry, dive lockers. Executive boardroom with seating for 14 delegates. Meals are available to guests by agreement with nearby Eats Café and Legendz Bar and Lounge. Diving and fishing with Fisheye or Captain Marvin's.

Rates per person per night, low/high season: studio US$130/195; deluxe US$150/220; one-bedroom US$170/240. Additional person US$20 per night, up to maximum of four (two in studio suites). Children under 12 stay free in parent's room. Limited maid service.

Treasure Island Resort PO Box 1817 GT, 269 West Bay Rd; tel: 949 7777; fax: 949 8672; email: admintir@candw.ky; web: www.treasureislandresort.net. US: 225 E Dania Beach Bd, Suite 210, Dania Beach, FL33004; tel: toll free 800 203 0775, 945 924 1515; fax: 945 924 1511; email: tir@vacationplaces.com (281 rooms)

At the southern end of Seven Mile Beach, just a mile from George Town, this rather functional-looking hotel is surrounded by artificial rock gardens complete with several waterfalls. All rooms have two double beds, or one king-size, with AC/ceiling fan, TV, telephone, safe, patio or balcony. Billy Bones snack bar. Hook's restaurant. Two swimming pools, one with swim-up bar; tennis and beach volleyball; bicycle hire. Watersports include diving through Bob Soto, with deep-sea fishing, sailing and windsurfing by arrangement. Duty-free, dive and souvenir shops, plus beauty salon. A steel band plays in the open-plan lobby Mon–Sat 6.30–8.00pm.

Rates per room, per night, based on single/double occupancy, low/high season: standard US$155/220; pool view US$170/240; partial ocean view US$190/260. Christmas season supplement. Additional person US$30 per night, up to maximum of four (two in studio suites). Children 17 and under stay free in parent's room. All rates subject to 10% gratuity.

All-inclusive resorts

Beach Club Hotel & Dive Resort PO Box 903 GT, West Bay Rd; tel: 949 8100, US toll free 800 482 DIVE; fax: 945 5167; email: cayresv@candw.ky; web: www.caymanresorthotels.com (41 rooms)

This complex of Caribbean-style villas on the beach is an all-inclusive resort, under the same ownership as Spanish Bay Reef (see page 149). Prices include breakfast, lunch, snacks and dinner, plus unlimited bar drinks (excluding wine and champagne), all non-motorised watersports and shore diving, dive equipment except wetsuits, taxes, gratuities and airport transfers. A shuttle service runs between here and Spanish Bay. All rooms have AC, TV, bath and shower, balcony or terrace. Superior and oceanfront rooms are also available. Small swimming pool, beach bar and restaurant (the latter both open to the public); tennis court. Wide range of watersports and diving. Evening live entertainment.

Rates per person per night, based on double occupancy, low/high season: standard US$180/375; superior US$200/420; oceanfront US$225/465. For single occupancy double these rates. Children under six free (maximum two per room); under 12 US$50 per night (boat dives not included). Extra person US$150 per night. Dive supplement: daily two-tank dive add US$66 per day. Wedding packages available.

Dive lodges

Most of Grand Cayman's dive lodges are located away from the bustle of Seven Mile Beach, just to the south of George Town where there is good shore diving. Most of the guests are here for the diving, and appreciate facilities such as dive lockers, rinse tanks and drying racks for their kit. See also Cayman Diving Lodge at East End, page 166.

Coconut Harbour PO Box 2086 GT, South Church St; tel: 949 7468; fax: 949 7117; US 1315 North Arlington Av, Indianapolis, IN 46219; tel: toll free 800 552 6281; 317 322 9920; fax: 317 322 1885; email: coccayman@aol.com (35 rooms)
A favourite with divers, Coconut Harbour is situated on the waterfront, approximately a mile or so south of George Town. Single and double en-suite studios each with their own entrance have AC/fan, TV, telephone and kitchenette. Swimming pool and jacuzzi. Dive shop in hotel grounds, and diving from the landing in front of the hotel – there's no beach. With Waldo's Reef just 20 yards (18m) offshore, shore diving is a must! Blue Parrot restaurant and bar.
Rates Two-tank dive packages in low season from US$378 for three nights with pool view, to US$1,077 for seven nights with sea view. Non-divers US$243–672. Prices subject to 10% gratuity. Airport transfers US$17 per person.
Seaview Hotel and Dive Centre PO Box 260 GT; tel: 945 0558; fax: 945 0559; email: seadive@candw.ky (15 rooms)
Built in 1952, and said to be 'the oldest and cheapest on the island', the Seaview has for years been popular with the diving fraternity, who come back time and again. In 2000, it was taken over and has since been given a new lease of life. A cheerful yellow and blue building, it is situated on the waterfront (no beach), approximately ten minutes south of George Town. There's easy access to the varied dive sites of the west coast, north wall and South Sound, with good shore diving from the resort itself. En-suite twin rooms have one double or two twin beds with AC and telephone. Spacious reception/bar area. Restaurant (Naked Fish). Large salt water pool. Live music Wed. Bob Soto's diving.
Rates per night low/high season: single US$90/100; double US$100/110. All-inclusive dive packages available on request.
Sunset House PO Box 479 GT, South Church St, George Town; tel: 888 281 3826; US toll free 800 854 4767; fax: 949 7101; email: sunsethouse@sunsethouse.com; web: www.sunsethouse.com (59 rooms)
Sunset House claims to be the only resort in the Cayman Islands 'designed by divers, operated by divers, for divers'. Be that as it may, it's certainly diver orientated, with a 95% diving clientele, many of whom return year after year. All rooms have private bathroom,

AC, TV, radio alarm and telephone. Courtyard rooms have two double beds or one king or two twin beds plus shared balcony; oceanview rooms have two double beds, ceiling fans, private balcony; suites also have living/dining area with sofa and fridge; apartments also have kitchenette and dining room (but no fan). Swimming pool, outside bar. Seaharvest restaurant and bar. And for photographers, this is the home of Cathy Church's Photo Centre (see page 135), so advice, equipment and film developing are right on hand. *Rates* per room per night (two people, low/high season): courtyard US$130/165; ocean view US$165/210; apartment US$185/250.

Two-tank dive packages low/high season from US$572/674.50 for three nights with courtyard view, to US$1,656/1,931.50 for seven nights with sea view. Non-divers from US$422/524.50 to US$1,226/1,501.50. All prices subject to 10% gratuity.

Guesthouses

Adams Guest House 84 Melmac Av; tel: 949 2512; fax: 949 0919 (6 rooms)
Mary Adams has for 11 years welcomed visitors to her guesthouse, offering simple accommodation with cooking facilities. Located just off South Church Street, it is about halfway between George Town and Smith's Cove. Each room has a private bathroom, TV and AC/ceiling fan. The three rooms with private entrance also have a fridge and toaster/microwave; those in the adjoining building share a kitchen with washer/dryer, dining room and living room, all with ceiling fans. Laundry, barbecue, picnic tables and telephone. Babysitting available on request.
Rates per room per night: low/high season US$85/95. No personal cheques. Maid service included.

Annie's Place PO Box 616 GT, 282 Andrew Drive, Snug Harbour; tel: 945 5505; fax: 945 4547; email: ampm@candw.ky; web: www.anniesplace.ky (2 rooms)
A few minutes' walk from Seven Mile Beach, and three miles from George Town, this comfortable home-from-home has rooms with en-suite bathroom, AC/ceiling fan, TV and safe. Guest laundry; use of telephone and fax by arrangement. Full European or American breakfast is included in the room price, and is taken in the dining room or screened courtyard.
Rates per room per night, low/high season: single room US$65–80/90, double room US$85–100/110.

Eldemire's Guest House PO Box 482 GT, Pebbles Way, South Church St; tel: 949 5387; fax: 949 6987; email: tootie@eldemire.com; web: www.eldemire.com (13 units)
Located close to Coconut Harbour, which was originally owned by Erma Eldemire and her late husband Wellesley, the guesthouse is just half a mile from Smith's Cove. All rooms, plus standard and deluxe studios and apartment, have a private bathroom and AC/ceiling fans; the studios and apartment have kitchen facilities.
Rates per night, low/high season: double room US$75/85; studio US$90/100; apartment US$100/110. Maid service included. No credit cards or personal cheques.

Self-catering villas and apartments

There are numerous villas, apartments and condominiums to let throughout Grand Cayman. Many of these are available through **Cayman Villas** (PO Box 681, Grand Cayman; tel: 947 4144, fax: 949 7471; email: cayvilla@candw.ky;

web: www.caymanvillas.com) whose office is on Owen Roberts Drive at the airport. Open Mon–Fri 9.00am–5.00pm. Others may be rented through various dive outfits, including **Ocean Frontiers** (PO Box 30433 SMB; tel: 947 7500; fax: 947 7600; email: oceanf@candw.ky; US tel: 561 477 6941; toll free 800 544 6576; fax: 800 886 1509; email: oceanf@adelphia.net; web: www.oceanfrontiers.com). Overseas, several tour operators feature a selection of self-catering accommodation (see pages 37–40).

The following is a small selection of the properties available on Seven Mile Beach:

Anchorage Condominiums PO Box 1589, West Bay Rd; tel: 945 4088; fax: 945 5001 (15 villas)
Located at the north end of Seven Mile Beach, these two-bedroom, two-bathroom villas each have kitchen, AC, TV, telephone and balcony or screened porch overlooking the beach; some also have a third room. Daily maid service and laundry facilities. Swimming pool, tennis.
Rates per night, low/high season: garden view US$160/255; oceanfront US$245/370. Additional guests US$20/30 per night. All rates subject to 5% gratuity.
Avalon Condominiums PO Box 31236 SMB, West Bay Rd; tel: 945 4171; fax: 945 4189; email: avalon_c@candw.ky (14 villas)
Also located at the north end of Seven Mile Beach, each of these seafront three-bedroom villas has three bathrooms, AC, kitchen, TV, telephone and screened balcony, plus private garage. Daily maid service. Swimming pool, fitness centre.
Rates per villa per night, low/high season: US$430–650 (one to four people), US$490–725 (five to six people). Christmas US$775. All rates subject to 6% gratuity.
Caribbean Club PO Box 30499 SMB, West Bay Rd; tel: 945 4099, US toll free 800 327 8777; fax: 945 4443; email: reservations@caribclub.com; web: www.caribclub.com (18 villas)
This colonial-style complex of individual pink villas or cottages running down to Seven Mile Beach was one of the first to be built here, and the emphasis is very much on peace and quiet. Each one- or two-bedroom villa is set in the gardens or on the beach, and offers AC, one or two bathrooms, living/dining area, kitchen, TV, telephone and barbecue. Laundry service. Bar, restaurant and tennis court.
Rates per villa per night, low/high season: one-bedroom patio US$180/260, one-bedroom garden US$230/315, two-bedroom garden US$280/375, one-bedroom ocean view US$280/375, one-bedroom ocean front US$335/460, two-bedroom ocean front US$375/525. Additional person US$25 per night. No children under 12 in high season, except at Christmas. All rates subject to 6% gratuity.
Coral Sands Resort PO Box 30610 SMB, North Church St; tel: 949 4400/3; fax: 949 4005; email: coralsand@candw.ky; web: www.coralsands.ky (12 flats/townhouses)
Situated within a short walk of George Town at the southern end of Seven Mile Beach, the units here are clustered around a small courtyard with swimming pool, leading directly on to the beach. Each two-bedroom unit has bathroom, living/dining area, kitchen with dishwasher, AC/ceiling fans, washer/dryer, telephone, TV. Deluxe flats have two bathrooms; deluxe townhouses face the sea. Maid service is included. Swimming pool, beach picnic area with barbecues, sundeck, boat dock, undercover parking.

Rates per unit per night, up to a maximum of six people, low/high season: standard US$232/290, deluxe US$264/350.

Harbour View PO Box 176 GT, North Church St, George Town; tel: 949 5681/4168; fax: 949 5308; email: harborvu@candw.ky; web: http://Cayman.com.ky/com/harview (9 units)

One of Grand Cayman's best accommodation deals, Harbour View is an exceptionally welcoming complex located just at the start of Seven Mile Beach, and within easy walking distance of shops and restaurants. The comfortable one-bedroom apartments and studios, all en suite, have separate living area, kitchen, AC/ceiling fans, TV and telephone. There is a beach with private jetty, and a separate guest laundry.

Rates for two people per night, low/high season: studio US$75/$99, deluxe studio US$99/125, apartment US$99/$149. Additional guests US$10 per night. All rates subject to 5% gratuity.

Plantation Village PO Box 30871 SMB, West Bay Rd; tel: 949 4199, US toll free 800 822 8903; fax: 949 0646; email: pvcres@candw.ky; web: www.cayman.org/pvbr (71 apartments)

This timeshare complex, one of the first to be built on Seven Mile Beach, has apartments for rent on a daily basis. Each apartment has two bathrooms, AC, kitchen, TV, telephone and screened patio. Laundry, maid service. Two swimming pools, tennis court, children's playground, gas barbecues, beach cabanas. Kayaks and bicycles available to guests. Diving (dive packages available).

Rates per night, low/high season: pool view (up to four people) US$185–210/310–340, ocean view (up to six people) US$210–265/340–405; oceanfront panorama (up to six people) US$265–335/405–505. Additional guests US$15 per night. Children 12 and under free. All rates subject to 5% gratuity. US$20 supplement payable per night at Easter and Thanksgiving, and US$50 per night at Christmas.

Seven Mile Beach Resort & Club PO Box 30742 SMB, West Bay Rd; tel: 949 0332; fax: 949 0331; email: smbrsort@candw.ky; web: www.7mile.ky. (38 condominiums)

Set back off the southern end of Seven Mile Beach, close to George Town, the resort's two-bedroom condominiums each have two bathrooms, kitchen, AC, patio or private balcony and satellite TV/VCR. Swimming pool with waterfalls, tennis courts, laundry, gift and dive shop, spa. Short-term membership of World Gym included. Maid service and babysitting available.

Rates per night, up to four people, low/high season/Christmas: US$250/450/675; children under 12 free; additional guest US$15 per night. All rates subject to 5% gratuity.

Villas of the Galleon PO Box 1797, West Bay Rd; tel: 945 4311/4433; fax: 945 4705/4659; email: vogcay@candw.ky. web: www.villasofthegalleon.com (78 apartments)

Just to the south of the Westin, these highly recommended apartments with all amenities, including AC/ceiling fans, sea view, free local phone calls and full maid service, are available for short-term rental. One- or two-bedroom units each have dining area, living room, barbecue grills.

Rates per apartment per day, low/high season/Christmas: one-bedroom (two people) US$235–250/$330–360/$395–435; two-bedroom (four people) US$270–300/

$420–450/$500–540; three-bedroom (six people) US$375–405/$575–610/$690–725; additional guest US$30/30/50 per night. Children under 12 free. All rates subject to 5% gratuity.

WHERE TO EAT

The standard of restaurant food throughout the island is excellent, although many locals reckon that some of the best food is to be had to the east and north of George Town (see pages 148, 159, 160, 163, 165, 166 and 168). Sunday brunch is something of an institution, too – for a real treat, try the Westin or the Hyatt.

For a preview of menus from a selection of Grand Cayman's restaurants, pick up of a copy of the free *Cayman Islands Menu Guide*, available from hotels and tourist venues islandwide, or look at their website, www.caymandining.com. It's an advertising tool, of course, but the menus are useful.

The geographical distinction between George Town and Seven Mile Beach is not particularly clear on the ground. For the purposes of this list, George Town is defined as the area up to and including Eastern Avenue to the north, and out towards Red Bay to the south and east.

George Town

What George Town lacks in hotels, it makes up for in restaurants. The capital's restaurants range from top-class seafood restaurants, with views (and prices) to match, to pizza houses and hamburger bars. Cayman-style food is a speciality of some, and well worth seeking out. Even outside the main town, towards the airport for example, there are gems to be found.

Restaurants

Almond Tree North Church St; tel: 949 2893. Once set back behind the Tree House (see below), the Almond Tree now shares the same beachfront premises, overlooking West Bay. Bar open daily, 5.30pm till late; meals served 11.00am–11.00pm.

Billy's see *Jerky's*, below

Blue Parrot Restaurant & Bar South Church St; tel: 949 9094. Set behind Coconut Harbour, the Blue Parrot is a large, easy-going establishment looking out over South Sound, with seating around the bar or on the deck. The fact that it is flanked by huge oil storage containers is turned to advantage when they are pressed into service as giant TV screens for the occasional big game: this is a popular sports bar. Cosmopolitan menu with fresh seafood and a US bias, with sandwiches and very good salads from US$5. Speciality nights include curries and Mexican.

Brasserie Cricket Sq, off Elgin Av; tel: 945 1815. Popular at lunchtime with local business people, the Brasserie also does a special deal on Sunday nights, with a three-course meal and a bottle of wine for CI$55 per couple, plus service. Open Mon–Fri 11.30am–2.30pm, 5.30–10.00pm; Sat/Sun 5.30–10.00pm.

Breadfruit Tree Café Eastern Av; tel: 945 2124. More of a diner than a restaurant, this is a good place to come for a light meal after a night out.

Casanova Old Fort Bldg, Fort St; tel: 949 7633. This small, intimate restaurant, with stunning views across West Bay, is particularly popular at lunchtimes for its excellent pasta, reputedly served by 'mad Italians'. Rumour has it that the restaurant is to move to Seven Mile Beach. Open Mon–Sat 11.30am–2.15pm; daily 6.00–10.00pm.

Champion House II 43 Eastern Av; tel: 949 7882. Tucked away on Eastern Avenue, but worth a visit for its authentic Cayman dishes at reasonable prices, Champion House also offers lunch-time buffets specialising in different world cuisines. For evening theme specials, call in advance. Open Mon–Sat 6.30am–midnight; Sun 8.00am–11.00pm. West Indian Sunday brunch 8.00am–2.00pm. Breakfast buffet Mon–Sat.

Crow's Nest South Sound Rd; tel: 949 9366. Situated on the right heading out of George Town on the coast road, approximately 1½ miles beyond Grand Old House. Owned and run by Caymanians, the Crow's Nest is an old Cayman house with beautiful views over to the tiny island of Sand Cay and across South Sound. Don't come in a hurry – the service is relaxed and friendly, the food traditional (though be prepared to be surprised), and children are genuinely welcome. Open daily 11.30am–3.00pm, 5.30–10.00pm.

Grand Old House South Church St; tel: 949 9333. Just a few minutes' drive south from George Town, on the waterfront, Grand Old House oozes old-world elegance. Its reputation for fine food makes it well patronised by business people. It is also a popular venue for wedding parties, as attested by the 'Wedding Gallery' in the grounds. Open Mon–Fri 11.45am–2.00pm, daily 6.00–10.00pm.

Hard Rock Café 43 South Church St; tel: 945 2020. Few introductions are necessary to this well-known US chain, where lively rock music accompanies huge portions of American-style food. Open daily from 10.30am; retail shop open Mon–Sat from 7.30am; Sun from 10.00am.

Jerky's North Church St; tel: 949 0470. Known until 2000 as Billy's Place, Jerky's (so-called after its parrot) has long been popular for Cayman-style food in simple, relaxed surroundings. Located just on the edge of George Town, near the cinema, it is easily accessible from both George Town and Seven Mile Beach. Complimentary appetisers such as conch fritters are a nice touch. And do try the home-made rum cake – a cut above the commercial variety. Jerky's is under new management from 2001 (although retaining the same ownership). Open Mon–Sat 5.30–10.00pm. 10% discount for divers on production of an accreditation card.

Landmark Cardinall Av; tel: 949 2582; email: landmark@candw.ky. This English-style pub, formerly known as the Cayman Arms, has pub-style food to match, including bangers and mash, or roast of the day at CI$13.95, and that great British institution, fish and chips in newspaper. It's also one of the few places on Grand Cayman where you can get British bacon. Very popular with expats, especially the Friday happy hour from 6.00pm to 9.00pm, it has a wide choice of imported draught beers, and shows major sports matches. The Pantry restaurant upstairs, overlooking the harbour, is more upmarket, with a wide variety of national dishes described as 'one-world' menus. Customers may be collected and taken back to their hotels free of charge – and in a London taxi to boot! Open daily 10.00am–10.00pm.

Lobster Pot North Church St; tel: 949 2736. The predominantly seafood menu here has a few alternatives for committed meat eaters and vegetarians, all at reasonable prices. Open Mon–Fri 11.30am–2.30pm, 5.30–10.30pm.

Maxin's Fort St; tel: 949 5747. An intimate town-centre restaurant, located just back from the harbour, with an excellent reputation. Maxin's revamped menu now focuses more on seafood and steaks. Specials include a Caribbean seafood extravaganza with live music on Tuesdays, live jazz on Thursdays, and a Saturday 'hangover cure' breakfast until 3.00pm. On Saturday, a three-course meal with wine is CI$55 per couple. Open for breakfast, lunch and dinner Mon–Fri 7.00am–1.00am; Sat 9.00am–midnight. Happy hour 5.00–7.00pm. Late-night tapas menu until midnight.

Naked Fish South Church St; tel: 945 0558. The restaurant of the Seaview Hotel was being revamped early in 2001 with a menu specialising in seafood and steaks. Restaurant open 11.00am–10.00pm daily. Bar open 11.00am–1.00pm Mon–Fri; 11.00am–12.00pm Sat and Sun.

On the Rocks North Church St; tel: 949 6163. Re-opened in November 2000, with a new chef, this British-owned restaurant has been refurbished and the menu overhauled, with both traditional British and US favourites and some innovative twists. Friendly service. Live music at weekends. Open daily 8.00am–10.00pm for breakfast (from CI$3.50), lunch and dinner.

Paradise Bar & Grill 96 South Church St, George Town; tel: 945 1444. This lively and relaxed establishment, with its inside restaurant, bar, open deck and stretch of beach, has great views of the harbour and is popular with cruise-ship visitors. American-style food of the burger and chips variety, plus separate children's menu. Snorkels and masks available for hire. Open Mon–Fri 7.30am–10.00pm; Sat/Sun 8.30am–9.30pm. Happy hour 5.00–7.00pm daily.

Rackams Pub Harbour Drive; tel: 945 3680. Despite the name, Rackams is also a restaurant, right in the centre of George Town on the waterfront. An upbeat, relaxed place, the service is friendly, the food varied and nightly tarpon feeding is a further attraction. Open daily 11.00am–10.00pm.

Seaharvest South Church St, tel: 945 1383. The restaurant at Sunset House is right on the waterfront, with seafood as its speciality and a self-consciously nautical menu. Nightly specials include an Indian night on Monday, while on Sunday there's an 'all you can eat' barbecue for just CI$14.95. Open Mon–Fri 11.30am–2.30pm, 5.30–10.00pm; Sat/Sun 5.30–10.00pm.

Shirley's Owen Roberts Dr; tel: 945 2100. Within walking distance of the airport, the restaurant at Sammy's has a simple menu featuring seafood and West Indian dishes. Open 7.00am–2.00pm; 6.00–10.00pm.

Smugglers Cove North Church St, next to Casanova; tel: 945 6003. Caribbean café/grill with dark wood décor and a cosy, old-world feel. Diners look out across the water from the indoor restaurant, which is particularly popular at lunchtime.

Tree House North Church St; tel: 945 0155. Casual beachfront bar and grill in an idyllic tree-backed location, offering grills, salads, sandwiches, etc. Daily happy hour, tarpon feeding, fresh seafood. Access to snorkelling. Open daily 11.00am to 'closing'. The more upmarket Almond Tree restaurant (see above) is moving to the upper-storey of the same premises.

Cafés and snack bars
Coffee & Bites Bodmer Bldg, opposite Edmar's Pharmacy behind the post office; tel: 945 4892

Craft Market Café Cardinall Av; tel: 945 7109. Simple, covered wooden café with friendly service close to the harbour and port terminals. Fruit punch from US$1.25;

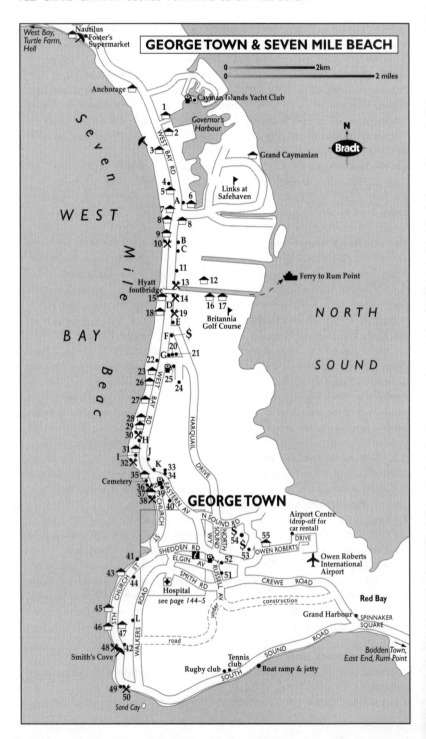

NUMERICAL KEY TO MAP OPPOSITE

Malls and squares

A Cayman Falls Centre
B Coconut Place
C The Strand
D Buckingham Square
E Regency Court
F Galleria Plaza
G West Shore Centre
H Seven Mile Shops
I Queen's Court
J Selkirk Plaza
K Merren Place
L Eden Centre

Hotels, restaurants and places of interest

1 Indies Suites
2 Holiday Inn/Mangrove Grill
3 Avalon
4 Governor's Residence
5 Westin Casuarina/Casa Havana/Ferdinand's
6 Sunshine Suites
7 Villas of the Galleon
8 Ritz Carlton (under construction)
9 Caribbean Club
10 Lantana's
11 Next Level

12 Annie's Place
13 Ottmar's
14 Decker's
15 Hyatt Beach Club/Hemingways/Bamboo
16 Hyatt Regency/Garden Loggia
17 Britannia Villas
18 Beach Club Hotel
19 Lone Star
20 Bed
21 World Gym/Planet Night Club
22 Royal Palms Beach Club/Reef Grill
23 Marriott/Peninsula
24 Harquail Theatre/Cayman National Cultural Centre
25 Cinema/Cimboco
26 Comfort Suites/Stingers
27 Seven Mile Beach Resort
28 Plantation Village
29 Treasure Island/Hook's Seafood Grotto
30 Big Daddy's
31 Sleep Inn
32 Wharf
33 Cardinal D's

34 National Trust
35 Harbour View
36 Almond Tree/Tree House
37 Coral Sands
38 Lobster Pot/Bob Soto's
39 Kirk Supermarket/Jerky's Restaurant
40 Bike rental/Naomi's Hair
41 Eden Rock Dive Centre
42 Pure Art
43 Seaview/Naked Fish
44 Adam's Guest House
45 Sunset House/Seaharvest/Cathy Church's Photography
46 Coconut Harbour/Blue Parrot
47 Eldemire's Guest House
48 Grand Old House
49 Dr Carey's
50 Crow's Nest
51 Farmer's Market
52 Cayman Islands National Archive
53 Foster's Supermarket
54 Tortuga Rum Cake Factory/Conch Shell House
55 Sammy's Airport Inn/Shirley's

ALPHABETICAL KEY TO MAP OPPOSITE

Malls and squares

Buckingham Square	D
Cayman Falls Centre	A
Coconut Place	B
Eden Centre	L
Galleria Plaza	F
Merren Place	K
Queen's Court	I
Regency Court	E
Selkirk Plaza	J
Seven Mile Shops	H
The Strand	C
West Shore Centre	G

Hotels, restaurants and places of interest

Adam's Guest House	44
Almond Tree	36
Annie's Place	12
Avalon	3
Bamboo	15
Beach Club Hotel	18
Bed	20
Big Daddy's	30
Bike rental	40
Blue Parrot	46
Bob Soto's	38
Britannia Villas	17
Cardinal D's	33
Caribbean Club	9
Casa Havana	5
Cathy Church's Photography	45
Cayman Islands National Archive	52
Cayman National Cultural Centre	24
Cimboco	25
Cinema	25
Coconut Harbour	46
Comfort Suites	26
Conch Shell House	54
Coral Sands	37
Crow's Nest	50
Decker's	14
Dr Carey's	49
Eden Rock Dive Centre	41
Eldemire's Guest House	47
Farmer's Market	51
Ferdinand's	5
Foster's Supermarket	53
Garden Loggia	16
Governor's Residence	4
Grand Old House	48
Harbour View	35
Harquail Theatre	24
Hemingways	15
Holiday Inn	2
Hook's Seafood Grotto	29
Hyatt Beach Club	15
Hyatt Regency	16
Indies Suites	1
Jerky's Restaurant	39
Kirk Supermarket	39
Lantana's	10
Lobster Pot	38
Lone Star	19
Mangrove Grill	2
Marriott	23
Naked Fish	43
Naomi's Hair	40
National Trust	34
Next Level	11
Ottmar's	13
Peninsula	23
Planet Night Club	21
Plantation Village	28
Pure Art	42
Reef Grill	22
Ritz Carlton (under construction)	8
Royal Palms Beach Club	22
Sammy's Airport Inn	55
Seaharvest	45
Seaview	43
Seven Mile Beach Resort	27
Shirley's	55
Sleep Inn	31
Stingers	26
Sunset House	45
Sunshine Suites	6
Tortuga Rum Cake Factory	54
Treasure Island	29
Tree House	36
Villas of the Galleon	7
Westin Casuarina	5
Wharf	32
World Gym	21

coconut water; ice-creams, etc. Patties US$1.25. Local specialities including jerk chicken, rice and plantain for US$6.25. Open daily 7.00am–4.30pm.

Daily Grind Edward St; tel: 945 1175. Located above Grannie Mae's and frequented predominantly by office workers. Freshly roasted coffee plus good selection of pastries, sandwiches etc. Open Mon–Fri 7.00am–4.00pm.

Every Blooming Thing 59 South Church St; tel: 945 1701. Just up the road from Atlantis, this tea room, complete with pink floral wallpaper, serves proper China tea and sandwiches. It also has a gift shop with English jams, notepaper and toiletries, including Crabtree & Evelyn and Woods of Windsor.

Grannie Mae's Fish & Chips Edward St; tel: 949 7175. Eat in or take away. Open Mon–Sat 10.00am–5.00pm.

Jailhouse Café Goring Av. Simple café close to the museum with open-air seating. Snacks include local meat patties at US$1.87; hot dog and soda US$2.50. Ice-cream cornets from US$2.50.

Seven Mile Beach

Bamboo West Bay Rd; tel: 94-SUSHI/948 8744. The telephone number at the Hyatt's grill bar says it all – this is indeed a sushi bar, with dark wood décor and an atmosphere more akin to downtown Tokyo or Manhattan than Cayman. Friendly service, music and cocktail menu. Open Mon–Fri 5.00pm–1.00am; Sat 5.00pm–midnight.

Bed Harquail Drive (next to World Gym); tel: 949 7199. Popular bar and restaurant with a rather sleazy bedtime theme which belies the excellent food. Comprehensive menu, with some innovative dishes and superb sea bass (flown in from Chile). Live music Wed, Sat. Ladies, watch out for the open-plan toilets! Open Mon–Sun 6.00pm–11.00pm; bar Mon–Fri 6.00pm–1.00am; Sat/Sun 6.00pm–midnight.

Bella Capri The Strand, West Bay Rd; tel: 945 4755; fax: 945 4968. Tucked away at the back of The Strand, this relaxed Italian restaurant with soft lighting also has tables on the open-air veranda. Lunchtime 'all-you-can-eat' soup and salad bar CI$5.95. Cocktail menu. Open Mon–Fri 11.45am–2.30pm; daily 5.00–10.00pm.

Benjamin's Roof Coconut Place, West Bay Rd; tel: 945 4080. A seafood restaurant and oyster bar with a reputation for conveyor-belt food and high prices – described by one person as 'tourist city'. If our welcome was anything to go by, give it a miss. Discount vouchers often available. German, Italian and Spanish spoken. Open 11.30am–3.00pm (high season only); 5.30–10.30pm.

Big Daddy's Restaurant & Sports Bar West Bay Rd; tel: 949 8511. The sports bar and restaurant above the liquor store by Seven Mile Shops has a friendly atmosphere – don't be put off by the garish signs. The large menu ranges across the UK, US and Caribbean, while nightly specials include steak night on Monday and West Indian curry night on Friday. For beer lovers, there are four different beers available from the micro-brewery (Old Dutch Brew Pub). Open Mon–Fri 8.00am–1.00am (breakfast 8.00–11.00am; lunch 11.30am–5.00pm); Sat–Sun 8.00am–midnight. Happy hour with free buffet Fri 5.00–7.00pm.

Billy Bones Treasure Island Resort; tel: 945 7069. An informal poolside bar and grill.

Café Mediterraneo (formerly Café Tortuga) Galleria Plaza, West Bay Rd; tel: 949

8669/7427. Dine indoors or out. Mediterranean menu and traditional Caribbean specialities. Good wine list.

Canton Chinese Restaurant The Strand, West Bay Rd; tel: 945 3536. Open daily 11.30am–3.00pm; Sun–Thu 5.00–10.00pm; Fri/Sat 5.00–10.30pm.

Casa Havana West Bay Rd; tel: 945 3800, ext 6017. Cayman's only AAA 4-diamond restaurant is based at the Westin Casuarina. This is a place for serious foodies, or for that very special treat, with a highly innovative menu (they call it Nuevo Latino), and a selection of tapas to make the mouth water. The opulence of the setting overlooking the Caribbean is matched by an extensive wine list, while the background music features a live South American harpist. Open daily 6.30–10.30pm.

Chicken! Chicken! West Shore Centre, West Bay Rd; tel: 945 2290. Good food based on wood-roasted chicken at affordable prices, with takeaway service available. Lunchtime specials CI$5–7.25. Open daily 11.00am–10.00pm.

Cimboco PO Box 30786 SMB, Harquail Drive; tel: 94 PASTA/947 2782; fax: 946 7112; web: www.cimboco.com. A new arrival on the scene, opened in late 2000, Cimboco is a small, colourful restaurant tucked behind the Esso station next to the cinema and within easy reach of Seven Mile Beach. Styled as a 'Caribbean café', it serves pasta and pizzas with a Caribbean twist at reasonable prices – pizza from CI$8.95. 'Phenomenal food', we're told. Open daily 11.00am–10.00pm to eat in or take away.

Decker's 269 West Bay Road; tel: 945 6600. The double-decker London bus and attendant pavement tables belie the smart but simple interior of this restaurant with white cloths and modern art décor. Particularly popular Thu–Sat, when local bands play, it is well patronised by staff from nearby dive schools. The international menu includes Eastern dishes as well as mesquite grills and steaks. Lobster special CI$34.00. Open daily 5.00–10.00pm.

DJ's Cantina Coconut Place, West Bay Rd; tel: 945 4234. Lively bar and restaurant featuring live music, including reggae. The Mexican-style menu caters for all tastes, from chips and salsa to jalapeno lime tuna. Open daily 5.00–10.00pm.

Eats Café Cayman Falls Centre, West Bay Rd; tel: 945 5288/1950. The term 'café' doesn't do justice to this place opposite the Westin. The good value American-style menu features a full breakfast at just US$6.95 (or US$10.95 for the 'hungry man' version), a varied lunch menu with salads and sandwiches, and a comprehensive dinner menu including pasta and steaks. Takeaway service available. Open daily 6.30am–11.00pm.

Edoardo's Coconut Place, West Bay Rd; tel: 945 4408. Cosy Italian restaurant with soft lighting and very reasonable prices by Cayman standards – pizza and pasta dishes start at CI$10.95. Open daily 5.30–10.30pm.

Ferdinand's Westin Casuarina, West Bay Rd; tel: 945 3800, ext 6017. The more casual of the two restaurants at the Westin has an interesting menu with international fare that includes selected healthy-eating options. But it's Sunday brunch that really draws the crowds. A firm favourite with both Caymanians and visitors, the atmosphere is that of an English garden party on the beach – tented shade and pure white napiery against a backdrop of miles of white sand. Disregard all previous notions of 'brunch'; this is something special, with dishes from around the world – Japanese sushi, old world roast beef, Chinese, seafood, French cheeses – not to mention a full-range of American breakfast food. Unstuffy waiters bring an unlimited supply of sparkling wine and orange juice, as well as soft drinks, tea and coffee. Open daily for breakfast, lunch and dinner; Sunday brunch, from 11.30am to 2.30pm, is US$42 per person, inclusive of 15% service.

Fidel Murphy's Queen's Court, West Bay Rd; tel: 949 5189. Not far north of George Town, Fidel Murphy's Irish pub and restaurant has a straightforward menu including Irish stew, roast chicken and steak and Guinness pie. Live bands play regularly; the place is said to be 'pumping' on Friday nights. Major sports events are shown live on big-screen TV. Open Mon–Fri 10.30am–12.45am; Sat 10.30am–11.45pm. Happy hour Friday 5.00–8.00pm, with drink specials and free buffet. 'All-you-can-eat' carvery Wed, Thu and Fri, midday–3.00pm, for CI$9.95.

Garden Loggia Café West Bay Rd; tel: 949 1234. Breakfast at the Hyatt Regency is reputed to be superb, with Sunday brunch particularly special. A full selection of dishes is accompanied by freshly squeezed orange juice, and it's waitress service to boot. Caribbean night is on Tuesday, with local entertainment from limbo dancing to fire eating. Open for breakfast 7.30–11.00am daily. Tuesday Caribbean night, 6.30–10.30pm, reservations only.

Gateway of India The Strand, West Bay Rd; tel: 946 2815; fax: 946 2816. Traditional Indian restaurant with comfortable décor and air conditioning. Varied menu and daily lunchtime buffet at CI$7.95 for all you can eat. Open Mon–Fri 11.30am–2.30pm; daily 5.30–10.00pm.

Golden Pagoda West Bay Rd (opposite Marriott Hotel); tel: 949 5475. Traditional Chinese cuisine to eat in or take away. Open Mon–Sat 11.30am–2.30pm; 6.00–10.00pm. Bar open Mon–Fri 9.00am–1.00am; Sat 9.00am–midnight; Sun 1.00pm–midnight.

Golden Turtle Queen's Court, West Bay Rd; tel: 945 1263. Closed for refurbishment at the end of 2000, the Golden Turtle is well recommended so watch for its reopening.

Hemingways Hyatt Beach Club, Seven Mile Beach; tel: 945 5700. The atmosphere at midday of this cool, pastel-decorated restaurant, with views over the sea, is rather like that of a summer garden party, with gourmet sandwiches that make the average lunchtime offering seem plain boring. In the evening, the Caribbean-influenced menu is popular way beyond just hotel guests, with seafood a speciality. Parking opposite. Open daily 11.30am–2.30pm; 6.00–10.00pm.

Hook's Seafood Grotto Treasure Island Resort, West Bay Rd; tel: 945 8731. Themed cavern re-creating a pirate's lair, complete with contraband, albeit with inappropriate background music. Cosmopolitan menu includes a couple of local dishes. Portions are huge and a complimentary appetiser is served; think twice before ordering a starter. Open daily 7.00am–midnight.

Lantana's West Bay Rd; tel: 945 5595. Situated next to the Caribbean Club, but with no connection, Lantana's has a reputation for excellent food and service to match, under the watchful eye of the friendly English maître d', Lisa Macaulay. The menu changes regularly, but is broadly a mix of southwest American and Caribbean food, with local fish and their 'world famous apple pie' (as featured on Discovery TV Channel!). The fixed price three-course menu at CI$25 plus 15% gratuity is particularly good value. Undergoing renovations at the end of 2000, the restaurant was set to re-open with capacity for 100 people downstairs. Upstairs, the area will be reserved for 'fine dining'. Open Mon–Sat 7.30–11.30am breakfast; 11.30am–2.00pm lunch, 5.30–10.00pm dinner.

Legendz Bar Cayman Falls Centre, West Bay Rd; PO Box 30932 SMB; tel: 945 1950. The bland exterior of Legendz opens into a surprisingly big, plush American bar with a rock theme and US sports TV, popular with the diving fraternity. Live music Mon, Tue and Fri. Open daily 6:30am –11.00pm. Bar open Mon–Fri to 1.00pm; Sat/Sun until midnight.

Links Restaurant West Bay Rd; tel: 949 5988. From the elegant upstairs restaurant of the Links golf course (see page 107) diners look out across the lake and lush green fairways to North Sound, a serene backdrop for a leisurely meal. International cuisine with salads, pasta, seafood and steaks takes the diner from the Caribbean to the Far East, by way of the US and Britain. Meals can also be served outside on the patio. Open daily 11.30am–2.30pm; Mon, Wed–Sat 6.00–10.00pm. Bar open daily 11.30am–4.00 or 5.00pm.

Lone Star Bar & Grill West Bay Rd; tel: 945 5175. Noisy Tex-Mex restaurant and sports bar popular with the diving fraternity and good for families. Themed 'all-you-can-eat' nights. Satellite TV, with all major games (and sometimes more than one) shown in the bar. Open Mon–Fri 11.30am–midnight; Sat/Sun 11.30am–11.30pm. Happy hour Mon–Fri 5.00–6.30pm.

Mangrove Grill Holiday Inn, West Bay Rd; tel: 946 4433. The blue-and-yellow polka dot banquette seating and heavy air conditioning make this more diner than restaurant, better for quick meals than serious eating. Open Mon–Fri 7.00–11.00am, 6.00–10.00pm; Sat/Sun 7.00am–1.00pm; 6.00–10.00pm.

Ottmar's West Bay Rd (junction with Palm Heights Drive); tel: 945 5879. Established in 1972, Ottmar's serves seriously good food in graceful surroundings. Particularly popular for business lunches and dinners, it also has facilities for banquets and conferences. The predominantly European menu specialises in the classics, alongside steaks and plenty of seafood, and the occasional Eastern dish. Open daily 6.00–11.00pm; bar open 5.00–8.00pm. Happy hour Fri.

Outback Steakhouse The Strand, West Bay Rd; tel: 945 3108. Large, Australian-themed restaurant with friendly service and 'Joey' menu for children under ten. The emphasis is on steaks and grills, with plenty of it. The range of beers is supplemented by a couple of Australian imports, with Aussie cocktails to complete the picture. Takeaway service available. Open Sun–Thu 5.30–10.30pm, Fri 5.30–11.30pm, Sat 5.30–11.00pm. Billabong bar open 5.30 till late. Happy hour Tue.

PD's Pub Galleria Plaza, West Bay Rd; tel: 949 7144. Don't be fooled by the exterior: behind the stark shopfront is a dark, pub-like environment (PD stands for 'pirates' den') offering good value food and fast, friendly service. Good selection of beer, including Stingray Dark. Surprisingly comprehensive menu from soups and salads at US$6 to burgers and steaks etc with very generous portions at CI$14. Internet access available at CI$0.12 per minute (no minimum charge). Open Mon–Sat 8.30am–10.00pm.

Peninsula West Bay Rd; tel: 949 0088. The Marriott's exclusive restaurant overlooking the sea is open for lunch and dinner, with evening entertainment. Don't go in a hurry – the menu alone takes some reading, and making a choice from such an eclectic range could take time! Friday night is Pirates' Night Buffet, with limbo dancing and Caribbean music: adults US$34.95; children US$15.95. Open daily 11.30am–2.30pm, 6.00–10.30pm.

Pizzeria Vesuvio Regency Court; tel: 949 8696. Open Mon–Sat 11.30am–10.30pm; Sun and holidays 5.30–10.30pm.

Ragazzi Buckingham Sq, West Bay Rd; tel: 945 3484. Don't be put off by the unprepossessing location – the food at this upmarket pizzeria is very good, as is the wine list. A wide selection of pizzas and pasta dishes from CI$10.95 is complemented by other Italian specialities. Particularly popular at lunchtime. Takeaway service available. Open daily 11.30am–11.00pm.

Reef Grill Royal Palms Beach Club, West Bay Rd; tel: 945 6358. The Reef Grill does indeed specialise in grills, but this is not the run-of-the-mill restaurant that the name suggests. Fish, lamb and steak are served with the emphasis on innovative accompaniments, such as charred onion aioli and Scotch bonnet vinaigrette. Indoor or patio dining. Open daily 6.00–10.00pm. For details of the beach club, see page 139.

Stingers Eating poolside at the Comfort Suites is, as you would expect, a relaxed affair, with simple meals available all day until 10.00pm. Bar open Mon–Fri 11.00am–1.00am; Sat 11.00am–midnight; Sun midday–midnight.

Tapas Bar and Grill West Bay Rd; tel: 949 0652. Opened at the end of 2000, this Spanish-style restaurant situated opposite the Comfort Suites is open daily 5.30–10.00pm.

Thai Orchid Queen's Court, West Bay Rd; tel: 949 7955. Thai cuisine may not be something you would immediately associate with the Cayman Islands, but this tranquil restaurant makes a welcome change and the food, including vegetarian dishes, is reputed to be extremely good. Open Mon–Sat 11.30am–2.30pm; daily 6.00–10.00pm. All you can eat lunch buffet Tue and Thu, CI$11.95.

Tortuga Tims Seven Mile Shops, West Bay Rd; tel: 949 8299. A very reasonably priced Caribbean bar and grill with a selection of stir fries and some local dishes as well. Full main courses from CI$8.95. Quick, polite service. Open daily 7.00am–9.30pm for breakfast, lunch and dinner.

Wharf West Bay Rd; tel: 949 2231/7729. The stunning location of this large waterfront restaurant and bar at the beginning of Seven Mile Beach ensures its enduring popularity among locals and visitors alike, particularly for that special meal. Predominantly seafood-based menu, with daily specials. Tarpon gather nightly in the shallows around the pier at 9.00pm to be fed by the restaurant staff. Live music Mon–Sat. Open Mon–Fri midday–2.30pm; daily 6.00–10.00pm. Bar open daily from 3.00pm.

Fast food

On the US front, there are branches of several fast-food chains:

Burger King has several branches: opposite Atlantis Department Store on Harbour Rd, George Town; West Bay Rd; and Eden Centre on Walkers Rd. Open daily 7.00am–late.

Domino's Pizza West Shore Centre, West Bay Rd; tel: 949 8282. Free pizza delivery service. Other outlets across the island are at West Bay, Savannah and North Side.

KFC The Strand, West Bay Rd; further south on West Bay Rd itself; Shedden Rd. Open Sun–Thu 11.00am–11.00pm; Fri 11.00am–2.00am; Sat 11.00am–1.00am.

Pizza Hut West Bay Rd by Harquail Drive; tel: 949 0404; 947 7333

Subway has three outlets, at West Shore Centre, West Bay Rd, tel: 949 6866; Andersen Sq, George Town; tel: 945 3568; and Industrial Park, George Town; tel: 945 7373

Wendy's West Bay Rd; tel: 949 0616

Cafés and snack bars

Coffee Grinder Seven Mile Shops, West Bay Rd. US-style café serving sandwiches, pastries and light meals etc. Open Mon–Sat 7.30am–6.00pm, Sun 7.30am–3.00pm.

Haagen Dazs The Strand, West Bay Rd; tel: 945 8707. Open daily for ice-cream, midday–11.00pm.

Merrens Merren Place, West Bay Rd. Ice-cream parlour. Open Sun–Thu 11.30am–11.00pm; Fri–Sat 11.30am–midnight.

TCBY at the Hyatt West Bay Rd; tel: 949 1234. Tropical frozen yoghurts, coffees and pastries are served from a vantage point that overlooks the Hyatt Beach pools and Seven Mile Beach. Open all day.

Self catering?

Don't miss out on good food just because you want a night in. Fine Dine-In (tel: 949 DINE; email: ken@candw.ky; web: www.finedine-in.com) works with a selection of local restaurants to deliver meals to hotels, condos, or even the beach, anywhere between West Bay and Prospect (that's effectively the whole of Seven Mile Beach and a little further east than the Stingray Brewery at Red Bay). Restaurants featured include Bed, Big Daddy's, Casanova, Champion House II, Chicken! Chicken!, Cimboco, Decker's, DJ's Cantina, Edoardo's, Gateway to India, Maxin's, PD's Pub, Ragazzi and Thai Orchid, so there's plenty of choice to whet the appetite. There is a minimum charge of CI$20, with delivery usually made between 30 and 45 minutes after placing your order. For an additional US$5 you can order a video at the same time. Open Sun–Thu 5.30–10.30pm; Fri/Sat 5.30–11.00pm.

BARS AND NIGHTLIFE

The nightclub scene on Grand Cayman is slowly evolving, but don't expect pumping music till dawn – most places close by 1.00am during the week, while local licensing laws insist that establishments close at midnight on Saturday and Sunday. Many of Grand Cayman's restaurants have separate bars, for which opening times are given under *Restaurants* above, and several establishments, including Bed and DJ's Cantina, feature live entertainment on different days of the week. Other bars and nightlife locations include:

The Attic Queen's Court, West Bay Rd; tel: 949 7665. This billiard lounge is situated on the second floor of Queen's Court, opposite Fidel Murphy's.

Bobo's Iguana Islander Complex, West Bay Rd; tel: 946 6900. A sports bar and lounge. Open Mon–Fri 5.00pm–1.00am; Sat 5.00pm–midnight.

Club Scene Selkirk Plaza, West Bay Rd; tel: 945 8950

Illusions The Strand, West Bay Rd; tel: 945 0707. Large bar and dancing area above Outback Steakhouse. Themed nights with live bands – see *Caymanian Compass* for details. Open Mon–Thu 7.30pm–1.00am; Fri 4.30pm–1.00am; Sat 5.00pm–midnight; Sun 7.00pm–midnight.

Jungle Night Club Trafalgar Place, off West Bay Rd; tel: 945 5383. Dark décor with a jungle theme. Popular with locals, with a good atmosphere and live DJ Tue–Sat. Karaoke night Tue. Bar snacks. Open Mon–Fri 11.00am–1.00am; Sat 11.00am–midnight; Sun 1.00pm–midnight.

Next Level West Bay Rd; tel: 946 6398. Located just north of the Hyatt bridge, this relatively new nightclub features regular live bands – see *Caymanian Compass* for details. Open 8.00pm–late.

Planet Arcadia Grand Harbour, Red Bay; tel: 947 GAME. Bar with billiards. Open Mon–Thu 5.00–10.00pm; Fri 3.00pm–midnight; Sat midday–midnight; Sun 2.00–10.00pm.

Planet Night Club Harquail Drive. Located above World Gym, this club with its new bar is particularly popular with expats on Thursday nights, with Caymanians for the most part preferring the weekends.

Rackams Pub Harbour Drive, George Town; tel: 945 3680. In addition to its US-orientated menu, Rackam's also has a friendly and relaxed bar. Open daily 10.00am till late.

Royal Palms A great place to be on Friday night, when live music features calypso and reggae. For details, see *Beaches* page 139.

Shooters Seven Mile Shops; tel: 946 3496. Dark, rather sleazy lounge bar with billiards table and internet café. Taped modern music. Plans are in hand to open a restaurant. Open Mon–Fri 10.30am–1.00am; Sat/Sun 10.30am–midnight. Over 20s only after 6.00pm.

Welly's Cool Spot 110 North Sound Rd; tel: 949 2541. A local watering hole frequented mostly by Caymanians, this is definitely off the normal tourist track. Open Mon–Sat 7.30am–9.00pm.

Wreck Bar North Church St, George Town; tel: 949 8060. An English-style pub said to serve the best pint of Guinness on the island. Major US football games televised. Open Mon–Fri 10.00am–12.45am; Sat/Sun 10.00am–11.45pm.

SHOPPING AND AMENITIES

Many shops, and particularly those catering for the tourist, are open seven days a week. Boutiques and duty-free shops abound in George Town. For shops beyond George Town and Seven Mile Beach, see *Chapter 6, Beyond George Town*.

Books, maps and games

Book Nook Galleria Plaza, West Bay Rd. Open Mon–Sat 9.00am–6.00pm.

Book Nook II off Cardinall Av (behind Kirk Freeport), George Town. Open Mon–Fri 9.30am–5.00pm; Sat 9.30am–2.00pm.

Hobbies and Books Piccadilly Centre, Elgin Av, George Town; tel: 949 0707; fax: 949 7165; email: hobbook@candw.ky. Tucked away in a modern building round the back of George Town, there's a wide variety of books and gifts here, including a good selection of books related to the Cayman Islands. Also at Grand Harbour, Red Bay.

Books may also be bought at both of the following:

Cayman Island National Archive, Printers Way, George Town; tel: 949 9809; email: cina@gov.ky. The archive houses a comprehensive series of records related to the islands, including a memory bank of non-written data. Books concerned with the islands' history are on sale. Open Mon–Fri 8.30am–5.00pm; reading room open 9.00am–4.30pm.

National Trust Courts Rd, Eastern Av; tel: 949 0121. This attractive building is not only an excellent place to find out more about the work of the Trust, but is also a good source of books on the natural history and culture of the islands. Open Mon–Fri 9.00am–5.00pm.

Cigars

Churchill's Cigar Store Anchorage Centre, George Town; tel: 945 6141. Also at Galleria Plaza on West Bay Rd.

Puro Rey West Bay Rd, opposite the Hyatt; tel: 945 4912/3; web: www.puroreycigars.com. Open 10.00am–10.00pm daily. Also at the Rent-a-Car Centre, Airport Rd. Open Mon–Sat 9.00am–6.00pm.

Coins

Gold Mine West Bay Rd (next to Deckers); tel/fax: 949 0620; email: goldmine@candw.ky; web: www.erols.com/landoc/cayman. Coins are a speciality here, mostly ancient, and all with a certificate of authentication. There are, too, original issue 1972 Cayman Islands coins in mint condition – the result of a chance find by owner Jim Rauch in a leased building. Also black coral and caymanite jewellery. Open Mon–Sat 9.00am–7.00pm.

Dive supplies

Divers Supply West Shore Centre, West Bay Rd; tel: 949 7621; fax: 949 7616. Rentals and sales of all equipment, plus dive tuition. Open daily 8.00am–9.00pm.

Divers World Seven Mile Shops, West Bay Rd; tel: 949 8128; mobile: 916 0028; fax: 949 7178; email: divworld@candw.ky. Fully comprehensive retail dive shop with everything a diver could possibly need, from equipment to books. Rentals available. Open Mon–Sat 7.30am–6.00pm.

Duty free

Traditional duty-free items – jewellery, watches etc – are to be found alongside glass and china, antique coins and other similar items in the numerous duty-free shops opposite George Town harbour and lining both sides of Cardinall Avenue. The following are some of the larger duty-free centres:

Anchorage Centre corner of Cardinall Av and North Church St, George Town. Various stores sell cosmetics and perfume, crystal, jewellery and watches; leather goods; designer clothes and T-shirts; cigars.

British Outpost Coconut Place, West Bay Rd; tel: 945 3835. Jewellery, watches and treasure coins. Open Mon–Sat 9.30am–9.30pm. Also at the Duty Free Centre.

Duty Free Centre Edward St, George Town. Another umbrella outfit with shops selling jewellery, treasure coins, watches, sunglasses, designer clothes, luggage and T-shirts.

Duty Free Ltd South Church St; tel: 945 2160. Jewellery, glassware, watches and treasure coins. Also at Galleria Plaza on West Bay Rd; tel: 945 5754/4055. Open Mon–Sat 9.00am–9.15pm.

Kirk Freeport Plaza Cardinall Av, George Town; tel: 949 7477; fax: 949 8124; email: kirkfree@candw.ky. Also at The Strand, West Bay Rd.

Food and drink
Food
Local produce and specialities, including homemade cakes and fruits such as soursop in season, are available from **Farmer's Market** on Thomas Russell Way near the airport, open Monday to Saturday, 8.00am to 6.30pm. There is also a daily hot buffet for about an hour from noon, with local dishes such as conch stew available to take away for around CI$5.99 a pound (CI$13.20 per kg).

Fresh fish is sold most days on the harbour in George Town, near the Port Terminal next to Don Foster's dive shop.

Grand Cayman's supermarkets are modern and efficient, with a wide variety of goods including US branded foods. Supermarkets don't sell alcoholic drinks - you'll have to go to a liquor store for these (see opposite).

Fort Street Market Fort St, George Town; tel: 945 0760. Mini supermarket which also serves buffet lunch food, including soup. Pavement tables. Open Mon–Fri 7.00am–7.00pm.

Foster's Food Fair Airport Rd; tel: 949 5155. Open Mon–Sat 7.00am–11.00pm; holidays 9.00am–6.00pm. Also at The Strand, West Bay Rd, tel: 945 4748 (in-store pharmacy open Sun 9.00am–6.00pm) and Republix Plaza, West Bay, tel: 949 3214 (bus stop 18).

Hurley's Marketplace Grand Harbour, Red Bay; tel: 947 8488. Also at Walkers Rd, George Town; tel: 949 8488. ATMs at both branches. Open Mon–Wed 7.00am–9.00pm, Thu–Sat 7.00am–11.00pm.

Kirk Supermarket Eastern Av, George Town; tel: 949 7022. Fresh produce, salad bar, in-store pharmacy, ATM. Open Mon–Fri 7.00am–10.00pm; Sat 7.00am–11.00pm. Closed public holidays.

Rum cake is a popular souvenir, with a variety of flavours available and tastings on offer in several tourist shops or indeed straight from the factory. More traditional to the Cayman Islands is coconut candy, which is sometimes available from Farmer's Market (see above).

Cayman Islands Rum Cake Centre North Church St, George Town; tel: 945 6895; email: cakesrum@candw.ky. The replica pirate ship in front of this large shop is an added attraction for children while you're sampling the cakes. Open Mon–Sat 7.00am–4.00pm.

Tortuga Rum Cakes Tel: 949 8866/949 2162. The company has several outlets on Grand Cayman, including two shops in the centre of George Town, and two factories

– one near George Town (see page 145) and the second next to the Turtle Farm (see page 153). All offer free samples of its different varieties of rum cake. The small duty-free shop opposite the port also sells patties, as well as coffee, liquor and cigars.

Drink
Rum is a popular choice to take home, with flavoured rum a speciality. There are numerous liquor stores (off licences) on the island, with opening hours almost universally Mon–Sat 10.00am–7.00pm. Contrary to popular opinion, liquor stores are not duty free – a bottle of rum that costs US$33.50 on the island would cost around US$8.50 duty free at the airport. In addition to the following, some branches of Tortuga Rum (above) sell liquor.

Big Daddy's West Bay Rd; tel: 949 8511
Blackbeard's, 236 Crewe Rd; tel: 949 8763; fax: 949 8764; email: info@blackbeardliquors.com; web: www.blackbeardsliquors.com. One of several shops on the island featuring speciality rums, including banana and mango flavours. Other outlets include Seven Mile Shops, Grand Harbour and North Sound Rd.
Jacques Scott 384 Shedden Rd, George Town; tel: 949 7600
Red Rabbit Liquor Store Red Bay; tel: 947 1536
Wine Cellar Galleria Plaza, West Bay Rd; tel: 949 5155

Gifts, souvenirs and beachwear
There are plenty of small shops in the centre of George Town near the harbour selling everything from local arts and crafts to good-quality T-shirts and other souvenirs. Most of these are open Mon–Sat, 9.00am–5.00pm unless otherwise indicated; for the most part they'll be open when the cruise ships are in port. The following is just a selection of these and others nearby:

Aquaworld Mall and Aquarium Harbour Drive, George Town. This modern first-floor mall houses a number of small shops selling clothing, gifts and souvenirs – a pretty good bet for something a bit different under one roof. The two nurse sharks in the central aquarium are fed at 11.00am and 1.00pm each day; you'd do better to take a submarine excursion and see them swimming free.
Casual Sports Bodmer Bldg, Shedden Rd, George Town; tel: 949 2199. T-shirts, souvenirs.
Cayman Islands National Museum (see page 144). The museum shop is an excellent source of good-quality gifts and souvenirs.
Craft Market Cardinall Av, George Town. A small group of shops with locally produced gifts, geared primarily to the cruise market and located just across the road from the two port terminals.
Flameworks off Cardinall Av, George Town. Small glass-blowing emporium behind Kirk Freeport with related gifts. Admission free.
Glass-blowing Studio North Church St, George Town; tel: 949 7020. Colourful glass ornaments, including fish, sailboats etc, plus live demonstration. Open Mon–Sat 8.00am–5.00pm. Admission free.
Heritage Craft Goring Av, George Town; tel: 945 6041. In spite of the name, most of the huge range of items on sale here fall into the bracket of cheap souvenirs,

though the occasional gem is to be found. At least it feels real, making a change from the rather sterile duty-free shops. Open Mon–Fri 8.30am–5.30pm; Sat 10.00am–5.00pm.

Hot Tropics Thompson Bldg, opposite the post office, George Town; tel: 949 7014. Large selection of T-shirts, plus other gift ideas.

Island Art & Framing Grand Harbour, Red Bay; tel: 947 2606. Local arts and crafts. Open Mon–Sat 10.00am–6.00pm. Also at Treasure Island Resort, West Bay Rd; tel: 945 2606; open Mon–Fri 9.30am–9.00pm; Sat/Sun 9.30am–5.30pm.

Kennedy Gallery, West Shore Centre, West Bay Rd, tel: 949 8077. Arts and crafts. Open Mon–Fri 8.00am–4.30pm, Sat 8.30am–1.30pm.

Pure Art South Church St, George Town; tel: 949 9133. Located in a small cottage on the left as you head south from George Town, Pure Art has a colourful selection of individually made arts and crafts within a wide price range. Woven baskets, wooden toys and other artefacts jostle for space with original paintings (including some by owner Debbie van der Bol) and a range of prints from modern to classical. There are even local food specialities. Open Mon–Sat 9.00am–5.00pm.

Rackams Harbour Drive, George Town. Souvenirs and gifts, including lots of pirate paraphernalia. Rackams is also the gift shop for Stingray Brewery. Open Mon–Sat 10.00am–7.00pm.

Shellections South Church St, George Town. Gifts and souvenirs are sold in small tourist shops on both sides of the street.

Treasure Hunt Craft Shop off South Church St, George Town (opposite North Terminal). A small, friendly shop with some of the cheapest T-shirts on the island at CI$8.95 each or three for CI$21. Also does hair braiding (see below).

Trifles Elizabeth Sq, Shedden Rd, George Town; tel: 949 6141. The mainstay of this shop is its pastries, but gifts are on sale as well.

Tropical l'Attitude Edward St, George Town; tel: 945 1233. Close to the post office, a classy gifts and clothes shop with a Caribbean theme. Open Mon–Fri 8.30am–5.30pm; Sat 8.30am–5.00pm.

Tropical Trader Galleria Plaza, West Bay Rd; tel: 949 8354. Also at the Duty Free Centre, George Town; tel: 949 6538. Arts and crafts, island music and casual clothes. Open Mon–Sat, 9.00am–9.30pm.

T-Shirts of Cayman Goring Av, George Town; tel: 949 7093. In addition to a wide selection of T-shirts, browse here for sarongs, swimwear and souvenirs, to a background of calypso music.

Hair braiding

Hair braiding is popular with visitors, whether it be single braids for around US$2 to a full head from around US$60. A full set of braids will take around 45 minutes to complete, depending on the length of hair. The following are just some of the many salons that offer this service:

Ebanks Beauty Centre Coconut Place, West Bay Rd; tel: 949 1995. As the name implies, this is a full beauty salon, with hair braiding just one of its many services. Open Mon–Sat 10.30am–8.30pm.

Iris Braids and Beauty Regency Court, West Bay Rd; tel: 945 3525

Naomi's Hair Affair Eastern Av (behind the bike rental place), George Town; tel: 949 8980

Spa Novell Harquail Drive; tel: 945 1810. Hair braiding is just one of the services here, which also include massage, skin care and hair care. Open daily.

Treasure Hunt Craft Shop off South Church St, George Town (opposite North Terminal). Hair braiding US$2.50 per braid, or special deal for whole head.

Pharmacy

Remember that pharmacies on the islands can only fulfil prescriptions that have been issued on the islands, so bring sufficient quantities of any regular prescription drugs that you need to last your stay. In addition to the following, there are pharmacies at the hospital and at both health clinics (see page 137).

Cayman Drug Kirk Freeport Centre, Albert Panton St, George Town. Open Mon–Sat 8.30am–5.30pm.

Edmar's Thompson Bldg, George Town; tel: 945 5042. Diagonally opposite the post office. Also sells newspapers etc. Open Mon–Sat 8.30am–5.30pm.

Grand Harbour Pharmacy Grand Harbour, Red Bay; tel: 947 3784. Open Mon–Sat 8.00am–10.00pm, Sun 10.00am–6.00pm.

Island Pharmacy West Shore Centre, West Bay Rd; tel: 949 8987. Open Mon–Sat 9.00am–7.00pm, Sun 10.00am–6.00pm

Strand Pharmacy The Strand, West Bay Rd; tel: 945 7759. Open Mon–Sat 7.00am–10.00pm, Sun 9.00am–6.00pm.

There is also a pharmacy at Kirk Supermarket, open Mon–Sat 9.00am–9.00pm.

Photography

There are some stunning prints of underwater life available at most gift shops on the island. For these, as well as photographic equipment and films, try the following:

Cathy Church's Underwater Photo Centre & Gallery Sunset House, South Church St; tel: 949 7415, US toll free 800 934 3661; web: www.cathychurch.com. The wide range of underwater prints, some signed, makes this place worth a detour. Good selection of cameras and film, including underwater equipment. Print and slide processing in just three hours. Underwater camera sales, and rental from US$10 per half day. Underwater photography courses include half-day beginners' course US$100; private sessions from US$50–125 per hour. Week-long package, including hotel, diving and some meals, approx US$3,000. Open daily 7.30am–6.00pm.

Cayman Camera South Church St, George Town; tel: 949 8359. Films, cameras etc.

Photo Centre, Bush Centre, North Church St, George Town; tel: 949 0030

Photo World Queen's Court, West Bay Rd; tel: 945 0351. Open Mon–Fri 8.30am–6.30pm; Sat 9.00am–5.30pm.

Rainbow Photo Elizabeth Sq, Shedden Rd, George Town; tel: 945 2046

Rapid Photo Merren Place, West Bay Rd; tel: 949 7514. One-hour processing for 35mm or APS films. Pick-up service available from various hotels on Seven Mile Beach. Open Mon–Fri 8.00am–6.00pm, Sat 10.00am–6.00pm.

Music and video

Blockbuster Video Outlets at Eden Centre, George Town, tel: 949 9500; West Shore Centre, West Bay Rd, tel: 949 4500, and Grand Harbour, Red Bay, tel: 947 9660. Rental of VCRs as well as videos.

Caribbean Rhythms Old Fort Building, North Church St, George Town; tel: 949 4094. Just north of the port, this waterfront shop specialises in CDs (from US$17) and tapes from US$10. Wide range of music, including reggae, steel band and calypso, with recordings of local bands and the Barefoot Man. Open Mon–Fri 8.00am–5.00pm; Sat 9.00am–2.00pm.

Hottrax West Shore Centre, West Bay Rd; tel: 949 9047; also at Grand Harbour, Red Bay; tel: 947 9040. CDs and tapes for every taste. Open Mon–Sat 10.00am–10.00pm.

OTHER PRACTICALITIES
Banks

Cayman National Bank (tel: 949 4655), has branches with cash machines throughout Grand Cayman. Visa, MasterCard etc are accepted. There is a 24-hour ATM near the port in George Town.

ATMs

Several banks on the island have ATMs, as do the major supermarkets. Machines can issue either US or CI dollars, so decide what you want first, but remember that there is a minimum withdrawal of CI$25. ATMs are available at the following locations:

Barclays Bank Shedden Rd, George Town
Cayman National Bank Elgin Av and Harbour Drive in George Town; Galleria Plaza on West Bay Rd; Mirco Commerce Centre, North Sound Road; Owen Roberts Airport

Also at:

Foster's Food Fair Airport and The Strand
Grand Harbour Pharmacy Crewe Rd, Red Bay
Kirk Supermarket Eastern Av; North Sound Rd
Republix Supermarket West Bay
Texaco Star Mart Poinciana Dr, Savannah

Money wiring

FIS Eastern Av (next to Old Champion House), tel: 945 5616, are agents for MoneyGram.

Communications
Telephone, fax and internet

There are numerous public telephones throughout the island. Most hotels have business centres with internet access, but many are very expensive. For an efficient, all-round service at a fraction of the price, visit:

Cable & Wireless Andersen Sq, corner of Elgin Av and Shedden Rd, George Town. Telephone and fax centre. Open Mon–Fri 8.15am–5.00pm; Sat 8.15am–1.00pm.

Communication Station Cardinall Av, George Town. Phone, fax and internet access (US$0.25 per minute; US$1 minimum), and photocopying service. Pre-paid phonecards available at US$12.50 and US$20, as well as Smart cards. Open Mon–Sat 8.30am–5.00pm.

For similarly priced but rather more convivial internet access, try one of the following:

Dickens Internet Café and Coffee Shop Galleria Plaza, West Bay Rd; tel: 945 9195. US$0.12 per minute. Open Mon–Sat 8.30am–10.00pm.
PD's Galleria Plaza, West Bay Rd; tel: 949 7144. Pub-like bar with internet access available at US$0.15 per minute (no minimum charge). Open Mon–Fri 7.00am–1.00am; Sat 7.00am–midnight; Sun 11.00am–midnight.
Shooters Seven Mile Shops, West Bay Rd; tel: 946 3496. US$0.18 per minute or US$11 per hour. Minimum charge US$2. Open Mon–Fri 10.30am–1.00pm; Sat/Sun 10.30am–midnight.

Post office and couriers
The main post office is on the corner of Edward Street in George Town, tel: 949 2474; fax: 945 1246. Post office boxes are located outside the building on Edward Street. Stamp collectors will find plenty of interest here, or at the philatelic bureau at Seven Mile Beach post office in West Shore Centre on West Bay Road. Open Mon–Fri 8.15am–5.00pm; Sat 8.30am–midday.

Medical facilities
George Town's Chrissie Tomlinson Memorial Hospital is on Walkers Road, tel: 949 6066. The recently renovated buildings incorporate a full range of medical facilities, including a decompression chamber for use by divers in an emergency. In the event of specialist treatment being necessary, patients are transferred to the Baptist Hospital in Miami.

There are also several private medical centres, including the Professional Medical Centre (tel: 949 6066) and Cayman Medical and Surgical Centre (tel: 949 8150).

Should you be in urgent need of a dentist, call one of the two private dental clinics in George Town: Cayman Dental Services, tel: 947 4447, or Cayman Medical and Surgical Centre, tel: 949 8150.

For details of pharmacies, see page 135.

Religious services
With over 50 Christian churches on the islands, there is no shortage of services to attend. The majority of these are Presbyterian, but there is also a Catholic church, St Ignatius, in George Town's Walkers Road. Most hotels hold a list of churches with service times. For services at Elmslie Memorial Church, see page 141.

The Lord's Church in West Bay offers a free island-wide pick up to visitors for their Sunday morning service at 10.30am. To arrange to be collected, call 949 1802 at least 24 hours in advance.

Travel agency

Cayman Travel Elizabeth Sq, George Town. Open Mon–Fri 8.30am–5.30pm; Sat 8.30am–midday.

ENTERTAINMENT AND ACTIVITIES

Grand Cayman offers a wealth of activities for all interests, both on and off the water. For details of these, see *Chapter 4, Diving and Other Activities*. For information about festivals, see pages 57–9.

Music

Many restaurants and hotels feature live music on a regular basis. These include a lively steel band at Treasure Island Resort, on West Bay Road, Mon 6.30–8.00pm; Tue–Sat 7.00–10.00pm.

Theatre and cinema

The **Harquail Theatre** (PO Box 30201 SMB; tel: 949 5477/5839; fax: 949 4519; email: cncf@candw.ky; web: www.artscayman.org), home of the Cayman National Cultural Foundation, is located on the left off the Harquail Drive bypass heading north from George Town. The 330-seat, purpose-built theatre features both specially commissioned plays and musical entertainment, including classical concerts, opera, dance schools and the annual local battle of the bands. It also stages the occasional fashion show and exhibition of local art.

There is a second theatre, the **Prospect Playhouse** just off Red Bay Road in Prospect (tel: 949 1998/5585). Home of the Cayman Drama Society, which is predominantly made up of expatriate workers, the Playhouse puts on a wide variety of plays from comedies and pantomime to serious drama.

The **cinema** on Harquail Drive, just off West Bay Rd (tel: 949 4011), has two screens, and shows new releases every day except Sunday. There is talk of building a second cinema at the newly opened Grand Harbour near Red Bay, but nothing has yet been decided.

For details of what's on, see the Friday edition of the *Caymanian Compass*, which includes a weekly entertainment guide.

Bowling

Bowling is on offer at the ten-lane Stingray Bowling Centre, The Greenery, West Bay Road (next to The Strand); tel: 945 4444; fax: 949 6900; web: www.stingraybowling.com. Cost CI$4 per person, per game; CI$24 per lane for one hour; CI$3 shoe rental. Open Mon–Thu 11.30am–11.30pm; Fri 11.30am–1.00am; Sat–Sun 11.30am–midnight.

BEACHES

Grand Cayman has no shortage of beautiful beaches, for every taste. Even within easy reach of George Town, visitors can opt for the sophistication of Seven Mile Beach or head for the more secluded coves of South Sound. Further afield, laid-back Rum Point beckons (see page 164), while choose carefully on the eastern or northern shores of the island and you could have the place to yourself.

Seven Mile Beach

Arguably the quintessential Caribbean beach, Seven Mile Beach (it's actually 4.6 miles, or 7.5km) runs the length of the western side of the island north of George Town. Hotels, villas and apartments line almost the whole of the beach, blocking any view of the sea from West Bay Road, although there are several access points to the beach, clearly marked with blue and white signs.

Just beyond the Westin, however, is one point where the builders have been kept at bay. The **public beach** (bus stop 15) is a tribute to a last vestige of commonsense, a relatively peaceful stretch of soft white sand with buoyed swimming area and natural shade provided by tall casuarina trees. Painted wooden beach shelters with barbecue grills provide ideal spots for a sand-free picnic, with toilets and telephones nearby. For children, there is a play area – and the ice-cream van pays regular visits. A little further north, **Cemetery Beach**, at the southern end of Boggy Sand Road (access is alongside the cemetery, opposite the fire station on West Bay Road) is another tranquil spot, with picnic benches located in the shade, and public toilets. A swim of five minutes or so brings you out to Cemetery Reef for some really good snorkelling, though the distance and relatively deep water means that this isn't for weak swimmers. Shoals of parrotfish and sergeant major fish may be seen, and even the occasional reef shark. The fish here are well used to their graceless human companions, and may indeed swim straight up to you, which can be quite unnerving.

Facilities all along Seven Mile Beach are numerous. All the hotels along the coast have bars and restaurants open to the public, so the choice is wide. Watersports, too, are easily booked: beach kiosks up near the Hyatt and Westin Casuarina hotels offer parasailing, and some of the six dive specialists that operate from here even have outlets on the beach.

For those looking for a good base, try **Royal Palms Beach Club** (West Bay Rd; tel: 945 6358; fax: 945 5360; email: rpalms@candw.ky) at the southern end of the beach, which has a beach bar, snack shop, barbecue, terrace and Reef Grill restaurant. A lively venue, this, there are local bands playing Monday to Saturday nights in season, or Wednesday to Saturday out of season. Most watersports are available on site, and diving can be arranged through Red Sail Sports. Admission is free to residents and those staying on the island; day-trip visitors pay US$2 per person. The bar is open Mon–Sat 9.00am–midnight; Sun 1.00pm–midnight. An alternative venue for the day is **Beach Club Hotel & Dive Resort**, where visitors, including cruise-ship passengers, are welcome Monday to Saturday. Here, the bar is open daily 10.00am–11.45pm, and the restaurant 6.30–9.30pm.

George Town and further south

On the other side of George Town is **Club Paradise** (also called Paradise Bar & Grill) in South Church St, tel: 945 1444 (see page 121). With its restaurant/bar and on-the-spot diving and snorkelling, this friendly venue is a good place to spend the day, whether you want to participate in active sports or just laze in the sun with a cool rum punch, though it does get busy when the cruise ships are in.

A little way beyond the centre of George Town lies the secluded **Smith's Cove**, a public beach that contrasts strongly with the flashier Seven Mile Beach. The small area of sand is surrounded by rocks and backed by trees under which picnic tables are set out. It is the perfect spot for snorkelling, or just to sit on the rocks and watch the sea.

Rum Point
See page 164.

GEORGE TOWN
George Town, at least at first glance, is more small-town resort than offshore banking capital. Painted wooden buildings nestle among smart shopping arcades overlooking the small natural harbour, where boats tie up to ferry their passengers to and from local beaches, or to the big cruise ships which anchor in the bay on an almost daily basis. Along the waterfront, and in the area behind, the streets are lined with shops where visitors can buy anything from tacky souvenirs to top-class jewellery and watches at duty-free prices.

Although the centre of George Town has no real beaches, it's only a short walk to the southern end of Seven Mile Beach, or to the south of town, or a quick bus or taxi ride to Smith's Cove or further up West Bay.

History
Once known as the Hog Sties, and overlooking what is still called Hog Sty Bay, George Town took over the role of capital from Bodden Town, some 12 miles to the east, in 1888, having been widely regarded as the capital since the 1830s. The town was probably renamed after George III in an attempt to bestow an aura of dignity on the place.

Hog Sty Bay is a natural harbour, sheltered from the prevailing winds and the only place on the island where ships of any depth may safely anchor. In 1796, George Gauld reported that the place was:

> a small village, near which is the only place where large vessels can come to. The water is so clear that you can easily see where it is most proper to drop the anchor but without the greatest precaution you are in danger of having your cables cut by the rocks.

For a brief period at the end of the 19th century, the port was the centre of a phosphate mining industry, with phosphate derived from the fossilised guano of seabirds. The formation of the Grand Cayman Phosphate Company in 1883, followed by the Carib Guano Company the next year, led to the export of tons of phosphate to the US. Within just a few years, however, large deposits of the mineral were discovered in Florida, and the industry was no longer economically viable. By the early 1890s, trading had ceased, with both companies suffering heavy losses.

Today, the harbour is a mecca for the cruise ships that bring countless passengers to the island almost daily.

What to see
A short walking tour of George Town

The following route takes in the major sites of George Town, starting from either South or North Terminal, close to the point at which cruise-ship passengers dock, and finishing at the nearby museum. Allow about 45 minutes for the walk, longer if you plan to stop for a drink or explore inside any of the buildings.

From North Port Terminal, turn left along Harbour Drive, with the sea to your left. Cross the road almost immediately to **Elmslie Memorial United Church**, named after the minister who brought the Presbyterian faith to the islands in the mid 19th century. The simplicity of this whitewashed church, built in the early 1920s, is accentuated by dark wooden pews and a stunning stained-glass window. Look up at the vaulted wooden ceiling: the rafters were designed like the upturned hull of a ship, reflecting Cayman's seafaring tradition. All are welcome to attend Sunday services, held at 9.30am, 11.00am and 7.00pm. For information, tel: 949 7923.

Just in front of the church is Cayman's **War Memorial**, a tribute to those Caymanians who lost their lives during two world wars.

Cross back to the sea side of the road, and just past the container depot on your left you will find the **Seamen Memorial**, a simple but chilling reminder of the almost total reliance on the sea of Caymanians through the ages.

Continue past various duty-free shops and restaurants to a small **glass-blowing studio**, where free demonstrations can be seen Monday to Saturday from 8.00am. A little further on, on the same side of the road, is **Fort George**, overlooking the harbour. This was never a fort in the sense of a protective building, but rather a simple enclosure surrounded by low stone walls housing just three small cannons. George Town's entire defence against late 18th-century Spanish marauders, it was later used as a look-out post in World War II, but was partially demolished in 1972. The area that you see today, with its replica guns, is all that is left of the 'not very well constructed' fort that met Edward Corbet in 1802. Admission is free.

Turn back across Harbour Drive into Fort Street, and walk up here past Fort Street Market (a good place to buy a cool drink) to the modern **Legislative Assembly** building on your left. Visitors may attend sessions of the assembly provided that they conform with the required dress code. Alternatively, if the assembly is not in session, it may be possible to have a short guided tour by the Sergeant at Arms. Outside stands a statue of Mr Jim, a popular politician – arguably a contradiction in terms – during the 1970s and 1980s who was the brains behind the hugely successful annual Pirates Week festival.

The **Town Hall** next door is designated the 1919 Peace Memorial, although it was not actually built until 1923. For many years, the building was a focal point of island life, but nowadays it is used effectively as an

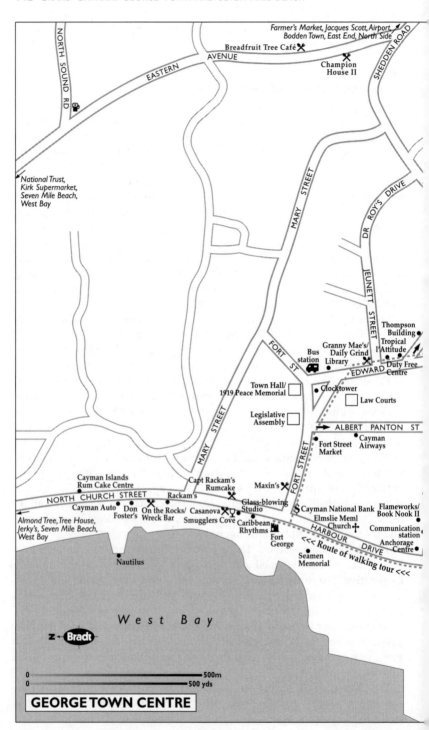

Farmer's Market, Jacques Scott, Airport,
Bodden Town, East End, North Side
Breadfruit Tree Café ✗
Champion
House II ✗

NORTH SOUND RD

EASTERN AVENUE

SHEDDEN ROAD

National Trust,
Kirk Supermarket,
Seven Mile Beach,
West Bay

MARY STREET

DR ROY'S DRIVE

JEUNETT STREET

Thompson
Building ●
Tropical
l'Attitude

FORT ST

Bus
station
Granny Mae's/
Daily Grind
Library ✗
EDWARD Duty Free
Centre

Town Hall/
1919 Peace Memorial ▢
● Clocktower
Law Courts ▢

Legislative
Assembly ▢

ALBERT PANTON ST
Fort Street
Market
Cayman
Airways

MARY STREET

Cayman Islands
Rum Cake Centre
Capt Rackam's
Rumcake ✗
Maxin's ✗

NORTH CHURCH STREET
Rackam's

FORT STREET

Cayman Auto
Don
Foster's
On the Rocks/
Wreck Bar
Casanova ✗
Glass-blowing
Studio
Cayman National Bank
Elmslie Meml
Church ✝
Flameworks/
Book Nook II

Almond Tree, Tree House,
Jerky's, Seven Mile Beach,
West Bay
Smugglers Cove
Caribbean
Rhythms
Fort
George
HARBOUR DRIVE
Communication
station
Anchorage
Centre ●

● Nautilus

Seamen
Memorial
<<< Route of walking tour <<<

West   Bay

z ◆ Bradt

0 _____ 500m
0 _____ 500 yds

GEORGE TOWN CENTRE

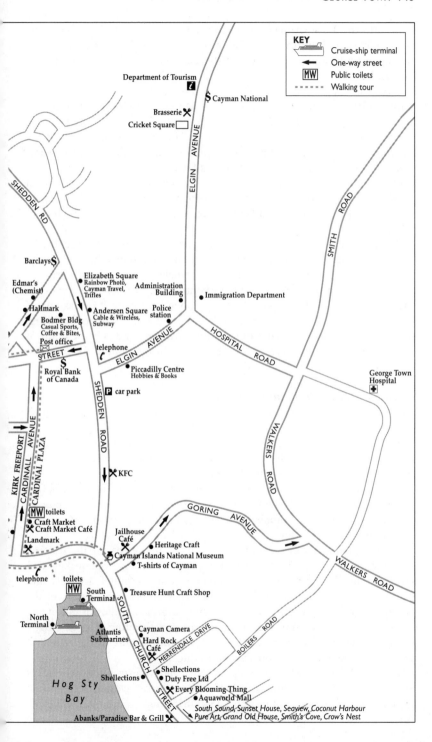

KEY
- Cruise-ship terminal
- One-way street
- MW Public toilets
- ········ Walking tour

Department of Tourism

$ Cayman National

Brasserie ✕

Cricket Square

ELGIN AVENUE

SHEDDEN RD

SMITH ROAD

Barclays $

Edmar's (Chemist)

Elizabeth Square
Rainbow Photo,
Cayman Travel,
Trifles

Administration Building

Immigration Department

Hallmark

Andersen Square
Cable & Wireless,
Subway

Police station

Bodmer Bldg
Casual Sports,
Coffee & Bites,

Post office

HOSPITAL ROAD

STREET

telephone

ELGIN AVENUE

$ Royal Bank of Canada

Piccadilly Centre
Hobbies & Books

George Town Hospital

SHEDDEN ROAD

P car park

KIRK FREEPORT

CARDINALL AVENUE

CARDINAL PLAZA

WALKERS ROAD

✕ KFC

MW toilets

Craft Market
✕ Craft Market Café

Landmark
✕

GORING AVENUE

Jailhouse Café

Heritage Craft

Cayman Islands National Museum
T-shirts of Cayman

WALKERS ROAD

telephone   toilets

MW South Terminal

Treasure Hunt Craft Shop

North Terminal

SOUTH CHURCH STREET

Atlantis Submarines

Cayman Camera

Hard Rock Café

MERRENDALE DRIVE

BOILERS ROAD

Shellections

Duty Free Ltd

Shellections

Every Blooming Thing

Aquaworld Mall

Hog Sty Bay

South Sound, Sunset House, Seaview, Coconut Harbour

Abanks/Paradise Bar & Grill ✕

Pure Art, Grand Old House, Smith's Cove, Crow's Nest

annexe to the **Law Courts** just round the corner in Edward Street. The steam-powered **clocktower** in front of the Town Hall was erected in 1937 for the princely sum of £140 (US$210) to commemorate the reign of King George V.

Diagonally opposite the Town Hall, on Edward Street, is George Town's public **library** (tel: 949 5159; open: Mon–Fri 10.00am–6.00pm; Sat 10.00am–1.00pm). The building dates to 1939, one of four in the town constructed by the shipwright Captain Rayal Bodden, during the tenure of Allen Wolsey Cardinall. Cardinall was commissioner to the Cayman Islands from 1934 to 1941, and it is after him that George Town's Cardinall Avenue is named. Further along Edward Street, on the opposite corner, is the rounded façade of the **post office**, another of Bodden's constructions, also built in 1939. As well as central postal facilities, the office boasts a philatelic bureau (see page 137).

Turn west from here back towards the harbour and you will be following Cardinall Avenue, with its array of modern duty-free shops. Just before the end, on the left, is the Craft Market Café, a homely place to stop for a drink or a quick snack. At the junction with Harbour Drive, turn left and cross over Shedden Avenue – the wooden buildings along here mark it out as one of George Town's older streets – to end the tour at the **Old Courts building**, one of Cayman's few surviving 19th-century structures and now the home of the National Museum. To return to the port, turn right out of the museum and follow Harbour Drive until you are opposite the terminal.

Cayman Islands National Museum

PO Box 2189, Harbour Drive; tel: 949 8368; fax: 949 0309; email: museum@candw.ky

Situated opposite Hog Sty Bay in the Old Courts building, the museum offers plenty to interest both adults and children. Don't miss the excellent 3D model, or bathymetric map, showing the Cayman Islands perched high above the sea bed of the Caribbean. A more graphic presentation of the famous walls that surround these islands would be hard to find. A laser-disc show focusing on the underwater world is complemented by interactive displays of undersea life and Cayman natural history.

Upstairs, a moving mannequin tells stories of the sea beside the restored 14ft (4.2m) catboat, the centrepiece of displays on turtling, rope making and shipbuilding. Alongside this are numerous other cultural artefacts and paintings from the national collection, all serving to bring the history of the islands to life. The old court room has been refurbished to allow for changing exhibitions of community life, including art and furniture. Heritage days, featuring one of the Cayman districts, are a regular feature of the museum. Downstairs, there is a good gift shop and a café.

Open Mon–Fri 9.00am–5.00pm; Sat and most public holidays 10.00am–2.00pm. Last admissions half an hour before closing. Closed first Monday of each month. Admission CI$4/US$5; concessions CI$2/US$2.50. Admission free first Saturday of each month.

For a more in-depth look at the town, get hold of a copy of the National Trust's **Historic Walking Tour**, which takes in the capital's historic buildings and monuments as well as several traditional homes and shops in the vicinity. The Trust's full walk takes approximately two hours, though of course you could cover just part of the route; the information in the leaflet gives considerable insight into the buildings on the route and the historical context in which they were set. For a copy of the leaflet, contact the National Trust (see page 27).

Near George Town

Grand Cayman is so small that, realistically, everywhere is within easy reach of George Town. The following suggestions are for trips starting from George Town itself, as well as focusing on one or two places on the outskirts of the capital. For organised tours covering the rest of the island, see page 77. For details of areas beyond here and Seven Mile Beach, see *Chapter 6, Beyond George Town*.

Within the George Town area, but beyond the scope of a simple walking tour, are the following:

Cardinal D's Eastern Av; tel: 949 8855. Over 60 species of birds, including Cayman parrots and West Indian whistling-ducks, inhabit this small zoo on a five-acre site just opposite Kirk's supermarket on Eastern Avenue. Also to be seen are the blue iguana, turtles and agoutis, as well as emus and miniature ponies, which are particularly popular with children. The souvenir shop sells food to feed the birds. Guided tours are available. Open Mon–Fri 10.00am–6.00pm; Sat/Sun midday–6.00pm. US$5 adult; children under 12 US$2.50.

Hidden behind George Town, next to the CUC electricity generating station on the industrial estate, is the extraordinary **conch shell house**. Originally built in 1935 from more than 4,000 conch shells, it later burned down but was subsequently rebuilt. A much-photographed private house, it is not open to the public. Nearby is the **Tortuga Rum Cake factory** (tel: 949 7701; fax: 949 6322; email: tortuga@candw.ky; web: www.caribplace.com/foods/tortuga.htm), where visitors can get an idea of the manufacturing process as they sample the various flavours, or stop for a drink or snack. Open Mon–Fri 8.00am–5.00pm, Sat 8.00am–2.30pm.

Boat trips
Submersibles, semi-submersibles and glass-bottomed boats

You don't have to be a water baby to experience the under-sea attractions of the islands. Even if you're not a diver, you can explore the fascinating reefs and shipwrecks that surround Grand Cayman, not just from the surface but in submersibles – a form of submarine that has to return to shore regularly for its batteries to be recharged. Grand Cayman played host to the world's first tourist submersible and with good reason – the reef is relatively shallow and the visibility is excellent.

For the less intrepid, semi-submersibles have a lower deck beneath the surface, enabling passengers to walk below and view the first few feet of the underwater world, as seen by a snorkeller, through large glazed windows, then to return to the fresh air on the top.

Atlantis Submarines PO Box 1043 GT, Harbour Drive, George Town; tel: 949 7700, US toll free 800 887 8571; email: atlantis@candw.ky; web: www.goatlantis.com/cayman
The first of the world's passenger submarine operators, Atlantis was established in 1984. Passengers are ferried out to the dive site by shuttle, then transferred to the submersible for a 40-minute trip down to around 100ft (30m). For the non-diver, this is a real opportunity to see the underwater world; even divers will find the running commentary fascinating. Up to six dives a day, Mon–Sat, depart from 8.30am. Night dives are also offered Wed, Thu, Fri at 7.00pm and 8.00pm in winter, or at 7.30pm Wed, Fri in summer. Adults US$79; children half price. No children under 3ft (0.9m) tall.

For the true – and well-heeled – adventurer, Atlantis boasts an altogether more serious craft capable of going to depths of up to 1,000ft (304m). The one-hour deep dive, the only one of its kind in the world, takes just two passengers per trip to depths of 800ft (244m) for US$345 per person, or to 1,000ft (305m) for US$450 per person. Under the bright lights of the submarine, the true colours of coral and other marine life are clearly visible. Videos of your trip are also available. Tours depart Mon–Sat (Mon–Fri in summer) at 8.30am, 10.00am, 11.30am, 1.00pm and 2.30pm.

At the other end of the scale, the semi-submersible ***Seaworld Explorer*** explores the harbour around George Town, including the area around two of the town's shipwrecks (departures Mon–Sat 10.00am and 2.00pm), while ***Stingray Explorer*** – as its name suggests – takes you out to Stingray City (departures from Morgan's Harbour Tue, Thu and Fri at 3.00pm). For information on both of these, call 949 8534. Adults US$35, children US$19.

Nautilus PO Box 10094 APO, Bush Centre, George Town; tel: 945 1355; fax: 945 3739; email: nautilus@candw.ky; web: www.nautilus.ky
Tours are run day and night in the semi-submersible *Nautilus*, named after Jules Verne's futuristic craft, from Rackam's dock (behind Rackam's Pub) in George Town. The hour-long trip with commentary offers the opportunity to see both marine life and shipwrecks, and to watch fish being fed by divers just outside the window. In the afternoons, the trip is followed by an opportunity to snorkel, either on the reef or over a nearby wreck. Mask, snorkel and fins are included, with tuition available if needed. One-hour trip: adults US$35, children US$19; two-hour snorkel trip: adults US$39, children US$19.

Nautilus can also be chartered at CI$500 per hour to take passengers on a sunset cruise, the ship-based equivalent of a night dive, with the chance to see octopus, squid and perhaps the occasional shark. Unlimited rum punch and substantial snacks come as part of the deal.

Cayman Submariners/SEAmobile Submarine Tours Tel: 916 DIVE
Trips to the reef for just two passengers in this small vessel with all-round visibility make this a pretty exclusive set up, even offering the opportunity to pilot the sub – under supervision, naturally. US$139 per person.

Red Sail Sports at Rum Point (see page 105) offers trips in glass-bottomed boats.

Other boat trips

Cockatoo Tel: 949 8100. A 2½-hour sail in this racing catamaran departs at sunset from North Sound on Fridays at 5.00pm. US$40 per person.

Jolly Roger Tel: 946 5232; email: jolroger@candw.ky. The replica of a 17th-century galleon that is moored off George Town provides an interesting and diminutive contrast to the multi-storey cruise ships that anchor alongside. Afternoon 'pirate encounters' offer two hours of fun and frolics, with departures at 2.30pm Mon, Wed and Fri. Adults US$30, children 3–12 US$20. In the evening, there are two sunset cruises – given a choice, go for the booze (cocktail) cruise rather than dinner. All cruises depart from Harbour Drive opposite the Hard Rock Café. Cocktail cruise US$40 (children 6–16 US$25); dinner cruise US$60 (children 6–16 US$35). Children under 6 free.

Outings on the *Jolly Roger* and the *Valhalla* (a 1934 tall ship) may also be booked through E&H Cruises. Tel: 949 8988 (*Jolly Roger*); or 945 7245 (*Valhalla*).

A day trip to **Rum Point** is a must, with a regular ferry leaving from the dock alongside the Hyatt Hotel on West Bay Road several times a day. For details, see pages 76–7 and 164.

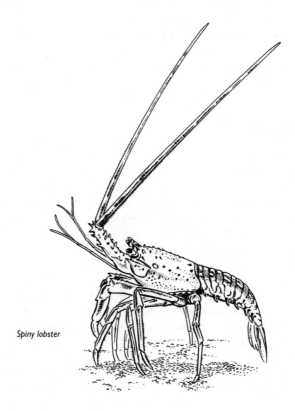

Spiny lobster

Beyond George Town

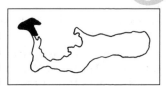

WEST BAY

Drive north past the last of the big hotels on West Bay Road, and you head back to an era when the island was rarely visited and the pace of life was slow. Painted wooden houses with airy verandas are set far back from the road in large gardens, many of them the traditional sand gardens that are so much a part of the Cayman heritage. Once a thriving fishing community, the focal point for everyday activities from shopping and schools to the making of turtle nets, West Bay is still the second largest residential district on Grand Cayman, and popular with visitors to the Turtle Farm and Hell.

Head for the northern coast of West Bay and you will find empty beaches and virgin mangrove forest. Here, casuarinas and sea-grape trees cast their shade over the narrow expanse of sand, and wild tamarind grows along the roadside, intertwined in season with the purple and white morning glory. Don't expect any facilities – that's the beauty of the place.

Where to stay

Cobalt Coast PO Box 159 H, 18 Sea Fan Drive; tel: 946 5656; fax: 946 5657; email: cobalt@candw.ky; US reservations tel: 800 992 2015, 305 670 4911; fax: 305 670 4948; email: iconmarketing@prodigy.net; web: www.cobaltcoast.com (18 rooms/suites/villas) Opened in 2001, this small new resort is in a secluded beachfront location at the north of West Bay, some two miles east of the Turtle Farm. Each hotel room and one or two-bedroom suite has one king or two double beds per bedroom, a living room with sofa bed, AC, TV, fridge, coffee machine, telephone and safe. In addition, villas have fully equipped kitchens. Duppies restaurant and bar. swimming pool, jacuzzi, diving (through Dive-Tech) and other watersports, boat dock, dive shop.
Rates per night (including complimentary breakfast) low/high season: garden view US$105/140 (two people); oceanfront US$120/160 (two people); one-bedroom suite US$185/250 (two people); two-bedroom suite/villa US$255/325 (four people). Each additional person US$20/25. All prices subject to 8% service charge. Dive packages available on request.

Nautilus Apartments PO Box 634 GT, 88 Boggy Sand Rd; tel/fax: 946 0464; fax: 949 2677; email: nautiapt@candw.ky; web: http://cayman.com.ky/com/nautilus/contact.htm (4 units)

Frank and Beth Roulstone's beachside townhouses, cottage and studio on one of
Grand Cayman's most historic roads offer a comfortable and personal alternative to the
hotels further south. With direct access to the secluded northern end of Seven Mile
Beach, each of the houses has two bedrooms, two bathrooms, kitchen and living room.
The townhouses also have a balcony with sea view, AC/ceiling fans, washer/dryer and
garden furniture with gas barbecue; the cottage has a screened porch and deck. The
studio, ideal for two people, has ceiling fans, basin/toilet, a fridge and a cooker.
Rates per night, low/high season (inclusive of tax): townhouse (up to four people)
US$220/330; cottage (up to four people) US$100/140; studio (up to two people)
US$65/75. Children under 12 free. Minimum stay three days in summer, seven days
in winter. No credit cards.

Spanish Bay Reef Resort PO Box 903 GT, Pikes Rd; tel: 949 3765, US toll free 1
800 482 DIVE; fax: 949 1842; email: spnshbay@candw.ky; web:
www.caymanresorthotels.com (66 rooms)
This all-inclusive hacienda-style resort is set in tranquil gardens on the north coast of
West Bay, not far from Pappagallo's restaurant. Particularly popular with families and
couples, the resort's rooms have AC, TV and balcony or patio with garden or sea
view. Standard and superior rooms are located in the main building, while additional
accommodation is available in cottage oceanview rooms or one-bedroom bungalows.
Spanish Main restaurant, Calico Jack's poolside bar, swimming pool, private harbour
and boat dock with full dive facilities. Entertainment includes sunset party and
barbecue.
Rates, quoted per person per night and based on double occupancy, vary almost from
month to month. Low to high prices are as follows: US$160–230 (standard);
US$185–255 (superior); US$205–280 (sea view); US$250–325 (one-bedroom
bungalow; US$200–275 (two-bedroom condominium). Single supplement US$100
per night. Third and fourth adults US$150 per night. Special rates for up to two
children when sharing with two adults: under six free; 6–12 US$50 per night; 12–17
US$75 per night. Free upgrade for honeymooners. Two-tank dive package, inclusive
of most equipment, additional US$50 per day.

Where to eat
Borden's Pizzas Morgan's Lane; tel: 949 3462. A popular place with locals, and the
pizzas look good, though the smell of cooking oil is a bit overpowering. Eat in or
takeaway pizzas from CI$7.50. Caribbean dinner at weekends. Open Mon–Thu
5.00–10.45pm; Fri 3.30–11.45pm; Sat/Sun midday–11.45pm.
Calypso Grill Morgan's Harbour; tel: 949 3948. Tucked away right on the
harbour on the east of West Bay, Calypso Grill opened in 1999 and was an instant
success. It's easy to see why – it's one of the most reasonable places to eat on the
island, and the combination of waterfront setting, friendly atmosphere and good
food is unbeatable. Mussels, fresh fish etc come straight from the dock, and sticky
toffee pudding's a speciality. Open Tue–Sat 11.30am–3.00pm and 6.00–10.00pm;
Sun 12.30–10.00pm.
Corita's Silver Sands Café Town Hall Rd; tel: 949 3301. Very simple breakfast,
lunch and dinner, as well as snacks to take out, all at very reasonable prices. Open
Mon–Sat 7.30am–9.30pm.

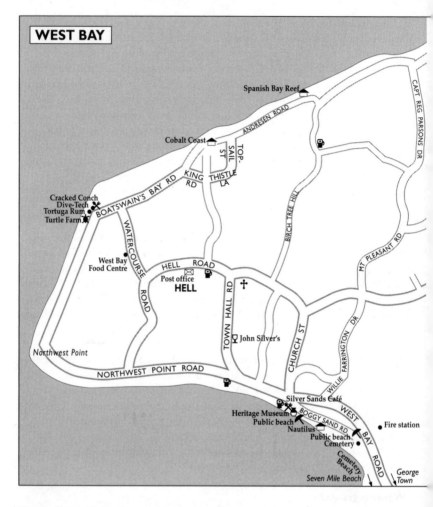

Cracked Conch by the Sea Northwest Point Rd; tel: 945 5217. Established in 1981, this nautical-themed establishment, owned by the wife of Bob Soto (of local diving fame), is just up the road from the Turtle Farm. Large waterfront balcony, bar area, and comfortable restaurant featuring a chronology of Cayman history. Very good traditional Cayman food, including turtle and conch, as well as a range of more cosmopolitan dishes, but slightly perfunctory service. Private room for up to 80 people, or parties for up to 250, plus catering and takeaway services available. Open daily, 11.00am till the last diners have left. Sunday Caribbean buffet 11.30am–3.00pm.

Domino's Pizza Birch Tree Hill Rd; tel: 949 6633. Open Mon–Thu 4.00–11.00pm, Fri and Sun 4.00pm–midnight; Sat 11.00am–midnight.

Liberty's Town Hall Rd, West Bay; tel: 949 3226. We didn't succeed in finding this family-owned restaurant in West Bay, but it is so well recommended for local dishes that it must be worth a try!

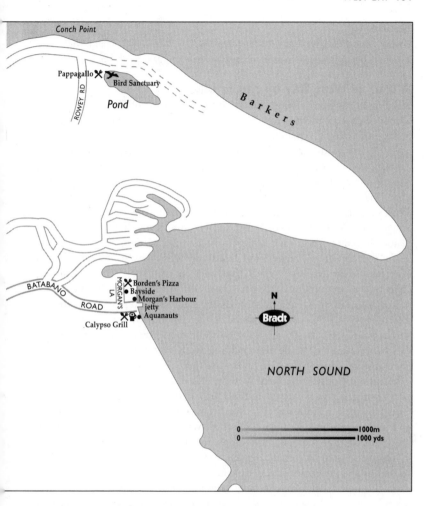

Pappagallo Barkers, tel: 949 1119/3479; email: pappa@candw.ky; web: www.pappagallo.ky. The romantic lakeside setting of the thatched Ristorante Pappagallo on the edge of West Bay is reason enough to visit. The food here is excellent, too, specialising in both Italian cuisine (the gnocchi is said to be unbeatable) and Caribbean seafood, with a noticeably creative hand behind the scenes. The comprehensive wine list affords plenty of choice. Open daily 6.00–10.30pm.

Bars

Silver's Canoe Noisy local bar well off the tourist trail with large open-air dance floor. Live music at weekends; loud juke box during the week. Open Mon–Fri 11.00am–1.00am, Sat/Sun 11.00am–midnight. Next door, John Silver's Inn (tel: 949 4264/4242) has basic rooms from CI$60, but be warned about the noise!

Shopping

Foster's Food Fair West Bay Rd (bus stop 18). Open 7.00am–11.00pm, Mon–Sat; 9.00am–6.00pm holidays. In-store pharmacy open Sun 9.00am–6.00pm.

A tour of West Bay by car or bike

Heading north from George Town, at the crossroads of West Bay Road with Church Street or by bus stop 19, stop a while to take on board a little of the heritage of Grand Cayman that is rapidly disappearing. The National Trust (see page 27) has produced a walking tour of central West Bay, covering historic Cayman houses and churches, including several in nearby **Boggy Sand Road**. Tucked away behind West Bay Road, and backing on to Seven Mile Beach, this quiet lane is worth a visit, even if you don't have time to do the whole walk. The Trust's tour takes about 2½ hours to complete, fanning out to encompass Church Street, Pond Road, Elizabeth Street and Henning Lane, but it can sensibly be divided into three parts, each taking no longer than an hour.

On the corner of Boggy Sand Road and West Bay Road is the so-called **Heritage Museum**, tel: 949 3477, and adjacent craft shop. More a ramshackle collection of documents and artefacts accumulated by one Prentice Powell than a museum, it is really only of passing interest. That said, the examples of different types of wood – ironwood, bullet wood, black mangrove used for smoke wood, and furstic, used for boatbuilding – shed light on a number of Cayman traditions, while the building itself was originally Mr Prentice's general store. Open Mon–Sat 9.00am–4.30pm. Small admission fee.

Continuing northwest along West Bay Road, the road follows the line of the coast, bringing you eventually to the Turtle Farm on the left, with the Cracked Conch by the Sea (see page 150) shortly beyond, a good place to stop for lunch.

Turtle Farm PO Box 645 GT, North West Point Road, West Bay; tel: 949 3893; fax: 949 1387; email: ctfl@candw.ky; web: www.turtle.ky. Bus stop 24.

The world's only commercial green sea turtle farm, established in 1968, is now owned by the government and welcomes visitors to observe green sea turtles, from the tiniest hatchlings to fully grown adults. The farm also has a small number of three other species of sea turtle: Kemp's ridley, loggerhead and hawksbill.

Originally set up in the natural environment of North Sound, the farm moved to its present site in 1971. Today, a breeding herd of 300 turtles produces some 45,000 eggs each year. A programme to release turtles back into the wild has been in operation since 1980. The annual 'turtle release' takes place in Pirates Week, at the end of October, and is run in conjunction with a recently launched interactive release programme. Under this, groups of up to eight people may have a guided tour of the farm, select a turtle, then accompany 'their' turtle out to sea, either diving or snorkelling. Since the scheme was started, 28,000 hatchlings and yearlings have been released into the wild, all tagged for subsequent identification.

Although the farm is hugely popular, some visitors are disappointed at the commercialism of the operation here. Do remember that it is first and foremost a working farm that is open to visitors, rather than a visitor attraction with farming on the side. There is a full-time marine biologist on the staff to look after the welfare of the turtles, some of which are second-generation turtles bred in captivity. Inevitably, work of this sort is controversial. It is too early yet to know whether released turtles will ever be able to contribute to the nesting population, as turtles do not start nesting until they are 25–30 years old. At that time, their instinct is to return to their hatching place to nest. Only time will tell whether the farm-reared turtles will be able to adapt to this intervention, but researchers are monitoring the situation closely.

In nearby pens, visitors can see the native parrot, iguana, agouti and hickatee. It seems rather incongruous to put these animals on display in the context of the farm, although it does afford the opportunity to see these relatively shy creatures close up.

An on-site café selling snacks, drinks and ice-cream is surrounded by a small exhibition on the history of turtling in the islands and marine conservation. The excellent gift shop across the way has a good selection of souvenirs and related merchandise, including books and jigsaws. For more about the history of the farm, pick up a copy of *Last Chance Lost*, which also addresses some of the conservation issues raised by the farm's programme.

Open daily, 8.30am–5.00pm. Adults US$6.00; children US$3.00. Turtle release Tue and Fri, 1.30–5.00pm. Snorkellers US$125; divers US$150.

Located just next to the Turtle Farm is the source of many of Grand Cayman's rum cakes, **Tortuga Rum Cake Factory**. Here you can see the bakery where some of the cakes are made and sample the various flavours before you buy. Open Mon–Fri 8.00am–5.00pm, Sat 8:00am–2:30pm. Admission free.

Follow the road on past the Turtle Farm and the Cracked Conch by the Sea, then turn right into Watercourse Road, with West Bay Food Centre on your right. Shortly after this is the turning left towards Hell.

The tiny village of **Hell**, about half a mile from the sea, probably acquired its name from the dark, rather evil-looking rock formations that lie behind the post office and are now much sought-after by photographers. A second, unsubstantiated story has it that a one-time British governor, intent on shooting birds in the vicinity, lost his temper when he missed a target and uttered a loud 'Oh, hell!' Either way, the name stuck. Not surprisingly, cards postmarked 'Hell' are popular among tourists, and a couple of shops alongside the post office oblige with a range of postcards. The village is also said to be the setting for scenes in Defoe's *Robinson Crusoe*.

This is truly a desolate place. The blackened landscape is at its most atmospheric in the early evening, when visitors are few and the light reflects off the still, dark water. The sharp formations of karst rock seen here are similar in structure to the rock found on the Mastic Trail. Over countless years, the underlying bedrock of limestone and dolomite, originally formed under the sea, was eroded both by the action of the waves and by microscopic algae, tiny marine organisms that ate away the calcium from the rock. Whereas the rock on the Mastic Trail is white, however, the rocks here have been stained black over the years by traces of algae that still cling to them.

The post office is open Mon–Fri 8.30am–5.00pm, Sat 8.30am–midday, and sells special stamps. If it's closed, the Devil's Den and Hades Hideaway alongside are open 7.00am–5.00pm; both sell stamps as well as postcards, so you can still post your correspondence here.

To return towards Seven Mile Beach, take the next turning right into Town Hall Road, which joins up with the northern end of West Bay Road. Alternatively, bear left on to Birch Tree Hill and make your way out towards Barkers, near Ristorante Pappagallo. The 14-acre pond and **bird sanctuary** here, overlooked by the restaurant, is a tidal lagoon that is home to tarpon. White egrets, ducks and numerous migrant birds gather here, particularly in winter. The road at this point becomes a rough track – for an idea of the seclusion that was typical of Grand Cayman 30 years ago, it's much nicer to leave your car or bike and explore the narrow shoreline lined with sea-grape trees on foot.

Turn back along the road to Captain Reginald Parsons Drive, then wend your way through to Batabano Road and east to North Sound at **Morgan's Harbour**. This quiet little backwater has a few places to moor small boats, and limited facilities including water, fuel and ice. Moorings may be booked through Aquanauts (see page 89). There's a minimarket with laundry next to Borden's Pizzas, just inland and to the right. Right by the harbour is the Calypso Grill, a friendly place for a meal or a drink with beautiful views across North Sound. To return to Seven Mile Beach, go back along Batabano Road to the crossroads, turn left into Church Street, and left again into West Bay Road.

GEORGE TOWN TO BODDEN TOWN

Following the coast road out of George Town to the south, the streets soon give way to a quiet and exclusive residential area. On the left as you leave the town is Pure Art (see page 134), a colourful celebration of Cayman art, from painting and ceramics to woven baskets 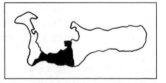 and wood carving. Follow the road past the Grand Old House (open Mon–Fri 11.45–2.00pm, daily 6.00–10.00pm) and continue on along the coast beyond Smith's Cove (the perfect place for a quick swim – see page 140). Stop, if you have time, to visit Dr Carey's small workshop where he produces black coral jewellery and engraved glass (open Mon–Sat 8.00am–6.00pm or later). Irrespective of your views on black coral, Dr Carey is something of an institution in his own right. Take him a marble or two and you'll make his day, adding to his huge collection (19,913 in November 2000) from all over the world.

As the road veers round to the east, even the larger houses thin out to reveal a narrow coastline fringed by mangroves and casuarina trees, looking out across **South Sound.** If it's around lunch time, try the Crow's Nest (see page 120) for a relaxing meal in an idyllic setting.

Further on to the right, sea kayaks are available for hire from the car park. There's a small public jetty here, too, and a couple of phone boxes.

Almost three miles after leaving George Town, the road links up with Crewe Road, coming in from the airport area. Just beyond here is the home of the **Stingray Brewery**, which lies on Red Bay Road, tel: 947 6699. Cayman's only brewery, which is open to visitors, has three beers, available at bars throughout the islands. Durty (3%) and Dark (6%) are both available on draught only; the more popular Premium (4%) is bottled. Brewing is normally on Mondays and Thursdays, with bottling on Wednesdays. Open Mon–Sat. Closed public holidays. Admission free, including beer-tasting for over 18s only. Small shop.

Just before the brewery, set back from the road on the left, is the Playhouse Theatre, home to the Cayman Drama Society (see page 138). Popular with theatre-goers as well as local residents, the nearby **Durty Reid's** in Red Bay Plaza is a lively bar that also serves ice-creams and main meals, including a daily special, such as dolphin, for around CI$9.50. It is open 10.30am–10.30pm.

Continuing east, new developments soon give way to a more verdant landscape. You could be forgiven for going through the village of **Prospect** without noticing it, though it is thought to have been one of the first settlements in Grand Cayman, dating from the latter half of the 18th century; at one time there was even a fort here. The village itself lies to the right off the main road, but has been abandoned since 1932, the church on the coast left in ruins. In the nearby 19th-century Watler family cemetery, now owned by the National Trust, the solid stone grave markers in the shape of small houses are testament to a former, more prosperous settlement. The sandy beach just round the point at Prospect is a good place for snorkelling and diving, though at weekends it can get quite crowded. There's a small car park, with beach shelters and toilets.

The Prospect road rejoins the main road and shortly after this you come to the village of Spotts, with its sandy public beach nestled between the rocks. There is a second cemetery not dissimilar to that at Prospect, though here the 18th-century grave markers are painted white.

For the **Governor Michael Gore Bird Sanctuary**, take Spotts Newlands Road to the left, and shortly afterwards turn right; the sanctuary is about a hundred yards further on the left-hand side. More than 60 species of both water and land birds, including over a quarter of Cayman's native birds, are attracted to the small freshwater pond at the centre of this two-acre site. Walkways enable the visitor to get around, while an observation post allows undisturbed viewing of the birds. The best time to visit is in the dry season, during the spring. Admission is free.

Entering the village of **Savannah**, there is a post office on the left shortly before you come to a crossroads; on the corner opposite is a petrol station, where there's an ATM. The 1940s schoolhouse in the village was renovated by the National Trust in 1995 and is now open to the public by appointment only (tel: 949 0121).

At the crossroads, the road to the left takes you to the Sunrise Golf Centre (see page 108). Turn right into Pedro Castle Road, however, and you'll be heading towards the historic house of Pedro St James.

Pedro St James

Savannah; tel: 947 3329; fax: 947 2611; web: www.pedrostjames.ky

This 19th-century plantation great house – categorically *not* a castle – is the oldest building in the Cayman Islands, having survived two earthquakes, three fires and over a dozen hurricanes. In fact, it was the only building on the island to remain standing after the 1785 hurricane.

Originally built by William Eden in the 1780s, Pedro (pronounced locally as 'Peadro') St James became the seat of justice during the early 19th century, and even served time as the island's jailhouse. In 1831, the decision was taken here to form the first elected assembly of the Cayman Islands,

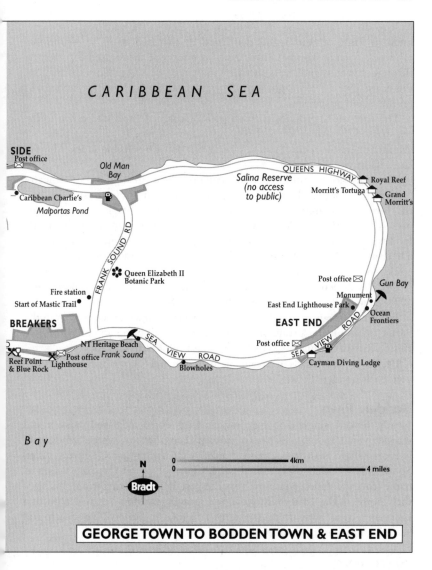

CARIBBEAN   SEA

SIDE
Post office ⊠
Old Man
Bay
QUEENS HIGHWAY
Salina Reserve
(no access
to public)
Morritt's Tortuga ⊔
Royal Reef ⊔
Caribbean Charlie's ●
Malportas Pond
Grand
Morritt's ⊔

FRANK SOUND RD

Queen Elizabeth II
Botanic Park
Post office ⊠
Gun Bay

Fire station ●
Monument
East End Lighthouse Park ●
Start of Mastic Trail ●
Ocean
Frontiers

BREAKERS
EAST END

NT Heritage Beach
SEA VIEW ROAD
Reef Point ⊠
& Blue Rock Post office ⊠ Frank Sound
Lighthouse
Blowholes
Post office ⊠
SEA VIEW ROAD
Cayman Diving Lodge

B a y

N
0 ——————— 4km
0 ——————————— 4 miles

Bradt

GEORGE TOWN TO BODDEN TOWN & EAST END

and four years later the proclamation ending slavery in the islands was read from its steps.

Towards the end of the 19th century, the house fell into disrepair, remaining more or less abandoned over the next 60 years or so. A misguided attempt to 'restore' it as a castle led to a new lease of life as a restaurant and hotel, but successive fires eventually put paid to this venture. It was not until the early 1990s that the government purchased the property and restored it to its former elegance.

The house today features shining mahogany floors and authentic polished furniture, giving a taste of the standard of living enjoyed by the well-to-do at the end of the 18th century. Across the yard is the separate kitchen, built of wattle and daub with a thatched roof. Its traditional caboose – a large wood-fired hearth – is typical of those used for cooking throughout the islands well into the 1950s. Well-placed plaques throughout the house give a real insight into the way of life for both owners and slaves on the island at the time.

The landscaped grounds with their air of colonial grace lead down to the sea, backed by ironshore, and with wonderful views. It's a great place for clambering on the rocks if you're careful, but do wear sensible shoes. There is also a short woodland trail.

The half-hour multimedia presentation held in the on-site theatre presents life on the islands from the time that the house was built through the birth of Cayman democracy and the abolition of slavery up to the present day. Allow at least an hour – considerably more if you're really interested – to visit the theatre and look right round the house and grounds. There's a well-stocked gift shop, but the chrome and plastic of the café could do with a rethink.

Open daily 9.00am–5.00pm; multimedia presentation on the hour from 10.00am to 4.00pm. Adults US$8; children US$3.75.

From the entrance to Pedro St James' car park, a track leads away from the village of Savannah. A walk of 15 minutes or so will bring you out on Pedro Bluff, some of the highest cliffs on the south coast of the island.

Back at the crossroads in Savannah, turn right and follow the road east until you reach Bodden Town.

Bodden Town

Neatly fenced single-storeyed houses with corrugated-iron rooves and wooden verandas line the roads of this small community, whose atmosphere is more village than town, more English than American. Originally called South Side, Bodden Town was the first capital of Grand Cayman, taking its name from the 'oldest and most respectable settlers' who first made this place their home in the 18th century. Today, though, Bodden Town is a bit of a backwater, well away from the tourist frenzy of Seven Mile Beach and retaining much of its traditional charm.

Where to stay

Turtle Nest Inn PO Box 187 BT, Bodden Town Rd; tel: 947 8665; fax: 947 6379; email: turtlein@candw.ky; web: www.turtlenestinn.com (9 apartments)
Located on the beach near the post office, the hacienda-style Turtle Nest Inn is something of a revelation in Grand Cayman. Small, quiet and personal, it is owned and run by a friendly Canadian couple. Each of the eight one-bedroom apartments and the one two-bedroom apartment has a bathroom, living room with sofa bed, TV/VCR, telephone, AC/ceiling fans. Business facilities are available on request, as are stereos. Each week, a Caribbean night and an Indian night are held for guests, as well as a barbecue. Diving through Ocean Frontiers.
Rates per room (low/high season): one bedroom US$155/195 (two people); one

bedroom beachfront US$175/225; two bedrooms: US$270/335 (four people). Additional guest US$25. Children three and under stay free. One night free per two-week stay. Maid service included.

Wild Orchid PO Box 31371 SMB, 116 Northward Rd; tel: 947 2298; email: orchidin@candw.ky; web: www.candw.ky/users/cay04917 (4 rooms)

This newly opened country inn will appeal to visitors with a genuine interest in discovering a little about the Cayman lifestyle. Owned by 'Mr Budd', it has a spacious garden with many exotic species. Located a short walk from the beach, the inn also has its own beach in Bodden Town, and has dive lockers on site.

Rates per room (two people) per night: US$75–100.

Restaurants

Edge Bodden Town Rd; tel: 947 2140; fax: 947 2108. Situated on the waterfront in Bodden Town, the Edge is popular with locals and visitors alike, recommended by significantly more people we spoke to than any other restaurant. The relaxed mood of the place is matched by generous portions which are served with salad, beans and rice, and fried plantain, as well as Cayman-style fried bread, all at reasonable prices. Do try the fresh fish. Open 8.30am–10.00am for breakfast; 11.00am–4.00pm for lunch, and 5.00–10.00pm for dinner.

Shopping

A number of small gift shops in Bodden Town cater for the tourist market. **K-Man Custom Pottery**, Bodden Town Road (tel: 947 7687), just beyond the post office, claims to have live demonstrations, but opening hours are erratic and we were unable to check it out. **One of a Kind** (tel: 949 5944/916 4340), affectionately known as Queen Anne's Tavern, is the setting for Mark Rice's individually made wooden crafts, from jewellery boxes and chests to items of furniture. All pieces are made from salvaged materials or renewable sources, and are signed and numbered. **Twyla's Creations** (tel: 947 3777) in Cumber Crescent Road, more or less opposite the Turtle Nest Inn, is the only outlet on the island for Twyla Varga's crafts based on calabashes and shells.

Set back from the road next to the pottery, **The Caves** has souvenirs, drinks, snacks etc, and will help with booking tours. This is also the entry point to Bodden Town's so-called 'pirate' caves, for which there is a small entry charge.

What to see

Guard House Park, which marks the entrance to Bodden Town from the west, was the location of a 19th-century security post. An information centre houses a small exhibition about the town. Admission is free. A little further east, beyond a monument to Queen Victoria, is **Gun Square**, its two 18th-century cannons a stark reminder of the town's need to defend itself against marauders from the sea.

A National Trust leaflet covering the historic sites of Bodden Town is available from the Trust (see page 27).

BODDEN TOWN TO EAST END AND NORTH SIDE

Just beyond Bodden Town on the left is the
small **Meagre Bay Pond**, once frequented by
hunters after teal and mallard for the pot, but
now a wildlife sanctuary that is popular with
birdwatchers. There is a bird hide here, but
the pond dries out in the winter months. Park

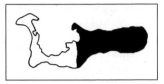

on the side of the road. From here, the roadside vegetation becomes denser as
you head for the village of **Breakers**, where there are two restaurants:

Reef Point Restaurant/Blue Rock Sports Bar Breakers; tel: 947 2183. A family-
owned Caymanian restaurant with simple décor and loud music, mainly frequented
by locals and with very reasonable prices. 'Catch of the day' on Friday nights from
6.30pm (CI$8.50); jerk pork and chicken Saturday and Sunday evenings (from CI$3
per piece); Sunday lunchtime barbecue from 11.00am (CI$8–11). In the evenings,
food is put out in front of the restaurant, attracting a regular clientele of lemon sharks.
Open Mon–Fri 9.00am–1.00am; Sat/Sun 9.00am–midnight.
Lighthouse Breakers; tel: 947 2047. Despite the name, the 'lighthouse' was in fact
built as a restaurant, and a pretty imposing one at that, with views out to sea from the
waterside terrace or the air-conditioned restaurant. The rather pricey menu specialises
in Italian dishes and seafood, with daily specials. The restaurant prides itself on a huge
range of wines – 275 at the last count, with a cellar numbering some 3,000 bottles.
Exclusive private room available for small parties. Taxis from George Town cost
about CI$40 for the round trip, which takes less than half an hour. Open daily
11.30am–4.30pm for lunch and 5.30–9.30pm (later in high season) for dinner.

The coast road continues from here through to East End. To the left, though,
is Frank Sound Road, which takes you direct to North Side and Rum Point,
passing both the entrance to the Mastic Trail and Queen Elizabeth II Botanic
Park.

Mastic Trail

The Mastic Trail was used from the late 18th century to enable people to
transport goods and logs from one side of the island to the other. Long disused,
it was restored by the National Trust and re-opened as a public right of way in
1995. The whole area covers some 1,000 acres. To date, 399 acres of forest are
owned by the Trust, which aims eventually to acquire the remaining 601 acres.

The best time to visit for birds is from October to early December, and for
tree orchids, June and July. That said, it's an intriguing place at any time of the
year, though note that it's subject to flooding during heavy rain.

The start of the trail is just off the Mastic Road, a turning to the left off Frank
Sound Road by the fire station. Those on a guided tour will be collected and
brought to this point. If you're in your own vehicle, park here; if the car park is
full, then you are asked to return at another time as it indicates that the trail is
operating at capacity level. A third option would be to get a bus to the junction
of Bodden Town Road and Frank Sound Road, then walk to the beginning of
the trail from there (see *Buses*, pages 75–6, for details).

Although the trail is relatively short – around 2.5 miles (4km) in total – don't underestimate the level of difficulty. The path passes through hazardous terrain, from wetland that is in part very boggy to ancient (two-million-year old) forest founded on treacherous and unforgiving karst rock. There is also a species of poisonous tree, the maiden plum, close to the path. Wear good strong shoes or boots (not sandals of any description), take plenty of water and stick to the path. There are no emergency facilities.

A **guide** may not be obligatory, but is strongly advisable, at least for a first trip, and infinitely more rewarding than tackling the trail alone. During our visit, we would undoubtedly have walked through the various habitats without any real understanding, and would probably have missed many of the birds and reptiles that were pointed out to us, including a nightjar and a stripe-headed tanager, as well as the Cuban tree frog, a couple of racer snakes and several land crabs. Just as interesting are the stories of island life that find their way into discussions about the surrounding flora and fauna, from the practical uses of a particular timber to the medicinal properties of an individual plant. And on a practical note, guided tours are usually one-way, with transport provided from the end of the trail to save you retracing your steps in the heat of the day.

Guided walks are run by Geddes Hislop, who worked for the National Trust during the restoration of the trail, and his wife, Janet. Their company, Silver Thatch Excursions (tel: 945 6588 – see also page 78), now takes guided walks on behalf of the Trust, each catering for a maximum of ten people, though groups are normally smaller. Walks cost US$30 per person, and it takes approximately two hours to cover the whole trail in one direction. The rugged terrain means that the trail is not suitable for young children, the elderly or the disabled.

The trail leads through an extraordinary diversity of landscape, from farmland and abandoned pasture alongside a quarry (the mahogany that once grew here has long since been felled for timber), through black mangrove swamp, across all that remains of the Mastic Bridge that once crossed the whole swamp area, and on to the bluff formation. Here, where there is no soil, trees have struggled for thousands of years to put down roots, taking advantage of periods of rain to force their way through holes in the rock and draw up moisture. This unforgiving substance is known as high rock, or cliffrock. Structurally it's the same as the evil-looking ground at Hell but here it is unstained by algae so is not the same distinctive black colour. It is probable that, as Grand Cayman emerged over time from the sea, this central ridge, effectively the backbone of the island, arose first, with the surrounding mangrove swamps following significantly later.

The Mastic Trail is the only place on the island to find the mastic tree, distinctive for the veins on its self-peeling bark. There are actually two different species, the yellow mastic, *Sideroxylon foetidissimum*, and the black mastic, *Terminalia eriostachya*.

Towards the end of the trail you will come to Grand Cayman's highest point. At just 60ft (18m), 'The Mountain' may not be on a grand scale, but on this terrain it's no mean feat going uphill. From here, the trail leads out into open farmland near the island's north coast.

Those on a guided trip will be collected from this northern point of the trail. If you are on your own, however, you'll have to retrace your steps to your vehicle at the start of the trail, then you could go on to visit Queen Elizabeth II Botanic Park, a little further north on Frank Sound Road on the right-hand side. If you're planning to leave by bus, continue on foot as far as the coast road on the north of the island and catch a bus from North Side.

Queen Elizabeth II Botanic Park

PO Box 203 NS, Frank Sound Rd; tel: 947 9462; fax: 947 7873; email: guthrie@candw.ky; web: www.botanic-park.ky

Set in 65 acres in the centre of Grand Cayman, less than an hour's pleasant drive from George Town, the park was opened in 1994 by Queen Elizabeth II and specialises in Caymanian flora. One of the best times to visit is in June when the native orchids are in bloom, but the design of the park and the local climate mean that there is always plenty to see.

The long avenue leading into the park is lined by logwood trees, and the smell is pervasive. Lofty royal palms guard the approach to the ticket booth.

The park is designed around a series of gardens and has a small visitors' centre and shop, plus a café. The heritage garden features a 100-year-old Cayman house, complete with separate cookhouse. Its traditional sand garden, lined by conch shells, is surrounded by local flowers, vegetables, medicinal plants and fruit trees. Here you can see such exotica as soursop and breadfruit, and learn about the traditional plants used by the islanders over the years to cure various ailments.

In the aptly named colour garden, native flowers and trees mingle with others from around the world to create ever-changing colour-themed gardens of red, blue, yellow and white. Plans are in hand for new orchid and cactus gardens, and a children's educational garden.

MEDICINAL PLANTS

The provision of modern medical facilities is taken as read nowadays, yet the use of traditional remedies is still recent enough to be remembered by many local people. Arguably the greatest cure-all, still rated highly by herbalists today, was the aloe, variously used as a laxative, a purgative and to treat worms, not to mention its application on cuts and scrapes to prevent infection. Indian mulberry was used to reduce a fever, while juniper was beneficial in easing toothache. Yellow limes served a dual purpose: not only were drops of juice used to remove cataracts and styes, but the lime was rubbed in to a wound to cure blood poisoning. The leaves of the soursop tree were boiled up to make a sleeping draught.

Cobwebs, although hardly plants, were also part of the armoury, used to stop bleeding. And even less everyday illnesses had their cure: diabetes, for example, was kept at bay by the simple periwinkle.

All of these plants and more are to be found in the heritage garden at the botanic park.

A woodland trail just under a mile long (1.25km) takes the visitor through Cayman's native trees, including the silver thatch palm and the interestingly named duppy bush, *Phyllanthus angustifolius*, so called because it shimmers like a ghost in the moonlight. Information panels along the trail explain about some of the birds and butterflies to be seen, as well as the trees themselves, while warning signs indicate poisonous specimens.

Not surprisingly, the park is a haven for animals, birds and butterflies, with all of Cayman's landbirds to be seen and most of the aquatics as well, attracted by numerous ponds that cover some ten acres of the site. The protected blue iguana is also present, the subject of a breeding programme at the park. Iguanas are frequently to be spotted in the grounds, while in the iguana pen the handsome resident male seems thoroughly at ease posing for the camera.

During weekdays, guided tours of the park are available, and well worth the time.

Open daily Apr–Sep, 9.00am–6.30pm (last admission 5.30pm); Oct–Mar 9.00am–5.30pm (last admission 4.30pm). Adults US$7.50; children 6–12 US$5; children under 6 free. Guided tours US$2.50 (children US$1.50). Discount of 10% for members of the National Trust for the Cayman Islands, on presentation of a valid membership card.

North Side

As you complete the south–north traverse of the island, a glimpse of the deep blue and turquoise sea acts as a gentle reminder of just how small Grand Cayman is. Old Man Bay is a small settlement in the sleepy district of North Side, which was once a major rope-making centre, yet was almost completely isolated from the rest of the island until Frank Sound Road was built in the early 20th century. Bear left here past a petrol station and a couple of small shops and you'll come to the slightly larger village of North Side.

Where to stay and eat

Driftwood Village PO Box 35 NS; tel: 947 9015; fax: 947 9138 (4 cottages)
The rustic complex that is Driftwood Village straddles the road on the way to Rum Point. The two-bedroomed cottages sleep up to four people. On site there is a sports bar, which is open evenings only, and on Sundays a barbecue is offered 3.00–7.00pm. *Rates* per cottage per night, low/high season: US$110/150 (two people). Each additional guest US$10 per night.

North Side Surf Inn PO Box 205 NS; tel: 947 1431; fax: 947 0704; email: chefrayl@ candw.ky; web: www.northsidesurfinn.com or www.divelodge.com (10 rooms)
This small, relaxed inn right on the beach is ideally suited to the non-diver (although divers appreciate the peace and quiet of the place too). Light, airy rooms, six overlooking the sea, each have en-suite facilities and AC. Staff will help with local transport on request. The pleasant **Red Ginger restaurant** is a popular haunt for overseas workers in the evenings, particularly on Friday when there is live music. Open daily for breakfast, lunch and dinner, and Sunday brunch, approx 7.30am–3.00pm, 5.30–11.00pm.
Rates per room, low/high season: sea view US$125/170; other rooms US$100/138.

There's a small supermarket just beyond North Side Surf Inn on the right, backing on to the sea. The beach here is rocky rather than sand, but it's quiet and not a bad place to stop for a cool drink.

On the left-hand side continuing west towards Rum Point, is a sign to **Caribbean Charlie's** (49 Uncle Bert's Lane, North Side; tel: 947 9452). Tucked away in a small lane off to the left, Caribbean Charlie's specialises in colourful wooden birdhouses and traditional *waurie* boards. Opening times are erratic, so it's best to phone first.

Down the same road is The Hut, where local farmer Willie Ebanks has a flock of West Indian whistling-ducks on **Malportas Pond**. He introduced the first pair of ducks and seven chicks in 1990; today there are 400 wild ducks at his farm. The pond, which is set in largely undisturbed land, also supports herons, egrets, moorhens and coots.

Rum Point

The real estate signs lining the approach to Rum Point are an indication of just how popular this area is becoming, although so far there is little building of any note – just a few scattered private villas. Rum Point itself, though, has developed into a popular venue for visitors, with plenty of opportunities for fun and relaxation both day and night.

The *Rum Pointer* ferry plies regularly across North Sound between the Hyatt Regency dock on the east side of Seven Mile Beach and Rum Point. For details, see pages 76–7. Tickets at Rum Point can be bought from the gift shop. By road, Rum Point is approximately 25 miles from George Town.

The beach at Rum Point is ideal for swimmers, being both sheltered and safe. Snorkelling here is pretty good, too, but walk just a few hundred yards to the east and it gets steadily better as the reef comes closer to the shoreline. With luck, you'll have the place to yourself. The underwater life at this point is wonderful, with swaying sea fans, colourful fish and much, much more.

There are changing facilities, with toilets and showers, on the beach behind the Wreck Bar.

On Saturdays, there is a Cayman-style beach barbecue, and live entertainment on the beach by Cayman's Barefoot Man from 2.00pm to 6.00pm.

The watersports operation at Rum Point is run by Red Sail Sports (tel: 947 9203). Various pieces of equipment are available for rent, from tubes, paddleboats and kayaks to sailboats and jetskis (waverunners), as well as snorkels, masks and fins. Waterskiing, banana boats etc are also on offer. Prices: snorkelling gear at US$15 per day. Hourly rentals: sailboats US$25; kayaks US$20–25; paddleboats US$20. Waterskiing US$40 per 15-minute session (tuition available at US$65 for 25 minutes); tubing US$15 for ten minutes; waverunners US$50 single, US$65 double.

Where to stay

Most of the visitors to Rum Point come over on the ferry from hotels along West Bay Road. Others take the opportunity to drive, perhaps exploring inland en route. Only a handful make the effort to stay away from the hurly burly of

Seven Mile Beach, but those that do are rewarded by a gentler pace of life, some stunning snorkelling and watersports, and a real opportunity to escape the crowds – for some of the time, anyway.

For the most part, accommodation here consists of condominiums and private villas. For details of the latter, contact Cayman Villas (see page 116). The following are also available for rent to visitors:

Retreat at Rum Point PO Box 46, North Side; tel: 947 9135; fax: 947 9058; email: retrumpt@candw.ky; web: www.retreatcondos.com (23 units)
It would be hard to better the location of this seven-acre complex, on a sweeping expanse of sandy beach with panoramic views to the north, yet close to all the facilities at Rum Point. Each of the one-, two- and three-bedroom beachfront apartments has a screened-in balcony, kitchen, washer/dryer, AC/ceiling fans and TV. Facilities include tennis, swimming pool and racquetball.
Rates per night (minimum three nights), low/high season US$225/275 (one-bedroom/two people), US$255/380 (two-bedroom deluxe/four people), US$360/505 (three-bedroom/four people). Additional guests US$20 per night. A maximum of three people may be accommodated in a one-bedroom apartment, with up to six people in the two- and three-bedroom apartments. Prices are subject to 6% gratuity. Maid service included.

Where to eat
Rum Point Restaurant Tel: 947 9412; fax: 945 5526. The colourful Caribbean-style restaurant at Rum Point specialises in seafood and has its own bar. On Saturdays, the set menu is US$42.50. From Monday to Friday, though, dinner is à la carte, with starters from US$5.30 and main courses from US$23.75. Look out for Thomas, the Rum Point cat adopted as a stray and now supposed to be on a diet to counteract the titbits doled out by diners. Thomas is an ardent supporter of the Cayman Islands' Humane Society, which looks after animal welfare (see page 66). Open Mon–Sat 5.00–10.30pm.
Wreck Bar Rum Point's beach bar is open daily 10.00am–7.00pm. On Saturdays, the popular Cayman-style barbecue, at a fixed US$12.50 for one visit (you serve yourself and the plates are large), draws numerous visitors and locals to the beach. The rest of the week, the menu offers a more mundane selection of burgers etc. The bar serves beer and a selection of cocktails, including the popular mudslide which is just US$5 if ordered with your barbecue.

Shopping
The **Treasure Chest** gift shop at Rum Point, run by Red Sail Sports, has a comprehensive selection of gifts and beach-orientated goods, as well as newspapers etc.

Cayman Kai
Retrace your steps to the entry to Rum Point and take the left fork to bring you to Cayman Kai, a narrow finger protruding into North Sound. Follow the road straight to the end to bring you out to Kaibo Yacht Club, where the

sheltered beach has plenty of shade. Snorkel and dive trips operate from here. Beach bar with lunch menu open Tue–Sun 11.00am–7.00pm in high season; in low season, the bar closes earlier and food availability is sporadic.

In high season, from Tuesday to Sunday, the *Kaibo Express* ferries diners from Safehaven at 6.30pm and 8.00pm, returning by 10.30pm. The CI$10 fare is refundable against dinner at Cecil's. For details, call 947 9975 (see also page 77).

Cecil's Restaurant Cayman Kai; tel: 947 9975. Kaibo Yacht Club's upstairs restaurant, pronounced 'Seasil's', has a club-like atmosphere with a nautical theme and screened veranda. The menu is typical of the southern United States. Open Tue–Sun 6.00–10.00pm.

East End

The approach to East End from Bodden Town brings with it a gently undulating landscape with low open vegetation, quite a change from the unbroken flat terrain of the west of the island. Instead of turning left on to Frank Sound Road, continue east on Sea View Road into the district of East End.

The village of East End may have been the earliest settlement on Grand Cayman. Originally called Old Isaacs, it has been dubbed the 'graveyard of the Caribbean' as a result of the large number of ships wrecked on its shores. The most famous of these shipwrecks, now known as the 'Wreck of the Ten Sails', took place in February 1794 (see opposite).

Until early in the 20th century, many of the villagers 'commuted' by catboat to one of the sister islands to work in the phosphate mines or the coconut trade. The village was also a trading port; indeed, until the 1940s it was the main port of entry to Grand Cayman. It was here that the *Cimboco* made its monthly visits, bringing post, passengers and cargo from Jamaica and Cayman Brac, and returning with exports of thatch rope, mahogany and turtle products.

Despite these visits, the village remained almost totally isolated until, in 1935, the road was extended from Bodden Town. Before then, journeys to George Town could only be undertaken on foot or on horseback, with goods ferried by canoe. Such were the difficulties of travel that many East Enders never went as far as the island's capital.

The quieter pace of this end of the island makes it an excellent place to come for the day and get away from the brashness of Seven Mile Beach. Countless small sandy beaches offer the perfect spot for a quiet picnic, and there are numerous little coves awaiting exploration.

Where to stay

Cayman Diving Lodge PO Box 11 EE; tel: 947 7555, US 800 TLC DIVE; fax: 947 7560; email: divelodge@aol.com; web: www.divelodge.com (11 rooms) This small, all-inclusive dive resort is idyllically located on its own on the southern shores of the island at East End, well away from any hint of mass tourism. One of the three dive operators based in the East End, Cayman Diving Lodge, also known locally as East End Lodge, offers a highly personal service. All rooms have AC and sea view; some are oceanfront. Meals are served in the open-air dining area on the sandy beach, overlooking a shallow lagoon ideal for snorkelling.

Rates per person based on double occupancy (low/high season): two-tank dive package three nights US$565/631; seven nights US$1,207/1,361. Non-diver three nights US$407/485; seven nights US$833/1001. Oceanfront rooms additional US$11 per night. Prices include government tax and airport transfers, but not alcoholic or soft (fizzy) drinks, dive equipment or certification courses. Additional afternoon dive US$40. BCD/regulator US$10 each per day. Gratuities optional.

Grand Morritt's With its first phase of 20 units opening in May 2001, this new timeshare resort adjacent to Morritt's Tortuga is almost an extension of the current

WRECK OF THE TEN SAILS

In the small hours of February 8 1794, a convoy of 58 merchant ships, most of them square-rigged sailing vessels bound for Europe, and led by *HMS Convert*, approached the reef off the district of East End from their Jamaican port of origin. The seas were rough and it was pitch dark. As the first ships struck the reef, the ensuing signal, warning the rest of the convoy of the danger, was misinterpreted, and one vessel after another foundered on the rocks. By the time that the captain of the *Convert* realised the danger, and signalled to the convoy to disperse, it was too late. Altogether, ten ships were wrecked that night, leaving their crew at the mercy of the waves, with 'the surf beating violently over the reef'.

In spite of the conditions, the villagers of East End managed to save almost all of the 400 or so people on board the ships, bringing them ashore in canoes. However, such a large contingent caused serious problems for the islanders, who were already suffering from a shortage of provisions. Captain Lawford of the *Convert* was petitioned to move the survivors, who were for the most part taken aboard the remaining the ships, which then regrouped off George Town. The remainder of the men, including Lawford himself, journeyed west across the island overland. According to records in the Cayman Islands National Archive, they found themselves on 'the most execrable road imaginable... hot burning sands and sharp-pointed coral rocks that would have foiled the attempts of the most dexterous animal to pass them without injury'. To have survived the storm for a land such as this must have seemed something of a double blow.

Legend has it that George III was so grateful to the people of Cayman that he granted the islanders freedom from taxes in perpetuity. Other stories tell that, rather than freedom from taxation, Caymanians were granted freedom from conscription in times of war. Sadly, there is no evidence to support either anecdote.

site. The building has been designed and built to be hurricane 'proof' but the result is singularly unattractive when compared with its elegant neighbour. The finished complex will have 130 units with restaurants, shops and other facilities. For information, contact Brewster McCoy, tel: 916 6453; fax: 947 4974.

Morritt's Tortuga PO Box 496 East End; tel: 947 7449/945 1571; US reservations (L&M Reservations, Florida) 800 447 0309 (177 rooms)

An upmarket timeshare in a quiet location at the eastern end of the island, Morritt's Tortuga is an attractive three-storey complex built in traditional style with wooden steps and verandas. Rooms may be rented, subject to availability, through their Florida agency (see above), who will quote prices on request. Options range from one-bed studios to penthouses/townhouses suitable for families with up to eight people, and there are three rooms for disabled guests. All have AC and TV, and some have a sea view. There are two restaurants – David's and Windows Bar (see below). Nightly entertainment includes comedy shows, and popular themed evenings, such as Thursday's Caribbean Night (US$18.95; children under 12 half price), are open to non-residents. Children's activities range from kids' parties to one particularly innovative idea, which involves a beach walk during which children are encouraged to collect rubbish from the beach in return for free ice-cream. Swimming pool with bar, dive school (Tortuga Divers), watersports, bicycles, car rental, souvenir shop, laundry.

Royal Reef PO Box 30865 SMB, Colliers, East End; tel: 947 3100, US 888 452 4545; fax: 947 9920; email: rental@royalreef.com; web: www.royalreef.com (82 villas)

Opened in 2000, the bright yellow and blue building of Royal Reef is quite a contrast to the more discreet Morritt's Tortuga next door. Like Morritt's, it's a timeshare operation. Each two-bedroom villa or 'flexivilla' overlooks the beach and has two bathrooms, jacuzzi, living area, kitchen, TV, AC/ceiling fans, balcony; each can be divided by its owner on a temporary or permanent basis into two one-bedroom suites. Full maid service available. Facilities include swimming pool, tennis, gym, bicycles, diving (Ocean Frontiers) and other watersports. There are also a convenience store, beauty salon and car rental, plus a restaurant and bar. A full on-site programme of social activities is on offer. Opportunities for rental come up occasionally.

Rates per night, low/high season: standard US$172/286; suite US$240/400; villa US$343/572.

Where to eat

David's Morritt's Tortuga; tel: 947 7449. The more formal of the two restaurants at Morritt's Tortuga hosts a series of themed evenings, from beach barbecues and comedy nights to Caribbean evenings and 'Steakorama'. In addition, there is a cosmopolitan à la carte menu, available at weekends. Open daily 6.00–10.00pm.

Portofino Sea View Rd; tel: 947 2700. The wooden construction of Portofino, with its simple blue and white décor, belies its reputation for good food. Italian and local dishes, including conch steak, are on the pricey side, with starters US$5.30–14.95, and main courses US$17.45 for pasta dishes to US$35. Tables are all indoors, with views across the sea to the south. Cocktail menu. Open daily 11.30am–5.00pm, 5.30–10.00pm; Sunday buffet with local specialities 11.30am–3.00pm.

Windows Bar Morritt's Tortuga; tel: 947 7449. Open daily for breakfast and lunch 8.00am–6.00pm.

Shops etc
Lil Hurley's Marketplace Tel: 947 7733. General food store. Open Mon–Wed 7.00am–9.00pm; Thu–Sat 7.00am–11.00pm.
Wreck View Art Gallery East End; tel: 947 6604/6512. Local crafts and paintings by Earl and Elsa Tomlinson. Open Mon–Fri 9.30am–5.00pm; Sun 10.00am–4.00pm.

What to see and do
Just beyond Frank Sound Road is the small **National Trust Heritage Beach**, with shade provided by trees, a couple of wooden cabanas and barbecue areas, making it a good spot for a picnic. The swimming is not great, but small boats may be launched here.

A none-too-obvious sign a bit further on points towards the **blowholes**, with steps leading down to the sea. When the sea is up, the blowholes come into their own, but even on a calm day the extraordinary rock formations are worth visiting. Formed from karst limestone, the place is almost eerily barren, more lunar landscape than Caribbean beach. Don't attempt to walk on the beach without good shoes – the rocks are sharp and unforgiving.

Opposite the steps is a small layby where, in the main season, drinks and snacks are available from a wooden hut. Try the chilled coconut water at CI$2 for a refreshing drink, or perhaps some guava juice.

Follow the road through the village of East End until you come to the tiny **East End Lighthouse Park**, set just off the road beyond the village on the left-hand side. Owned by the National Trust, it contains the two lighthouses that have stood on this spot since 1919, with signboards explaining their historical importance. The small gravel courtyard is a miniature nature reserve, a tranquil place where birds and butterflies dart in and around the fruit trees, and wild flowers are intermingled with traditional medicinal plants.

There are several secluded beaches around this area where you could be in another world to that of Seven Mile Beach. Look closely among the rocks and you may find the odd piece of caymanite – though please don't take it away. East End public beach is one step up, a tranquil, shady site overlooking a small sandy beach with its own dock. Equipped with picnic benches and wooden beach shelters, it also has recently installed toilets and public phones.

To complete the circuit, follow the road right on to Old Man Bay, past Morritt's Tortuga and the Royal Reef. You can rent sailboats, kayaks and windsurfers at Cayman Windsurf, which is based at Morritt's, so it's worth a stop if you're into watersports. Then continue to Rum Point via North Side, or return along Frank Sound Road at Old Man Bay to rejoin Bodden Town Road just east of Breakers.

Part Three

The Sister Islands

Hawksbill turtles

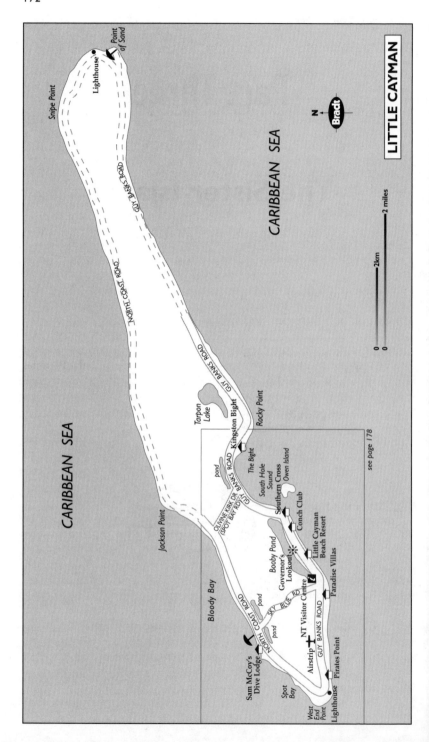

Snipe Point

Point of Sand

Lighthouse

GUY BANKS ROAD

NORTH COAST ROAD

CARIBBEAN SEA

CARIBBEAN SEA

LITTLE CAYMAN

N

Bradt

0   2km

0   2 miles

Jackson Point

GUY BANKS ROAD

Tarpon Lake

pond

Kingston Bight

Rocky Point

The Bight

South Hole Sound

Southern Cross

Owen Island

Conch Club

see page 178

Bloody Bay

OLIVINE KIRK DR / SPOT BAY RD / GUY BANKS ROAD

NORTH COAST ROAD

pond

SKY BLUE RD

pond

pond

Booby Pond

Governor's Lookout

NT Visitor Centre

Little Cayman Beach Resort

Paradise Villas

GUY BANKS ROAD

Sam McCoy's Dive Lodge

Spot Boy

Airstrip

Pirates Point

West End Point

Lighthouse

Little Cayman

Permanent home to over 20,000 red-footed boobies and just 115 humans, Little Cayman is surely the jewel in the crown of the Cayman Islands. You don't need to be an avid birdwatcher to be enthralled by the morning exodus from the booby colony, as thousands of birds head out to sea at dawn, with frigatebirds wheeling in the current overhead, anticipating their evening raid. Nor do you need to be a scuba diver to see the brightly coloured corals and sponges just below the surface of that crystal clear water, enlivened by myriads of fish of all hues. Little Cayman is a place to take time out, to relax, simply to be.

The smallest of the Cayman Islands, lying 89 miles (150km) northeast of Grand Cayman at 19°4' north, 80° west, Little Cayman is only 10 miles (16km) long and just over a mile and a half (2.7km) at its widest point. Its total land area is barely 10 square miles (26km²). Like the larger Grand Cayman, the island is more or less flat, rising to just 40ft (12m) in the centre.

Probably only 25 to 30 of the island's inhabitants – eight to ten households – are true Caymanians, the remainder being long-term residents from the US and elsewhere. There are very few children on the island; of those that do live here, most go to school during the week on Cayman Brac, though recently a teacher has been flown in daily from the Brac to teach two of the island's children. Visitors account for a further 500–600 people each year.

Considered by many to be one of the three best dive areas in the world, Little Cayman is also a haven for photographers, nature lovers and those in search of real peace.

HISTORY

When Edward Corbet prepared his report on the Cayman Islands for the governor of Jamaica in 1802, Little Cayman, like Cayman Brac, was uninhabited, although fishermen regularly sailed along its shores to catch turtles and a number of isolated groups had resided here over the years. It was only in 1832, however, that the first permanent settlement began, when a small group of families came over from Grand Cayman in a deliberate move to populate the island.

Until the early 20th century, the small community on Little Cayman was augmented by labourers from Grand Cayman who commuted to the island by catboat every Sunday evening to start work in the phosphate mines at daybreak on Monday morning. As the phosphate was extracted from the mines, it was loaded on to a small-gauge train which was hauled by mules to Salt Rocks Dock on the north side of the island. Here, it would await transfer on to a ship ready for export. On Friday nights, they would make the long and frequently dangerous journey back home, with the whole process repeated week after week, month after month.

Although not hit as badly as Cayman Brac, Little Cayman suffered considerable damage during the **1932 storm**, with severe flooding and many homes destroyed. The few buildings that did survive, including the house behind the church whose second storey acted as a shelter for some of the islanders, were later pulled down. The oldest building on the island today was erected just after the storm, opposite the Village Inn in South Town (since controversially renamed Blossom Village). The only structure on the island that predates the storm is the mule pen by Salt Rocks Dock, which was constructed around 1885.

The storm destroyed more than buildings of course. Prior to 1932, coconuts were a major export crop, but damage to the trees, together with a lethal yellowing blight, effectively put paid to this trade. Today, the island is dependent on tourism for its income.

It took a considerable time for the 20th century to catch up with the island. Even when the runway was finally cleared for incoming planes, in 1959, it was achieved singlehandedly by one Captain Woody Bodden, using just an axe and a handmade cart. Until 1990 there was no electricity here, and it was only in 1991 that telephones were installed; prior to this VHF radios were used. It's not surprising, then, that the islanders have a strong sense of community, and some older people are extremely suspicious of the outside world. It is said that when Neil Armstrong first walked on the moon, the islanders were firm in their belief that it was a television show, rather than a live event!

Today, pretty well all the food that is consumed on the island is imported, with the exception of fish, some of which is caught locally, and a few plantains, limes and coconuts that are grown on the island.

NATURAL HISTORY

The flattest of the three islands, Little Cayman consists essentially of mangrove swamps, with the land along the southern coast – and much of the north as well – lined with ponds. In summer, severe storms may cause the ponds to overflow, bringing the extraordinary phenomenon of tarpon swimming down the road. Little Cayman is host to a wide variety of flora, fauna and birdlife. It also has its own bird reserve, Booby Pond (see pages 188–9), which is a designated site under the Ramsar Convention.

No matter where you go on the island, you're likely to come across one of Little Cayman's most intriguing inhabitants, the Little Cayman grey iguana, which to all appearances is in charge here. These anachronistic creatures are frequently to be seen sunning themselves on porches or making the most of the quiet roads across the island in the heat of the day, perhaps secure in the knowledge that they have right of way over vehicles. One particularly cheeky specimen has been known to lie by the airstrip waiting for incoming planes – and presumably a tasty morsel!

Over 100 species of coral grace the reefs that fringe the island, with more than 500 species of fish to be found in Little Cayman's unblemished waters. Sea turtles, rarely seen on the surface elsewhere, are easily spotted from boats here, as well as beneath the waves, while the abundance of all manner of marine creatures seems just that much greater in these relatively tranquil seas. Interestingly, the shallow reef is the result of countless storms over the years. One of the local fisherman, Castro, remembers that a couple of generations ago there was some 65ft (20m) of water inside the reef, but a gradual build up of sand during the intervening years has left the shallows that you see today. At least some of the islanders believe that nature should be given a helping hand with digging it out again.

GETTING THERE
Island Airways has five flights a day from Grand Cayman, taking 35 minutes (or an hour if it stops in Cayman Brac), and two a day from Cayman Brac, taking just seven minutes, making Little Cayman very accessible. Planes are either 19-seater de Havilland DHC 6-300 Twin Otters, or 8-seater Piper Navahos. Prices are as for Cayman Brac (see page 196).

The first hint of the mood of the island comes at the approach to the grass airstrip at the westernmost point of the island. As the plane touches down, it turns across the road and parks in front of the 'airport' – a small group of wooden buildings housing the local fire station, post office and airline office. Baggage is weighed outside by the local fisherman, Castro – the office is too small for the scales. Don't be surprised if your luggage is not on the same plane as you – this is normal; it will usually arrive on the next one (but as that may be the following morning, it would be sensible to hang on to your toothbrush and swimming things). Sometimes, passengers are asked to take just one bag on their flight, with the other to follow, or to send a piece of luggage in advance of their departure.

There are controversial plans in hand to move the airport nearer to the middle of the island, towards the north side. It is understood, though, that the proposed new tarmac airstrip will be no longer than the existing grass strip, so with luck the move will have little impact on traffic, noise or environmental pollution.

The Island Airways office on Little Cayman is at the airport, tel: 948 0021.

GETTING AROUND
You have three choices if you wish to remain independent – walk, cycle or hire a jeep. Most of the hotels and guesthouses have **bicycles** for loan or hire and, with so little traffic, cycling on the paved roads is a real pleasure. Don't try to cycle right round the island, though – roads at the eastern end are unpaved and very bumpy. Add to this drifting sand, and a bike can prove treacherous, particularly one with no gears and back-pedal brakes.

The rule on bikes on the islands is to lock them when unattended. Although theft is not a problem, bikes have been known to 'walk' when visitors leave them outside a restaurant then take the wrong one after a drink or two. Hire bikes are not really an option after dark – they don't have lights and only a short stretch of road east of the airport is lit. If you want to go out in the evening, most of the restaurants will collect you if you ring them in advance.

Jeeps are available for hire from McLaughlin Enterprises, PO Box 46 L; tel: 948 1000; mobile: 916 3755; fax: 948 1001; email: littlcay@candw.ky. Their office/shop is on the small shopping parade within walking distance of the airstrip; they have a courtesy phone at the airstrip which rings directly through for visitors to be picked up on arrival.

Open Mon–Sat 8.30am–midday, 3.00–6.00pm; Sun 8.30–10.30am, 4.00–6.00pm. Rates per day: CI$60 (US$75). Additional charges: insurance CI$14 (US£17.50); second driver CI$12 (US$15).

Note that the jeeps are not four-wheel drive, so they should not be driven on soft sand. Since theft is not an issue, you'll be asked to leave the keys in the vehicle at all times.

The speed limit right across the island is 25mph (40km/h). Permits are required as on Grand Cayman (see page 73), and the same regulations apply. And do take note of the signs stating that iguanas have right of way. Fuel is available both near McLaughlin's and on the north of the island at McCoy's Lodge. Prices are approximately CI$3.00 per imperial gallon, but may vary.

There is also an island snorkel/**tour bus** run by Little Cayman Beach Resort. Prices start from US$20 per person, with group rates available. Phone 948 0133 for details.

WHERE TO STAY
Accommodation on Little Cayman is for the most part limited to the western end of the island, with a few private houses dotted here and there to the east. The majority of the accommodation is on an all-inclusive basis, in many cases with drinks as part of the package.

Resort hotels
Little Cayman Beach Resort PO Box 51 LC, Guy Banks Rd, Blossom Village; tel: 948 1033, US reservations: 800 327 3835; fax: 948 1040; email: lcbr@candw.ky; web: www.littlecayman.com (40 rooms)
A sense of light and air pervades this upmarket all-inclusive resort just a mile or so from the airport. All the rooms are in two-storey wooden buildings in a stunning beachside location, and each has one king or two double beds; AC, fan, TV; patio or balcony and pool view. Luxury oceanfront rooms also available. Air-conditioned Bird of Paradise restaurant (see page 181), beach bar, private beach with wide range of watersports. Facilities include floodlit tennis court, fitness centre, games room, library, gift shop, health and beauty spa. Dive centre run by Reef Divers (see page 185). Evening entertainment includes a rum punch party on Mondays, and a Friday karaoke night. The resort operates a no-smoking policy except outside and at the bar. Bar open Mon–Sat 11.30am–11.00pm; Sun midday–11.00pm.

Rates per person per night, based on double occupancy (low/high season): US$138.51–204.99/$171.75–238.32. Rates do not include 10% government tax, 12% gratuity, meals or transfers (US$10 per person).
All-inclusive rates per person for seven nights, based on double occupancy (low/high season): Divers (three dives per day) US$1,523–1,807/$1,665–1,949. Non-divers US$1,013–1,297/$1,155–1,439. Rates include transfer from airport, service charge and government tax, but not dive equipment rental. Children under five free. Rates also available for half board (breakfast and dinner), and all-in (inclusive of drinks).

Pirates Point PO Box 43 LC, Guy Banks Rd; tel: 948 1010, US: 800 327 8777; fax: 948 1011 (10 chalets)
This all-inclusive and somewhat idiosyncratic resort is ideal for both certified divers or those on holiday packages, with a prime beach setting on the southwestern tip of Little Cayman, just minutes from the airstrip. Run since 1986 by the inimitable Gladys B Howard, a larger-than-life Texan lady with a Cordon Bleu qualification and a reputation for getting things done, the resort has something of a family atmosphere, and appeals to a slightly older clientele than others on the island. Indeed, most of them return time after time, aided and abetted by various incentive schemes. Accommodation is in well-appointed individual chalets, six with ocean views (ask for room 5) and four further back with air conditioning. Comfortable dining room for meals, which include wine, and cosy, wood-panelled bar. Barbecue nights Thursday and Saturday.

The staff at Pirates Point are all part of the dive team, taking it in turns to work in the resort dining room etc. Personal interviews are held with individual divers to ascertain their status and interests, thus ensuring that each guest will get the most out of his or her stay. Courses include PADI referrals and are available up to Divemaster. Nature trail and fishing guides are also on hand.

Rates All-inclusive rates per person (low/high season): Divers (two dives per day) US$290/330 single, US$210/250 double, US$185/230. Non-divers US$230/275 single, US$150/195 double, US$135/175 triple. All rates subject to 15% gratuity and US$8 per room per day hotel tax. Rates include drinks, but not dive equipment rental. Children under 12 stay free when sharing with parents; meal prices available. No children under five.

Sam McCoy's Dive Lodge PO Box 12 LC; tel: 948 0026, US: 800 626 0496; fax: 948 0057; email: mccoy@candw.ky; web: www.mccoyslodge.com.ky or www.cayman.com.ky/com/sam (13 rooms)
Sam McCoy and his wife Mary opened McCoy's Lodge in 1988, having been the first to introduce diving to Little Cayman. An all-inclusive resort based on the north coast (opposite Bloody Bay Wall), the lodge offers packages based on diving, fishing or simply R&R, including all meals, and transfer to and from the airport. Rooms with AC and bathroom are large and comfortable, with sliding doors leading directly outside. Home-cooked meals are served at a large communal table in the dining room decorated with family photographs and mementos. The patio bar overlooks the sea, with a swimming pool, jacuzzi and hammocks nearby. As with many of the resorts on Little Cayman, most of their clientele come back year after year.

Saturday night is barbecue night at 7.00pm, with plenty of traditional Cayman fare. Non-guests are welcome at US$15 per head (though do book in advance) – the

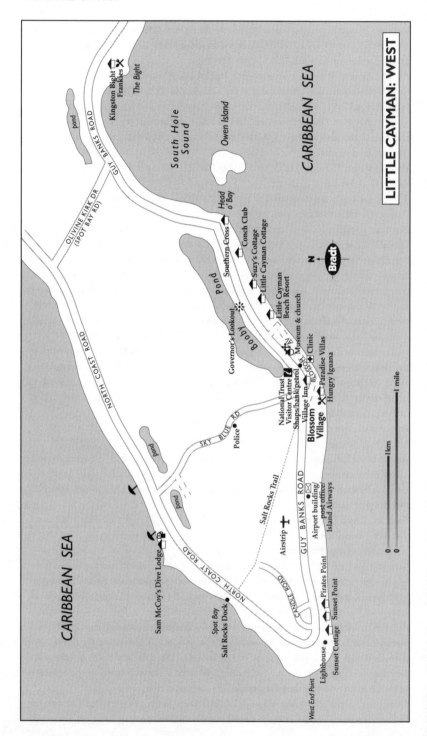

LITTLE CAYMAN: WEST

McCoys will pick you up if you don't have transport.

McCoy's has two dive boats and a fishing boat, all based at Little Cayman dock just to the east of the lodge. There's a maximum of ten divers per trip, with flexible schedules. Dive courses can be arranged on request, as can snorkel trips around the island. Shore diving from here brings you almost directly on to Jackson Point. Fishing for wahoo, dolphin and marlin is just 100ft (30m) off the wall.

Rates per person per night, based on double occupancy and inclusive of all meals (low/high season): Divers US$160/180 (includes two-tank morning dive, unlimited shore diving and optional night dive). Dive equipment is charged extra at US$10 each for BCD and regulator per day (a full set of equipment including mask and fins is US$25 a day). Hire of tanks and weights is included in the dive package. Non-divers US$105/115. Note that McCoy's defines the low, summer season as June 1 – Oct 15, and winter as Oct 16 – May 31.

Southern Cross PO Box 44 LC, Guy Banks Rd; tel: 948 1099; US reservations: 800 899 2582; international: 619 563 0017; fax: 948 1098; email: scc@candw.ky; web: www.southerncrossclub.com (11 chalets)

The first resort on Little Cayman, Southern Cross was opened in 1958 then taken over in 1995 by the current owner, Peter Hillenbrand, who has ensured that it retains every bit of its natural appeal. The club's popularity is self-evident. Over two thirds of its visitors have been before, and most of the rest have come through personal recommendation, with around 15% hailing from the UK.

Named after the constellation, which can be seen here in the winter at its most northerly point, the resort has an 800ft (243m) sea frontage on the southern side of the island, with uninterrupted views across to Owen Island and the reef just beyond. Each room is an individual, freshly painted chalet with en-suite facilities, separated from its neighbours by yards of sand, and looking out to sea. Visitors at Southern Cross stay on an inclusive basis, with three separate packages available for diving, fishing and holiday visitors. Breakfast and lunch are served as a buffet in the spacious restaurant, with plate service at dinner. The bar is open all day, with service available from 4.00pm to non-residents. Friday night is barbecue night out on the deck, at US$18.75 inclusive, with outside bar. Plenty of locals gather here then; if you meet up with Obie (Edward Obadiah Scott, that is), tell him you read about him – he'll be chuffed!

Diving, fishing and other watersports are available, including guided fishing trips (see page 185). In fact, the resort is one of only two on the island that offers fishing, and has two fishing boats, one deep-sea and one flat, moored at their own fishing dock. There is also a separate dive dock with two boats, each taking a maximum of 12 divers. Guests on a diving package who would prefer a day's fishing or sailing to diving can on occasion interchange the options subject to availability. Kayaks and bikes are provided free to guests, while sailboats are available for rent at US$25 per hour.

Rates Inclusive rates per person for seven nights, based on double/triple occupancy (low/high season): Divers (up to three dives per day) US$1,687/1,992. Non-divers US$1,323/1,579. Rates include transfer from airport, three meals per day, service charge and government tax, but not dive equipment rental (see page 185), nor drinks. No under fives as a rule. Other packages available on request.

Villas and apartments

Conch Club Condominiums PO Box 51 LC, Guy Banks Rd; tel: 948 1033; fax: 948 1045; US tel: 800 327 3835; fax: 813 323 8827; email: refz79a@prodigy.com; web: www.conchclub.com (20 townhouses)

In joint ownership with Little Cayman Beach Resort, and very close by, the Conch Club features luxury self-catering two- and three-bedroom townhouses, each with patio, balcony and sea view. Ideal for families or small groups. Swimming pool. Other facilities shared with Little Cayman Beach Resort (see page 176).

Rates per night high season: two-bedroom (4 adults) US$300; three-bedroom (6 adults) US$350; each additional adult US$25 per night. 10% government tax, cleaning and transfers (US$10 per person) extra. Meal plans available in conjunction with Little Cayman Beach Resort.

Kingston Bight Lodge PO Box 17 LC, Guy Banks Rd; tel: 948 1015; fax: 948 0006

Re-opened in 2000 with four apartments, and a further six rooms with en-suite showers under construction, Kingston Bight is co-owned by Little Caymanian resident Frankie and his US business partner Henry. The beachfront location overlooking the bay and Owen Island is stunning; it's not surprising that the place is popular with locals visiting from Grand Cayman or the Brac. Restaurant and bar (see below), with separate beach bar. Free transfer from airport. Fishing through Castro; diving by arrangement.

Rates low/high season: US$100/140.

Paradise Villas PO Box 48 LC; tel: 948 0001, US: 877 3CAYMAN; fax: 948 0002; email: iggy@candw.ky; web: www.paradisevillas.com (12 villas)

Marc and Sabine have run these idyllic beachside villas and their affiliated dive school for a couple of years, with a laid-back approach that is disarming in its efficiency. Located just a short walk across the grass from Little Cayman's airstrip, but there's no need to worry about aircraft noise – the few planes that fly in each day are completely unobtrusive. Each one-bedroom villa has AC/fans, bathroom, kitchenette and lounge area, together with its own veranda back and front, a sea view and shady hammock and – if you're lucky – semi-resident iguana. Bike hire US$10 for the duration of your stay. Swimming pool; restaurant (Hungry Iguana). Dive school (Paradise Divers). Fishing with the Iguana Fleet. Babysitting by arrangement.

Rates per night: winter US$143.75/161 per person; US$155.25/184 (2 people); US$178.25/207 (3 people). Office open Mon–Fri, 9.00am–5.00pm.

Village Inn Blossom Av; reservations through James Little at the Village Stores, tel: 948 1069; fax: 948 0069; email: james_l@candw.ky (8 efficiencies, 3 apartments)

Opposite the clinic just a hundred yards or so from the sea, and almost as close to the airport, the blue-and-white painted Village Inn offers good-value monthly rentals for two people in a quiet location close to the shops. All units have AC and kitchenette.

Rates per month: efficiencies US$550; one-bedroom apartments US$875 per month.

New condominiums are under construction to the west of Little Cayman Beach Resort. The traditional-style wooden building on the seafront will house two- and three-bedroom luxury units. For details, phone (US) 809 947 4388/4428; fax: 809 945 2063.

There are a small number of individual **privately owned** houses and cottages available for rent on the island. Suzy's Cottage, right on the beach opposite Booby Pond, is a small white-and-blue painted wooden house with its own sand garden. It has two bedrooms with ceiling fans (one with AC), bathroom, living area, small kitchen and seafront patio, plus washer/dryer, telephone, barbecue and bicycles. Other rental properties on the island include Little Cayman Cottage, Sunset Cottage and Sunset Point, all to the southwest. Cottages may be booked through the local agent for Cayman Villas, Tranquil Realty (PO Box 9 LC, Blossom Village; tel: 948 1077 fax: 948 0178; email: bettyboo@candw.ky), who have the advantage of local knowledge. Alternatively, you can go direct to Cayman Villas on Grand Cayman (see page 116).

RESTAURANTS AND BARS

In order to have a liquor licence, establishments on Little Cayman must have at least ten rooms, so all bars and restaurants are linked to hotels or villa complexes. If transport is a problem, do give your chosen restaurant a ring – many of them, including McCoys and Frankies, will collect you from your accommodation and take you back after your meal.

Bird of Paradise Little Cayman Beach Resort; tel: 948 1033. Meals are served in the elegant, air-conditioned dining room, on a screened veranda or on the patio. Buffet service. The menu changes nightly, and the resort will cater for individual requirements on request. Open 7.00–8.30am, 12.30–1.30pm, 6.30–8.00pm.

Frankies Kingston Bight; tel: 948 1015; fax: 948 0006. The no-smoking restaurant at Kingston Bight is a simple, no-frills place, with a separate bar. Frankie himself is from Little Cayman, although his business partner, Henry, is from the US. Cooking is basically good-value grills and Cayman specialities – turtle steaks cost CI$15. Beer at CI$3 a bottle is boasted as the cheapest on the island. Friday night is happy hour, 7.00–9.00pm, when beer is CI$2.50, and rum & Coke CI$3.50.

Hungry Iguana Restaurant and Sports Bar Tel: 948 0007. Set in the grounds of Paradise Villas, the interior of this wood-panelled restaurant with its long bar makes no concessions to the bright Caribbean sunshine. By contrast, the shady veranda, with its view of the sea framed by sea-grape trees, is a relaxing place for lunch in the company of a couple of cheeky bananaquits. The broad-spectrum menu ranges from burgers, sandwiches and pizza to fresh seafood and Caribbean/American dishes, with a daily special. Open daily 11.30am–2.00pm, 5.00–9.00pm; Sunday brunch 8.00am–10.30am. Bar open Sun–Thu 11.00am–11.00pm; later on Fri and Sat. Takeaway food is available to eat in your own villa.

McCoys Saturday night is barbecue night – for details, see page 177.

Pirates Point For non-guests, dinner at this resort should be booked 24 hours in advance. The food is said 'to stand comparison with some of the best in New York' – certainly the breakfast was good (albeit pricey), with plenty of fresh orange juice and unlimited coffee. Dinner US$37.50 plus 15% gratuity includes wine. Transport to and from your place of accommodation is also available.

Southern Cross The Friday barbecue out on the dock is open to all comers, and is good value at US$18.75, with beer at US$3 and rum punch US$5. See page 179.

SHOPPING AND AMENITIES

Almost all Little Cayman's shops are to be found in the grandly named Little Cayman Mall, a handful of shops on the right just a few hundred yards from the airfield as you head east on Guy Banks Road.

Food, drink and general supplies

Village Square Tel: 948 1069. The ultimate one-stop shop, the Village Square may not have a huge variety, but it does seem to have something of everything, including groceries, beer, hardware, fishing stuff, household goods, chandlery, camera films, newspapers and video rentals. Remember that everything on the island is brought in by boat, so prices are correspondingly high – you can expect to pay nearly US$4 for a loaf of decent bread. Open Mon–Sat 8.30am–6.00pm.

Gifts and clothes

Iguana Crossing next to the car hire place in Blossom Village sells T-shirts, beachwear, sandals, jewellery, souvenirs, as well as wine and liquor, Cuban cigars, coffee and rum cake. Open Mon–Sat 8.30am–midday; 3.00–6.00pm; Sun 8.30–10.30am, 4.00–6.00pm (but no alcohol is served on Sunday).
Mermaids Tel: 948 0097. The gift shop at Little Cayman Beach Resort sells souvenirs, clothes, postcards and treasure coins. Open Mon–Sat 10.00am–6.00pm.

Hairdressing/spa

Nature Spa Health & Beauty Tel: 948 0058. Owned by Little Cayman Beach Resort, and located just opposite, the spa offers a full range of services including hairdressing, manicure and pedicure, facials and massage. Open Mon–Sat, 10.00am–6.00pm; Sun 1.00–6.00pm. Appointments necessary.

Photographic supplies

Reef Photo & Video Centre at Little Cayman Beach Resort; tel: 948 1323. Daily processing, photo coaching, custom underwater videos, equipment sales and rentals from US$10 per half day. Half-day rental with basic lesson from US$39. Photography tuition from US$50 per hour.

For **dive equipment**, see Reef Divers, page 185.

OTHER PRACTICALITIES
Banks

Cayman National Bank, next to the shops at Little Cayman Mall, is open at least once a week from 9.15am to midday and again from 1.00pm to 2.30pm. A notice outside the bank gives precise dates for the coming month.

Church services

See page 180.

Communications
Post office

The only post office is by the airfield and is open Mon–Fri 8.00–11.00am and 1.00–3.00pm; Sat 8.00–11.00am.

Above Blue iguanas are frequently seen in Queen Elizabeth II Botanic Park. (TH)

Left Iguanas on Little Cayman have right of way, even by the airstrip. (TH)

Below Little Cayman iguana basking in the sun (KS)

Above The banana orchid, Cayman's
national flower (KS)

Right The Grand Cayman parrot, occasionally
spotted in the centre of the island (CITB)

Below Ironshore beach, typical of parts
of Cayman (TH)

Telephones
There is a public phone at the airport, one outside the clinic on Blossom Avenue, and one at the Hungry Iguana. Both Little Cayman Beach Resort and Southern Cross also have public phones. Phonecards can be bought at the Island Airways office at the airport.

Internet/fax
Internet and fax facilities are available at McLaughlin Enterprises, which is next to the general store in Blossom Village. Costs for internet use are CI$5 for 15 minutes on line. The cost of faxes varies according to the destination: Grand Cayman, CI$1 per page; US CI$4 for 1–5 pages; UK CI$7 for 1–5 pages.

Health and medical facilities
There is a nurse based at the **clinic** (tel: 948 0072) on Blossom Avenue, behind the shops on Guy Banks Road. The clinic is open Mon, Thu and Fri 9.00am–1.00pm; Tue 1.00–5.00pm; Wed 10.00am–2.00pm. A doctor visits the clinic from Cayman Brac every Wednesday.

In an emergency, the nurse can be contacted out of hours on 948 1073. The nearest **hospital** is Faith Hospital on Cayman Brac, tel: 948 2225. Should there be a need for urgent hospital treatment, patients are put on the first flight off the island, but do note that the patient still has to pay for the ticket, so make sure that you are properly insured. In the unlikely event of a diving accident with a need for decompression, the plane flies to Grand Cayman at a maximum height of 500ft (150m).

There is no natural source of fresh **water** on the island. Drinking water is produced by desalination, with each of the resorts having its own reverse osmosis plant. This means that tap water is safe to drink, but it also means that water is very expensive, so conservation is the watchword here. Rain water is also collected in cisterns. Water for showers etc comes from wells and is mostly brackish.

Police
The police station was opened in autumn 2000 as a base for the island's lone police officer, who you will regularly see on his beat. Before he came, the role was handled by immigration and marine officers. To contact the police in an emergency, dial 911.

ACTIVITIES
Diving, snorkelling and fishing
Diving and Little Cayman are pretty well synonymous in the minds of most visitors. Renowned worldwide for the attractions of Bloody Bay Wall, the island has a total of 57 designated dive sites, and countless places that are good for snorkelling.

The Bloody Bay Marine Park, incorporating the area between Bloody Bay and Jackson Point, is a regulated diving zone, in which only licensed vessels are permitted. Most of the dive sites around the island are either in the marine park or in replenishment zones (see map page 26). Under the rules that govern marine park status, boats are limited to a maximum of 20 divers on board at any one time. Even the resorts themselves are limited to the number of boats they may operate. It is therefore important to book diving in advance if you don't want to be disappointed.

On Bloody Bay Wall, each operator is limited to one visit per day by the Cayman Tourism Alliance Watersports Committee, and may dive no deeper than 100ft (30m).

Fishing was the original basis of tourism on Little Cayman (diving came later), and remains a strong lure, with fishing packages run by several of the resorts. The biggest draw – aside, of course, from the relaxed pace of the island and the lack of pressure from boat captains – is that of bonefish, which are to be found in sheltered shallow waters such as surround Owen Island. Tarpon, too, are much sought after, particularly in Tarpon Lake just east of Kingston Bight. Offshore, deep-sea fishing focuses on blue marlin, dolphin, wahoo, tuna and barracuda. As on Grand Cayman, bring your own tackle if you plan to go fly fishing.

Dive/snorkel/fishing operators

All of the island's resorts offer various diving, fishing and snorkelling opportunities to their guests. The following also welcome other visitors, space permitting:

Captain Castro's Fishing Excursions c/o the Village Square; tel: 948 1069/0092; email: james_l@candw.ky (this is via the Village Store, so use the phone if you can) If you want to go fishing, have a word with the guy at the airport with the pink sunglasses. Castro – his full name is Fidel Castro Christian – was born on the Brac, but has run fishing charters on Little Cayman for several years. His other job, checking the bags for departing passengers, means that he is available all day Tuesday and Wednesday, and 11.00am–2.00pm the rest of the week. Charters in his 17ft boat can be organised to go bonefishing, deep-sea fishing, night fishing, or after shark or grouper – basically, whatever your interest, Castro will organise it.
Rates US$150 per half day for one person for any type of fishing (including bonefishing). For two people, most trips cost US$200, but for deep-sea fishing the price is US$250 for two or three people. Night fishing for shark or grouper is US$150 per person.
Conch Club Divers PO Box 42 LC; tel: 948 1026; fax: 948 1028; email: ccdivers@candw.ky; web: www.conchclub.com
Next to Little Cayman Beach Resort, Conch Club Divers use the resort's boats, but limit the number of divers to 15 per trip. PADI and SSI courses up to advanced standard. Many of their visitors rent their equipment.
Paradise Divers PO Box 48LC; tel: 948 0001, US: 877 3CAYMAN; fax: 948 0002; email: iggy@candw.ky; web: www.paradise-divers.com
There is something very appealing about a dive boat that comes right up on the sand to collect its passengers, then anchors alone just a few hundred feet offshore above one of the most beautiful dive spots in the world. A relaxed and friendly outfit where

group dives are kept small and confidence is the watchword – it's not surprising that it regularly rates highly in surveys of dive operators. PADI and NAUI affiliated, with several PADI courses available, usually requiring advance reservation.

Rates Two-tank dive US$75; Resort course US$58; Open Water US$460; snorkel trip US$25. BCD/regulator US$10 each, but note that gear rental is a maximum of US$30 per day. Dive packages available on request for booking of five days or more.

Reef Divers Little Cayman Beach Resort; PO Box 51 LC, Blossom Village; tel: 948 1033; US reservations: 800 327 3835; fax: 948 1040; email: lcbr@candw.ky; web: littlecayman.com

Established in 1993, Reef Divers has three 42ft custom-built boats and up-to-date equipment. Range of PADI courses, including nitrox. Night dives Tue and Thu, provided that there are at least six divers. Dive shop with sailboat and kayak rentals.

Rates Two-tank dive US$75; Resort course US$100; Open Water US$450. BCD/regulator US$12 each. For dive packages, see Little Cayman Beach Resort (page 176).

Southern Cross (see page 179) Diving, fishing and other watersports are open to non-guests subject to availability.

Rates Two-tank dive US$75; Resort course US$125 (includes gear); Open Water referral US$300; snorkel trip US$25. BCD/regulator US$12 each.

Fishing: Guided flats fishing trips, ideally for two anglers, with a maximum of three, US$150–180 for 3–4 hours; guided fishing on Tarpon Lake US$110. Deep-sea fishing prices on request.

On the north side of the island, there is a sign proclaiming 'Bloody Bay Divers', an enterprise to be set up by Sam McCoy's son, though it is unlikely to be operational until at least the end of 2002.

Dive sites

Most of Little Cayman's 57 permanent moorings are located in or around Bloody Bay and Jackson Bay, to the northwest of the island.

Bloody Bay Wall to the north of the island drops almost vertically down to 1,200ft (365m) from a depth of a mere 18ft (5.4m). Giant sponges rise up from beautifully formed coral gardens, offering the perfect camouflage for any number of reef fish, while off the wall eagle rays glide gracefully by and the occasional shark lurks in the shadows.

Anchored dive sites on the wall include Randy's Gazebo, also known as Chimneys, which had us trying to formulate an underwater signal for 'wow'! A favourite with photographers, the site features corals of all shapes, sizes and hues, and so many marine creatures it's hard to focus on everything at once. Hawkshead turtles make their lazy way across the reef, while nearby stingrays glide effortlessly by. At Great Wall West, the shallow reef drops suddenly off into a seemingly endless abyss; the sensation of floating in space is amazing. You may be lucky enough to see the occasional nurse shark on patrol, completely uninterested in your presence. Other popular sites on the wall include Great Wall East, Fisheye Fantasy and Three Fathom Wall (also known as the Mixing Bowl) – this last being the home of Freddie, the Nassau grouper.

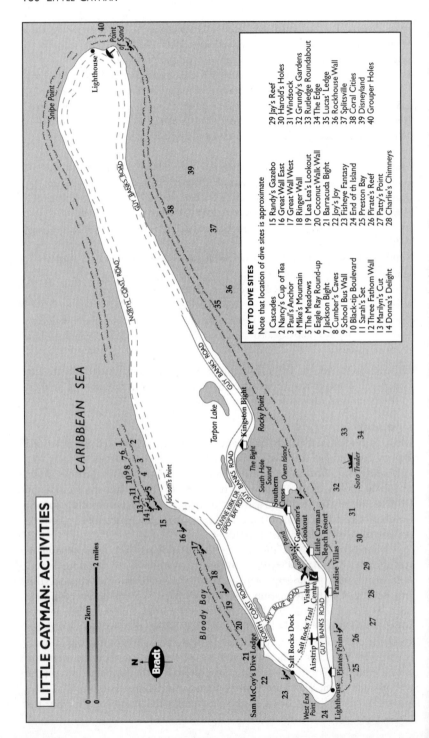

LITTLE CAYMAN: ACTIVITIES

CARIBBEAN SEA

KEY TO DIVE SITES

Note that location of dive sites is approximate

1 Cascades
2 Nancy's Cup of Tea
3 Paul's Anchor
4 Mike's Mountain
5 The Meadows
6 Eagle Ray Round-up
7 Jackson Bight
8 Cumber's Caves
9 School Bus Wall
10 Black-tip Boulevard
11 Sarah's Set
12 Three Fathom Wall
13 Marilyn's Cut
14 Donna's Delight
15 Randy's Gazebo
16 Great Wall East
17 Great Wall West
18 Ringer Wall
19 Lea Lea's Lookout
20 Coconut Walk Wall
21 Barracuda Bight
22 Joy's Joy
23 Fisheye Fantasy
24 End of th Island
25 Preston Bay
26 Pirate's Reef
27 Patty's Point
28 Charlie's Chimneys
29 Jay's Reef
30 Harold's Holes
31 Windsock
32 Grundy's Gardens
33 Rutledge Roundabout
34 The Edge
35 Lucas' Ledge
36 Rockhouse Wall
37 Splitsville
38 Coral Cities
39 Disneyland
40 Grouper Holes

As Bloody Bay Wall is renowned for boat diving, so **Jackson Point** is an excellent place for shore diving and snorkelling. If you're not staying at McCoy's (the only resort on the north of the island), you'll need to take all your equipment, including tanks, as there are no independent dive operators based here.

There are several places on the island where the snorkelling is superb. One of the most popular is reputed to be about half way to Point of Sand to the south of the island.

Wrecks

On the southern side of the island, the *Soto Trader* was sunk in 1975 after it caught fire. A 120ft (36.6m) cargo freighter, it lies today at a depth of around 50ft (15m).

Kayaks

Both Southern Cross Club and Little Cayman Beach Resort have kayaks for hire by non-guests. Single kayaks cost US$15 per hour (or US$30–60 per day); two-person kayaks US$20 per hour (US$40–90 per day).

Tennis

The tennis court at Little Cayman Beach Resort is open to non-residents. Contact the resort on 948 1033 for the current fees. The best times to play are early morning or after 4.00pm, when it is cooler.

Hiking

There are plenty of places to explore Little Cayman on foot, though sadly two of the three trails established across the island some 200 years ago – the Spot Bay Trail and the Lighthouse Trail – have recently been paved for vehicles. Of course, you can still walk these, and with considerably greater ease than before. The Spot Bay Trail (now renamed Sky Blue Road) across the western side of the island will take up to half an hour one way. The Lighthouse Trail (now called Candle Road) is a paved road with a dead end, and a loop that returns you to Guy Banks Road near Pirates Point. If you go up here, you may be rewarded with the sight of a rather larger iguana than you've seen elsewhere. The mile-long Salt Rocks Trail that links the North Coast Road with Guy Banks Road near the airstrip is the only one left in its natural state, but it's not easy to find. You'll need strong shoes and plenty of water, and to be able to recognise (and thus avoid) the highly poisonous manchineel tree, which grows along the trail.

For guided nature walks on the island, contact Gladys Howard (see Pirates Point, page 177).

ROUND THE ISLAND TOUR

The best way to see the island is undoubtedly by bike or, if you want to go right to the eastern tip, by hired jeep. Allow a couple of hours to do the shorter circuit by bike, which gives you time to complete it at leisure; you'll need longer if you're going to combine this with a visit to the museum or National

Trust. The full tour of the island by jeep could be completed in not much more than an hour, but anything less than half a day wouldn't do it justice. Take a hat and plenty to drink.

The circular tour here is based on starting at the airport and heading east, but it could of course be started anywhere.

Blossom Village to Kingston Bight

The paved road heading east from the airstrip is lined by dense vegetation, occasionally broken by ponds and mangrove swamps. Flowering trees enliven the wayside, bringing splashes of red and yellow at the end of the year.

Just a short walk east from the shops, set back from Guy Banks Road, is **Little Cayman Museum** (tel: 948 1033). The immaculately painted green and white building with its wooden veranda is surrounded by lawns, and flanked by artefacts from the collection. The museum houses personal and public memorabilia dating back 150 years or so. Originally the collection of Linton Tibbetts, a Bracker who went to the US with just $45 and returned a multi-millionaire, it tells the history of Little Cayman, as well as something of Cayman Brac. Tibbetts' collection is augmented by individual donations from the islanders, from a grandmother's sewing machine and plates to one of the turtle nets that were once effectively the lifeblood of the island. Open Mon–Fri 3.00–5.00pm.

Next to the museum, and opposite Booby Pond, is the tiny **Little Cayman Baptist Church** with its simple white walls and padded pews. All are welcome to attend the services at 11.00am and 7.30pm on Sunday, or the Wednesday Bible study at 7.30pm.

On the other side of the road is the recently built **National Trust Visitors' Centre**. Overlooking Booby Pond, the centre was built as a result of the almost single-handed effort of Gladys Howard, a Texan-born woman who bought Pirates Point (see page 177) and fundraised tirelessly until the building was finally completed. The centre is staffed entirely by volunteers. Gladys now leads nature walks and knows a considerable amount about Cayman history – contact her on 948 1010. Open Mon–Sat 3.00–5.00pm.

Inside the centre are panels featuring the natural history of the island, with a particular focus on the birds. Outside, telescopes on the porch enable visitors to watch the boobies across the pond, and above this is an observation area. A number of local books and prints by local artists are for sale.

The centre is also home to Little Cayman's **library**. Housed in a small room off the main centre, the library mostly comprises paperback fiction, although there are some reference books as well. Visitors and residents alike may swap a book for a fee of just CI$1, or buy one for CI$3, with all proceeds going towards the National Trust.

The peaceful setting of **Booby Pond** is a haven for wildlife and has been designated an animal sanctuary and wetland of international importance under the UN Ramsar Convention. Like the other ponds on the Cayman Islands, Booby Pond is Crown land, while the land to the north is now owned by the National Trust. The natural beauty of the place can be somewhat deceptive, however. At the beginning of winter, the pond may look deep but has in fact just a few inches of water. By May, before the summer rain, much of the water has evaporated leaving a pretty smelly brackish residue.

The ancient breeding colony of well over 5,000 pairs of red-footed boobies and the attendant magnificent frigatebirds is the largest in the Caribbean. In the past, booby eggs formed part of the local diet, effectively checking the growth of the colony since boobies raise just one chick per year. Now, however, the colony is fully protected and numbers are rising fast.

At dawn, the sky is alive with boobies heading out to sea for their fishing grounds, attaining speeds of up to 40mph (64km/h). Frigatebirds glide effortlessly overhead, easily distinguished in flight by their forked tails. In the mating season (late November to January), the males display their distinctive red pouch. Known to locals as the 'man o' war', the frigatebird may co-exist with the booby, but it is also its arch enemy, hovering menacingly above the coastline as dusk approaches to terrorise the boobies as they return into releasing their day's catch.

Overlooking the pond, not far from Little Cayman Beach Resort, is the Governor's Lookout, a small hide built for birdwatching.

Owen Island

Probably the nearest most of us will ever get to a desert island, Owen Island is located in the bay just a short kayak trip (or even a swim) from Southern Cross or – a little further – from Kingston Bight. The water here is very shallow and mostly thick with turtle grass; except at high tide it is actually quite possible to walk across. The small beach on the island is, quite simply, idyllic, with soft white sand backed by trees, and the odd piece of driftwood. Beyond is the edge of the reef. If you're planning to walk rather than wade out towards the reef, though, do take good shoes as this end of the island is rocky and it's tough going. The stretch of water between the island and the reef beyond is not deep, but watch out for currents around the tip of the island. There's plenty of underwater life here for snorkellers to observe, including young coral formations (take care not to knock them with your fins) and spiny lobster; you may even catch a glimpse of the occasional nurse shark as it slips through the narrow channel.

Further east

The road east from Kingston Bight is paved to about half way, then turns into a sandy track, rough in parts, all the way to Point of Sand and back along the north coast. The road is pretty flat, but drifting sand makes cycling particularly hazardous. That, coupled with the likelihood of punctures on the sharp stones and the lack of manoeuvrability of the island's rental bikes, makes it inadvisable to cycle beyond this point. It makes more sense, therefore, for cyclists to backtrack 500 yards or so (457m) from Kingston Bight to the paved crossover road, Olivine Kirk Drive, also known as Spot Bay Road, and head for the north side of the island, then west to complete a circuit of some eight miles (13km).

Continuing east along the unpaved road, you'll be following the coast. Inland, ponds line the roadside, many offering habitats to a wide variety of birds, including the West Indian whistling-duck. The largest of these ponds is the 15-acre Tarpon Lake, which lies on the left just past Kingston Bight. Popular with fisherman in search of the beautiful silver fish that make this their home in significant numbers, it is accessed via a wooden boardwalk from the road.

As the road becomes rougher, the vegetation becomes less dense, coconut palms rise high above and rough tracks to the right offer tantalising glimpses of the Caribbean. Some six miles (10km) from Kingston Bight, the road veers to the left, with a track off to the right leading through to Point of Sand.

Point of Sand, marked as Sandy Point on some maps, is almost at the extreme east of the island, looking over towards Cayman Brac, five miles (8km) away across the channel. The water here is as clear as anywhere on the island, and sheltered by the reef. Snorkelling is excellent, but watch out for strong currents. The white sandy beach shifts with the changing tides and seasons, meaning that no map is ever quite accurate. It is backed by low bushes that offer little or no protection against the midday sun. Although there is a purpose-built wooden shelter back off the beach, the place is stacked with broken benches, so take an umbrella and/or sunhat, plus water and suncream, if you're heading out this way. The nearest place to get a drink is at Kingston Bight.

To complete the circuit of the island, return down the track to the point at which you forked off, then turn right and follow the road right round the coast. After approximately eight miles (13km) the road is again paved, and shortly after this it passes the northern side of the road across the island. There is little along this road apart from trees, beaches and the occasional private house – the choice of picnic spots is all yours.

Just beyond Sam McCoy's on your right is Salt Rocks Dock, where ships tie up each week to bring provisions to the island. Hidden in the undergrowth is the old mule pen, built in 1885 and the oldest surviving structure on the island. There is no diving from the docks, and no beach, but several of the resort boats are moored here, giving them easy access out to Bloody Bay Wall.

Almost at the western tip of the island is the lighthouse, not accessible to the public. Continue past here and Pirates Point and you'll find yourself back at the airstrip, with luck in time to enjoy a relaxing siesta in a tree-shaded hammock.

Zebra butterfly

Cayman Brac

On first acquaintance, Cayman Brac seems the poor relation of the Cayman Islands – more stepsister than true family. Short on soft sandy beaches and with an apparently impenetrable interior, this Caribbean island lacks the clichéd Caribbean attractions. But appearances can be deceptive. Whereas Grand Cayman and, to a far lesser extent, Little Cayman are effectively ensnared by tourism, Cayman Brac very much retains its own personality. Here, you will meet the local people, or Brackers, in hotels, in restaurants, in the shops. Cayman food is the norm, not something to be sought out like a rare commodity. In fact, the whole ethos is that of Cayman – a gentler pace of life, a deeper sense of reality.

The Brac, so called after the Gaelic word for 'bluff', is 12 miles (19.3km) long from west to east, and nearly two miles (3km) across at its widest point, to the east. Located at 79° west, 19°41' north, the island covers an area of just 14 square miles (36km²). It may be similar in size to Little Cayman, but there the similarity ends. Like some great fossilised whale, the bluff dominates almost the entire length of the island, seemingly impenetrable, and with only the western tip untouched by its presence. To the east, looming straight up from the sea, the highest point of this stark rock, at 144ft (43.9m), must have been a forbidding sight for sailors in days gone by. Cruel ironshore lies underfoot at the top, but beneath is a veritable labyrinth of limestone caves that have not only offered full rein to the imaginations of countless children over the years, but rather more soberly have served as shelters to generations of Brackers from the fierce storms that are occasionally meted out to the island.

There are four main settlements, all on the west or north of the island: West End, Stake Bay, Creek and Spot Bay, housing the island's 1,800 or so population. A considerable number of expatriate workers also live on the island, mostly from Jamaica and Honduras, swelling the population by almost double. Unlike on Grand Cayman, however, few foreigners here are employed in the tourism industry. Aside from the construction industry, some work in one of the island's three primary schools or the high school, and others in the local hospital. The few tourist venues are at the westernmost point of the island, where the land is flat, and wide sandy beaches are lapped by the blue waters of the Caribbean.

THE '32 HURRICANE

On that fateful morning, it came with no warning,
Crashing waves sweeping o'er the land

From '1932 Hurricane' in
Traditional Songs from the Cayman Islands

The lives of the islanders have been shaped across the years by the various hurricanes that have hit the Brac and the other two islands in the group. In 1980, the tidal surge caused by Hurricane Arlene brought the sea some 300ft (100m) inland, throwing great stones against the bluff. Then, as so many other times, the islanders took refuge in the labyrinth of caves that lie within the bluff – a tough climb up to 80ft (24m) or so took them to a place of relative safety.

Undoubtedly the hurricane that caused the most damage in living memory was that of November 8 1932, which changed the lives of Brackers for ever. The Brac took the hurricane head on, with winds of 200mph (320km/h) and water crashing inland up to 800ft (244m). Indeed, the seas were so rough that some waves went right over the bluff. Later, as the storm died away and the waters subsided, a shark was found inland in the grounds of Spellman McLaughlin's house in the Creek, a rare light moment at a time of real tragedy.

One hundred and nine Brackers lost their lives that night, 40 of them in three separate ships at sea. Whole families were wiped out, from babies to grandparents. A mass gravesite for many of the victims of the hurricane lies near the sea on White Bay Road (see page 213).

A little-known venue for discerning divers, and gaining popularity with keen climbers, the Brac is also ideally situated for the nature lover, with a number of designated hikes of varying degrees of difficulty. Safe and stress free, it is a welcoming place with no frills.

Locals will tell you that Cayman Brac is getting more crowded, with a lot of building. It's hard to take this on board by comparison with Grand Cayman, but clearly the Brackers like their island the way it is, and have no intention of letting the rest of the world spoil its natural beauty.

HISTORY

The first permanent settlers on the Brac, in 1833, were boatbuilders, sailors and turtle fishermen who came over from Grand Cayman to people this previously uninhabited island. Trade links were soon established with Jamaica, Cuba and Central America. Sixty years later, the population had risen to 528, and by 1934 it stood at 1,317.

Until 1968, one of the major exports from Cayman Brac was turtleshell, together with coconut, cattle and rope. Alongside these, from the early part of the 20th century until 1939, Cayman Brac traded in relatively low-quality phosphate, which was blasted out of the rock on Cotton Tree Land in the interior and transported by rail to waiting ships.

Time in Cayman Brac is effectively measured from the 1932 hurricane, which brought death and destruction to the Brac in devastating fashion. At the time of the hurricane, life on Cayman Brac was pretty primitive by Western standards. Without electricity or telephones, and with very few cars, the islanders were cut off from the outside world except by sea. The few products that were imported were brought in by boat, traded in exchange for turtleshell and rope.

Electricity came late to Cayman Brac. Until the 1960s, nobody had a stove either. Instead, every house had a hearth in a separate caboose – a shed off the main house with a walkway between the two. Each day, one of the islanders would carry a live coal by hand to his neighbours until every fire was lit.

NATURAL HISTORY

Vegetation on the bluff is dense, in spite of the precarious existence that is the lot of trees whose roots penetrate deep into the limestone in search of water. Tall, pale-green cacti stand alongside large succulents, overshadowed by dense trees, from mastic and wild sapodilla to red birch, silver thatch and coconut palms. Fruit trees grow wild, including vine pears, wild figs and some 20 varieties of mango, which may be picked in season. Where sunlight penetrates, bougainvillaea tumbles down the rockface, and from November to January, the roads are lined with 'Christmas flowers' – yellow elders or shamrock that decorate the trees right across the island.

Almost 200 species of birds have been identified on the Brac, making it a wonderful place for birdwatching. High up on the southern side of the island, a small colony of brown boobies nests in the bluff. Like their cousins, the red-footed boobies, these are pelagic birds, to some extent at the mercy of the magnificent frigatebirds that swoop down and steal their catch. All around, on both sides of the bluff, white-tailed tropicbirds may be seen, distinctive for their long white tails, like streamers.

Inland is the only place in the world where the Cayman Brac parrot nests. With a population of just 350, it is seriously endangered. Among other birds endemic to the Brac are the red-legged thrush, the loggerhead kingbird and the vitelline warbler.

While the exterior of the bluff hosts several bird species, the network of caves that meander through the bluff is home to a multitude of different creatures. Barn owls nest in dark corners, and five species of bat, of which the most populous is the Jamaican fruit bat, have colonised the caves. That unexpected squeaking isn't a bat, though, it's probably a land crab. Watch out for them on the floor of the caves – it's easy to tread on them by mistake. The caves themselves are a seemingly endless series of interconnecting tunnels. Stalactites and stalagmites reach out to touch each other, formed from calcium carbonate as a result of the slow and incessant drip, drip of water over countless centuries. Leggy tree roots dangle into nothingness, seeking out sufficient water to eke out their precarious existence.

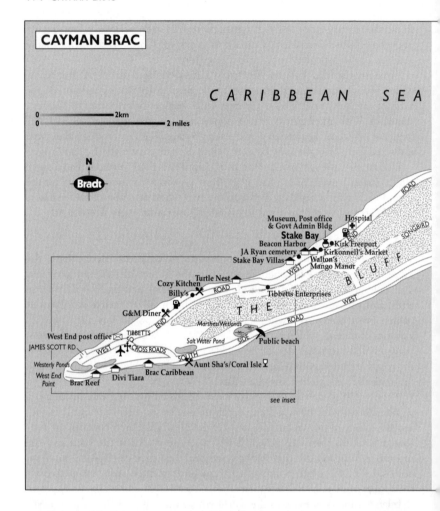

While the bluff dominates most of the island, to the west is a very different landscape. Here, herons, egrets and numerous other waterfowl are attracted by the flat wetland terrain, as are numerous migrant birds on their passage south.

The National Trust is engaged in long-term projects to preserve the unique wildlife and flora indigenous to Cayman Brac. Members of the trust visit the Divi Tiara Beach Resort on Monday evenings with displays of local crafts and information on local projects. For details, contact Wallace Platts on 948 2390.

GETTING THERE
By air
The flight from Grand Cayman to Gerrard Smith International Airport, at the westernmost tip of the island, takes between 40 minutes and an hour, depending on whether it's a direct flight or via Little Cayman. There are also

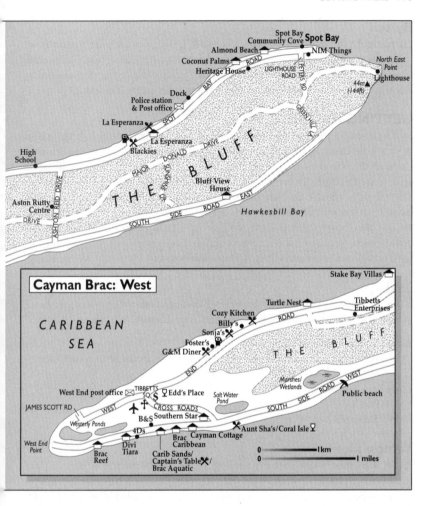

flights from Miami to Cayman Brac, with a short stopover in Grand Cayman. Note that passengers are not allowed to get off the plane in Grand Cayman when booked on a direct flight from Miami to Cayman Brac.

Cayman Airways (tel: 948 1221) has five flights a week on Boeing 737s to Cayman Brac from Miami, with a short stop in Grand Cayman. Fares US$376 (with three-day advance purchase).

Island Airways (tel: 948 1656) has four return flights a day from Grand Cayman, taking 40 minutes for direct flights, or an hour with a short stop in Little Cayman. Planes, as to Little Cayman (see page 175), are either 8 or 19 seater. Day trip: adult US$105, child US$84; standard return trip: adult US$149, child US$119; one-way adult US$75, child US$60.

Two flights a day operate from Little Cayman, taking just seven minutes. Day trip/standard return: adult US$40, child US$32; one-way adult US$20, child US$16.

By sea

Surprisingly, there is no ferry service between Little Cayman and Cayman Brac, although the distance between the two islands is just 5 miles (8km). That said, most of the boat operators here run snorkel and dive trips to Little Cayman, so day trips by boat are straightforward to organise (see pages 205 and 208).

GETTING AROUND

In a nutshell, getting around Cayman Brac is a problem. Although the island is small, there is no road that runs right round so those at the easternmost point of the island have to cover a significant distance to get just a mile or so around to the south. There is no public transport (don't be deluded by the 'bus stop' signs – they're for school buses only) and though walking is fine in daylight, it's not ideal on unlit roads at night. The options are therefore taxis, some sort of hire vehicle – car, scooter or bike – or to hitchhike. On the positive side, some of the restaurants and dive operators will collect you from your accommodation and take you home afterwards – it's always worth asking.

Taxis

Taxis are few and far between, and not always available when you want them, even at the airport, so do book in advance. Contact numbers are as follows:

Anton Foster Tel: 946 4279
David Hurlston & Osmond Knight Tel: 948 2307/0435/0523. Airport US$7 per person one way; island tour US$15 per person.
Elo's Taxi Tel: 948 0220
Hill's Taxi Tel: 948 0540
Maple Edwards Tel: 948 0395

Vehicle hire

As on the other islands, drivers need an international driving licence or their local licence plus a Cayman Islands driving permit. If you buy your permit on Cayman Brac, it is slightly cheaper than on the other islands, at US$5/CI$4. The speed limit is 25mph (40km/h) in the vicinity of schools and the hospital, 30mph (48km/h) in residential areas, and 40mph (64km/h) elsewhere.

Fuel prices are a little higher than on Grand Cayman. Petrol is CI$2.25 (US$2.81) per gallon. There are three fuel stations on the Brac – one opposite Salt Water Pond Walk on the north side of the island (open Mon–Sat to 8.00pm; Sun 3.00–5.00pm); a second opposite Kirk Freeport at Stake Bay (open Mon–Sat to 5.00pm), and the third at Watering Place, near La Esperanza (open Mon–Sat to 7.00pm).

Cars

All car-hire companies will meet incoming flights by arrangement, and most offer a free pick-up service.

Avis PO Box 89, Stake Bay; tel: 948 2847, US 800 228 0668; fax: 948 2329. Located at the airport, Avis has four-, five- and six-seater vehicles, with child safety seats available. Open daily 8.30am–5.00pm, but will meet any flight for confirmed incoming reservations. Rates per day low/high season: US$40/45 for four-door automatic. Collision damage waiver US$17.75. Discount of 20% to members of AAA and AARP, travel agents and airline employees.

B&S Motorventures PO Box 48 STB, 422 Channel Rd, South Side; tel: 948 1646/2517; fax: 948 1676; email: the_rock@candw.ky; web: bandsmv.com. Steve and Nola Bodden run this place on the southwest side of the island as if they were your friends, and offer a wealth of useful information along the way. Cars US$40 per day, US$35 per day after two days; US$210 per week (6/7 days). Jeeps US$40–45 per day; US$240–270 per week. Vans US$50 per day, US$300 per week. Weekly rates are applicable to six- or seven-day rentals. For bicycles, see below.

Brac Rent-a-Car PO Box 87 STB, Tibbetts Square; tel: 948 1515/0277/1380; fax: 948 0345; email: scottaud@candw.ky; web: bracrentals.com. Nissan Sentra US$42; Suzuki jeeps US$40; Ford van US$55. Fully comprehensive insurance additional US$18 on all vehicles. Open Mon–Fri 8.30am–5.00pm; Sat 8.30am–midday.

Four Ds Car Rental Kidco Bldg, South Side; tel: 948 1599; fax: 948 0459. US$35 per day, with fully comprehensive insurance. Seventh day free. Open Mon–Sat 8.00am–midday, 1.00–5.00pm; Sun 8.00am–midday.

Scooters and bicycles

For many visitors, scooters offer the ideal compromise between the high cost of car hire and the freedom of a bike, giving the opportunity to explore almost everywhere on the island except the unmade-up roads on the bluff.

Bikes are an ideal form of transport in the daytime, with quiet flat roads all along the coast, and the main road across the west of the island an easy cycle road. Don't try cycling up on the bluff, though – the bikes aren't geared for it. Some of the hotels have bikes available for guests.

Both bikes and scooters may be hired from **B&S Motorventures** (see above). Scooters US$27.50 per day, US$165 for 6–7 days. Bicycles US$10 per 24 hours. Unlike the hotel bikes, these ones have gears and proper brakes! If you phone from your accommodation, someone from B&S will drive out to collect you.

Hitchhiking

One of the bonuses of having no transport is the opportunity to meet local people. Giving and taking of lifts is not uncommon: during a walk along Stake Bay Road, two separate vehicles stopped to offer us a lift in as many minutes. Women on their own should obviously avoid any potentially threatening situation.

WHERE TO STAY

Cayman Brac has less choice of hotel accommodation than the other two islands in the group, although there are plenty of secluded villas and condominiums for the more independent minded. The two resort hotels are located on the southwest point, close to the airport. Don't worry about noise, though; there are very few planes and those that there are are small and quiet.

Resort hotels

Brac Reef Beach Resort PO Box 56 WE, South Side; tel: 948 1323; fax: 948 1207; US reservations: tel: 800 327 3835; fax: 727 323 8827; email: bracreef@candw.ky; web: www.bracreef.com (40 rooms)

A relaxed resort situated at the southwest of the island, Brac Reef is the most upmarket of the island's hotels. All rooms overlook the pool, most with either a patio or private balcony, plus en-suite bathroom, AC/ceiling fan, TV, telephone and radio/alarm. Luxury oceanfront rooms are also available. Meals are taken either in the air-conditioned restaurant (Coral Gardens), or at the terrace bar (Channel Lounge). There are also a conference/banquet centre, swimming pool, games rooms, fitness centre, floodlit tennis court and health and beauty spa (tel: 948 1323), plus Polly's Landing boutique and gift shop; dive and photo shops. Evening entertainment.

A beautiful private beach with hammocks and high shady 'lookout' – a perfect spot to relax in the cool breeze with a book – is also the place for a wide range of watersports. There is excellent snorkelling from the jetty. Diving is through Reef Divers, who are based on site. Bicycles and kayaks are available for guests.

Rates per room per night, low/high season: US$116/133. All rates are subject to 22% tax. Packages are available for divers and non-divers alike.

Divi Tiara PO Box 238 STB, South Side; tel: 948 1553, US toll free: 800 367 3484; fax: 948 1316; email: tiarares@candw.ky; web: www.divitiara.com (71 rooms)

The majority of guests at this slightly faded Canadian-owned resort are from the US, although a few come from the UK, and most are either divers or honeymooners (or both!). It's also a good bet for families, with a relaxed atmosphere and friendly, mostly Caymanian, staff. Standard, deluxe (with sea view and cable TV) and luxury (with jacuzzi) rooms, plus 12 one-bedroom timeshare apartments. Buffet-style restaurant. The bar is open 10.00am–midnight, with snacks available all day. In addition, a rustic beach bar overlooks a sandy beach where egrets and herons abound. Other facilities include a conference centre, swimming pool and tennis court. Shops with jewellery, coins and cigars, clothes, drinks and snacks are open 8.30am–5.30pm. Diving with Dive Tiara, and on-site dive and photo shop. Bikes available for guests.

Rates per room per night, low/high season: standard US$105/125; deluxe US$130/165; luxury US$150/195. Children 16 and under free if sharing with adults (maximum four people per room). Apartments US$200/245 per night. Prices are higher at Christmas. All rates subject to 10% service charge. Various meal plans available.

Guesthouses

Walton's Mango Manor PO Box 56, Stake Bay; tel/fax: 948 0518; email: waltons@candw.ky; web: www.waltonsmangomanor.com (5 rooms)

George and Lynne Walton's home away from home is conveniently located on the north of the island, just opposite the bluff, close to the museum, and with an ironshore beach almost at the bottom of the garden (though the house under construction on the land overlooking the sea may block this access). The model boats that adorn the house were built by George's brother, Albert, a further example of whose work is on display in the museum in George Town.

Rates per room, per night low/high season: US$80–90/$90–100, including an excellent home-cooked breakfast.

Above Hammocks slung between sea-grape trees are a great place to relax. (TH)

Left Little Cayman Museum (TH)

Below Wooden boat shelters, a reminder of Cayman's seafaring tradition (TH)

Top Peter's Cave on Cayman Brac (KS)

Above Brown boobies nest high up in the bluff on Cayman Brac. (KS)

Left First Cay walk, Cayman Brac (TH)

Below Juvenile brown booby (KS)

Self-catering apartments and villas

There are several small cottages and villas both to the north and south of the Brac, and the following is just a selection. For other properties, contact either **Trevor Foster**, tel: 948 1382, or **Tranquil Realty Sister Islands Ltd**, PO Box 90, South Side; tel: 948 1577; fax: 948 1578; email: tranquil@candw.ky; web: www.tranquilrealty.com. Agents for Cayman Villas, Tranquil Realty have direct knowledge of several properties on the island.

Almond Beach Hideaways Spot Bay; tel: 948 0336; US tel: 800 972 9795; fax: 541 426 4863; email: brac@almondbeach.com; web: www.almondbeach.com (2 villas) These two-bedroom individual villas on the beach each have a seafront patio, two bathrooms, kitchen, AC , laundry, phone, TV/VCR and barbecue. An additional three-bedroom house, The Retreat, is located below the bluff and sleeps up to nine people.
Rates per villa per night: US$205 (two adults); US$235 (three adults); U$265 (four adults); children under eight free; children aged 9–16 US$20 per night. Seven nights: US$1,275 (two adults); US$1,450 (three adults); US$1,650 (four adults). Three-night minimum stay. From August 1 to October 31, deduct 10%. All rates subject to 10% government tax. Maid service available US$10 per hour.
Beacon Harbor Foster's Rd, Stake Bay; US tel/fax: 956 544 4396; email: info@beaconharbor.com; web: www.beaconharbor.com (2 condominiums) These large two-bedroom condominiums look out over the north side of the island near Stake Bay. Custom-built for divers, the units lie opposite three good dive sites and have downstairs toilets, outside showers and washdown facilities for scuba gear. Upstairs, each unit sleeps up to six people, with living room, kitchen, bathroom, AC/fans, TV/VCR, telephone and laundry.
Rates for two people: US$190 per night; US$1,150 per week. Each additional guest US$35 per night, US$205 per week. All rates include 10% government tax. Minimum stay five nights.
Bluff View House For reservations contact John Byrnes, 46246 Weld CR #13, Ft Collins, CO 80524, USA; tel: 970 493 5801; fax: 970 493 2283; email: jbyrnes@frii.com; or Susie Lawton, tel: 970 482 1228; email: slawton@greyrock.org (2 units) Owned by the climbing fraternity on the Brac, Bluff View is on the south road towards the east end of the island. Backed up against the bluff, it's just 50yds (45m) from the sea. The house, built in 1993, has two independent one-bedroom units, one on each floor, each with lounge, bathroom, fully equipped kitchen and AC. Separate laundry and downstairs shower.
Rates per night: US$70 (two people), US$80 for (three people), US$90 (four people). Every seventh night is free. Rates subject to 7% tax.
Brac Caribbean Beach Village PO Box 4, Stake Bay; tel: 948 2265, US: 800 791 7911; fax; 948 2206; email: bracarib@candw.ky; web: www.brac-caribbean.com (16 condominiums)
These luxury one- and two-bedroom beachside apartments in the southwest each have private balcony, living room, cable TV, phone, kitchen and three bathrooms. There is a swimming pool and restaurant (Captain's Table) on site. Diving is through Brac Aquatics, also on site. Laundry facilities.

Rates (two-bedroom apartment) per night: US$185 (two adults); US$215 (three adults); U$245 (four adults); children under 11 free; children aged 12–17 US$35 per night. All rates subject to 10% government tax. Maid service US$35 per day.
Carib Sands PO Box 4 SPO; tel: 948 1121; fax: 948 1122; email: caribsan@candw.ky; web: www.caribsands.com (35 condomiumums)
The one-, two- and three-bedroom condominiums in this complex each have sea view, kitchen, AC/ceiling fans and cable TV.
Rates per night: US$185 (two adults); US$215 (three adults); U$245 (four adults); children under 11 free; children aged 12–17 US$25 per night. Dive packages available.
Cayman Cottage PO Box 100 WPO, South Side; tel: 948 1617, US 505 898 6854; email: caymancottage@yahoo.com; web: www.caymancottage.com
This private house in the grounds of the owner's home is just 25yds (24m) from the beach in the southwest of the island. Bedroom, bathroom, living room, kitchen, with AC/ceiling fans and TV/VCR.
Rates per night: US$120 (two adults); US$130 (three/four adults). Children under 12 free. All rates subject to 10% government tax.
Coconut Palms PO Box 132, Spot Bay; tel: 948 0470, US (K&M Rentals) 503 474 3708 or 800 484 3907 (ext 2722); fax: 503 472 6394; email: kbryan@candw.ky; web: www.coconutpalms.com (2 units)
These small, two-bedroom beachfront villas located on the northeast shore sleep up to six people. Each villa has a living room, two bathrooms, kitchen, AC, TV/VCR, barbecue and beach cabana with hammocks.
Rates per night, inclusive of government tax: US$200 (two adults); US$240 (three adults); U$265 (four adults); children under nine free; children aged 9–16 US$25 per night. 15% discount from August to October. 10% discount on car rental and diving.
La Esperanza PO Box 28, Stake Bay; tel: 948 0591; fax: 948 0525; email: lodging@candw.ky (4 apartments, 2 houses)
Located opposite the restaurant of the same name, La Esperanza is Caymanian owned and run and is arguably the most friendly place on the island to stay. Four comfortable two-bedroomed apartments (sleep 4–6) and two three-bedroomed/two-bathroom houses (sleep 6–8) are set in shady grounds; each has a kitchen, living room, TV, radio/cassette and AC/ceiling fans. There is a small shop next to the restaurant with basic groceries, T-shirts etc, and on the south side of the island is a private beach. Car rental for guests only is US$30 per day. Bicycles are also available.
Rates per night for two people: two bedrooms US$70; three bedrooms US$90. Each additional person US$15 per night.
Southern Star PO Box 90 WE; tel: 948 1577; fax: 948 1578; email: tranquil@candw.ky (5 units)
Overlooking a small pond near Captain's Table in the southwest, these two-bedroom townhouses have two bathrooms, kitchen, living room, laundry, AC/ceiling fans, TV/VCR, telephone and barbecue. Bicycles available.
Rates per night: US$125 (up to two people), US$90 (three/four people); per week US$750 (up to two people), US$850 (three/four people); children under 13 free. Studio apartment US$65 per night. All rates subject to 10% government tax.
Stake Bay Villas PO Box 48, Stake Bay; tel: 948 1646/2517; fax: 948 1676; email: sbvilla@candw.ky (2 villas)

Down a lane to the left, just before the Stake Bay sign when coming from the airport, these two brand new one-bedroom villas with screened balconies are right on the beach. Each villa sleeps up to four people (with sofa bed) and has AC, satellite TV, kitchen and laundry facilities.

Rates US$120 per night; US$700 per week.

Turtle Nest PO Box 50, Stake Bay, tel/fax: 948 1370; email: thetnest@candw.ky; web: www.badmen2000.com/rental

This privately owned house lies on the north coast, on the boundary between Cotton Tree Bay and Rock, next door to the owner's accommodation. Just 100yds (91m) from the sea, it sleeps up to four people. Modern bedroom, lounge, bathroom, kitchen with AC/fans, telephone and TV/VCR.

Rates for two people: US$100 per night; US$600 per week; additional adult US$15 per person per night; children under 12 free. All rates subject to 10% government tax. Maid service available.

Timeshare

Divi Tiara (details above) has 12 one-bedroom timeshare apartments in its resort complex, sharing the same facilities.

RESTAURANTS AND BARS

The Brac is not endowed with an enormous range of restaurants, but what it lacks in variety and style it makes up for in good traditional cooking. Both Captain's Table and La Esperanza will usually collect diners by arrangement.

Aunt Sha's Kitchen (at the Coral Isle) Tel: 948 1581. It's difficult to miss the bright pink building that is Aunt Sha's, situated all on its own on the southern side of the island. Good Cayman-style food, including turtle stew, at moderate prices (Cayman-style fish CI$9). If asked, they will also prepare sandwiches to take away – chicken CI$3.50. Even on windy days, the open-air area overlooking the sea is sheltered, making it a better bet at lunchtime than the rather dark restaurant. At night, look out to sea – you may be lucky enough to spot the odd shark. Lively bar, pool room. Dancing on the outside terrace Wed, Fri and Sat. Open 7.30am–11.00pm. Happy hour Fri/Sat 6.00–7.00pm (with special cocktails and snacks, plus 50 cents off beer).

Brac Reef Resort South Side; tel: 948 1323. The resort's Coral Garden restaurant features a fixed-price meal, although an à la carte menu is also available. Open for breakfast 7.00–9.00am (CI$13.80), lunch 12.30–1.30pm (CI$17.25), and dinner 6.30–8.00pm (CI$28.75). The shady Channel Lounge terrace bar has snacks from CI$4.50, and fruit punch at CI$2. Open Mon–Thu 11.00am–11.00pm; Fri–Sat 11.00am–midnight; Sun midday–11.00pm. Happy hour Fri 5.00–7.00pm.

Captain's Table South Side; tel: 948 1418; email: captable@candw.ky. Captain's Table is located in the southwest of the island, in front of Brac Caribbean Beach Village and near the resort hotels. The most cosmopolitan restaurant and bar on the Brac, it offers a wide-ranging menu including seafood, steaks and American-style dishes. The pleasant, airy restaurant has friendly service, or diners may opt for one of the tables by the pool. If you're short on transport, ring and they'll pick you up. Open Mon–Sat 11.30am–3.00pm, 6.00–10.00pm; Sun midday–3.00pm, 6.00–10.00pm. Happy hour Fri 7.00–9.00pm (but check times – they do change).

Coral Garden See *Brac Reef*, above.

Cozy Kitchen Cotton Bay; tel: 948 1339. Just after Billy's supermarket on the left as you head east, this place has local dishes from CI$8. Open Sun–Fri 11.30am–2.30pm.

Divi Tiara (details above). Simple food, including a choice of main course, is served buffet-style. Menus are changed daily. Open for breakfast, lunch and dinner, 7.00am–9.30pm.

G&M Diner West End; tel: 948 1272. This unlicensed restaurant serving local food, including turtle stew, is well patronised by church groups on Sundays. Open 7.30am–2.30pm, 6.30–9.00pm.

La Esperanza Stake Bay; tel: 948 0531. The pontoon at Bussy's, as this popular restaurant is widely known, has to be the best place on the island for a drink or meal as the sun goes down. Turn up on a Wednesday or at the weekend and you'll see Bussy or his wife slaving over a huge barbecue with mountains of jerk chicken prepared to their own recipe. Join the queue of locals for this unmissable treat, either to eat in or take away. At other times, try one of the fish dishes, including *akee* (salt fish) and dolphin. On Friday and Saturday nights, there is often live music; the rest of the week the juke box is as loud as the bar staff will allow! If transport is a problem, give them a ring – Bussy will usually collect you and take you home at the end of the evening. Restaurant open daily 9.00am–2.00pm, 6.00pm–10.00pm. Bar open all day till late.

Sonja's White Bay Plaza; tel: 948 1214. Local food is served at lunchtime only, with dishes around CI$7 each. Open Mon–Sat 11.45am–1.00pm.

Fast food/snacks

Blackies Drive Thru Open in the evenings for fast food and ice-cream.

Domino's Pizza Tibbetts Sq; tel: 948 1266. Open daily from 5.00pm, with free delivery service.

Quick Service by the police station at Creek is a snack bar with burgers and breakfast.

Soft-serve ice-cream, Tibbetts Sq. The name says it all.

Bars

Both the resort hotels and La Esperanza have good bars, as has Aunt Sha's (the bar is called Coral Isle). In addition, there is **Edd's Place** on Tibbetts Square, a rather dingy bar that, in spite of the signs, does no food except jerk chicken on Wednesdays and at weekends. Open Mon–Fri 9.00am–1.00pm, Sat 9.00am–midnight, Sun midday–midnight.

SHOPPING AND AMENITIES
Dive equipment

Both **Reef Divers** and **Dive Tiara** have shops selling dive equipment. See *Dive operators*, page 205, for details.

Food/general stores

Billy's Supermarket and Appliance Centre Cotton Tree Bay; tel: 948 1321. Next to Foster's, below. Open Mon–Fri 8.00am–9.00pm; Sat 8.00am–10.00pm.

Foster's Superette Opposite Salt Water Pond Walk. Open Mon–Sat 8.00am–midday, 2.00–6.00pm.

Kirkconnell's Market Stake Bay. Just after Walton's Mango Manor on the left, a newly opened supermarket with plenty of variety, reasonable prices and even a television for children to watch. Open Mon–Fri 8.00am–7.30pm; Sat 8.00am–8.30pm.
Marketplace Tibbetts Sq; tel: 948 1296. Groceries, hardware, electrics and fishing tackle. Open Mon–Thu 8.00am–9.00pm; Fri/Sat 8.00am–10.00pm.
Tibbetts Enterprises Cotton Tree Bay; tel: 948 1322. A general store on the bluff side of the road. Open Mon–Sat 7.30am–9.00pm.

Hair braiding
Sharon's Hair Clinic Tibbetts Sq; tel: 948 1387. Hair braiding from CI$80.

Liquor stores
Brac Freeport Tibbetts Sq; tel: 948 1332. Open Mon–Sat 9.00am–6.00pm.
Steve Foster's South Side; tel: 948 1537. Also known as **Brac Distributors**, this is just west of Captain's Table, in the same building as 4-Ds Car Rental. Open Mon–Sat 8.00am–6.00pm.

Photographic supplies and courses
All three dive operators on the Brac have shops supplying photographic equipment and offering daily on-site E-6 film processing.

Brac Aquatics Dive and Photo Centre Tel: 948 1429. Based at Brac Caribbean Beach Village, the centre offers camera and video rentals and instruction, as well as underwater videos.
Photo Tiara Dive Tiara's photo shop has camera rental from US$35 per half day. Underwater photography courses from US$85 include two hours in the classroom followed by a dive with an instructor. The six-day Nikon School of Underwater Photography course, the only one in the Caribbean, costs US$600; an all-inclusive package is available. For details, US tel: 800 661 3483. Open 8.00am–5.00pm.
Reef Photo & Video Centre Tel: 948 1320. Based at Brac Reef, the centre offers equipment sales and rentals, photography tuition and underwater videos. Open 7.30am–12.30pm; 1.30–5.00pm.

Souvenirs/gifts
It has to be said that Cayman Brac is not a mecca for shopping, but gifts and souvenirs are still to be found. Most of the general stores sell T-shirts and small nick-nacks.

Kirk Freeport PO Box 893 GT, Stake Bay; tel: 948 2612; email: kirkfree@candw.ky. This small shop next to the museum has a surprisingly wide range of glass, silver, gold, black coral, china, jewellery etc, as well as T-shirts and casual clothing. A good place for gifts of all prices. Open Mon–Sat 10.00am–6.00pm.
NIM Things Spot Bay; tel: 948 0461. Tenson Scott's local craft shop is an acronym for 'Native Island Made': everything here is handmade on the Brac, or painted by his daughter, Simone, whose gallery is next door. Don't go looking for sophistication – items on sale include shell crafts, straw bags and polished caymanite. And if you've time for a chat, Tenson can certainly fill the gap. Open Mon–Sat 9.00am–6.00pm.

Treasure Chest Tibbetts Square; tel: 948 1333. Probably the best shop on the island for gifts and souvenirs, Treasure Chest is also within easy walking distance of the airport. So check in your bags, then wander back here for a last browse – it's much more convivial than sitting in an airport lounge. Open Mon–Sat 9.00am–5.00pm.

OTHER PRACTICALITIES
Communications
Post office
The main post office is in the government administration building at Stake Bay, open Mon–Thu 8.30am–4.00pm; Fri 8.30am–3.30pm; Sat 8.30am–midday. Four sub post offices, located near Tibbetts Square in West End, and at Watering Place, Creek and Spot Bay, are open Mon–Fri 9.00–11.00am, 1.00–3.00pm; Sat 9.00am–midday. First-day covers can be bought at Stake Bay, or ordered from the sub post offices.

Telephones
There are 13 public telephones located on the island, including at Reef Divers, Salt Water Pond Walk, Stake Bay (government administration building) and the Aston Rutty Centre – the only one on the bluff.

Health and medical facilities
Cayman Brac Clinic, tel: 948 1777, is open Mon–Sat 8.00am–midday, and Mon, Wed, Thu and Fri 3.00–6.00pm. The government **Faith Hospital** is at Stake Bay, tel: 948 2243–5. For dental services, tel: 948 2618.

Water is produced by desalination from the island's reverse osmosis system, and is safe to drink from the tap.

Library
The modern public library is opposite the government administration building in Stake Bay. Open Mon, Wed–Fri 1.00–6.00pm; Tue 10.00am–3.00pm; Sat 10.00am–1.00pm.

Money and banking
The local branch of Cayman National Bank is at Tibbetts Square in West End, and has an ATM. It is scheduled to move into a new building across the road shortly. Open Mon–Thu 8.30am–2.00pm; Fri 8.30am–1.00pm, 3.30–5.00pm.

Brac Rent-a-Car (see page 197) are agents for MoneyGrams. Open Mon–Fri 9.00am–4.30pm, Sat 9.00–11.30am. Minimum fee US$12.

Tourist information
Cayman Brac Tourist Office (PO Box 194; tel: 948 1649/1849; fax: 948 1629) is tucked away on the north coast, to the east of the airport and next to the park. Open Mon–Fri 8.30am–midday, 1.00–5.00pm.

Cultural and natural history information is also available from **Heritage House Interpretive Centre** (tel: 948 0563), open Mon–Sat 10.00am–6.00pm. For details, see page 215.

ACTIVITIES
Beaches and snorkelling

The only wide sandy beaches on the island are on the southwest tip, where the two resort hotels and most of the villas are situated, and the public beach on the southern side of the island. The public beach, on the south coast, is a lovely swimming beach with gentle rollers in front of the reef. Unfortunately, the place is completely ruined by the wire enclosure that surrounds the picnic area. The showers don't work, the water smells and the toilets are filthy. Find your own stretch of the Caribbean!

Of course, you don't need expanses of white sand to go snorkelling. In many areas there are small stretches of sand and, with a pair of old shoes to clamber across the rocks, you can set off pretty well anywhere. The reef on the Brac is far less extensive than on the other two islands. In the southwest, there is a long stretch running almost continuously through to the area beyond Salt Water Pond, with another stretch further east at Hawkesbill Bay. In the north, however, the only place with a reef is just to the west of Spot Bay. Other good locations for snorkellers include Buccaneer's Barcadere, accessed along Robert Foster Lane near the airport, and Radar Reef, to the centre of the island, both on the north coast. Note that strong currents at each end of the island make snorkelling at these points potentially hazardous, with the rocks to the east adding to the risks.

Diving

Diving off Cayman Brac is consistently rated among the best in the Caribbean, with calm conditions almost all year round, and most dive sites within five to 15 minutes' boat ride. All the dive operators on the island also visit Little Cayman, just five miles (8km) away, a boat trip of some 50 minutes.

Dive operators

There are just three dive operators on the island, all based in the southwest near the two resort hotels.

Brac Aquatics PO Box 89 WE, South Side; tel: 948 1429; fax: 948 1527; email: bracdive@candw.ky; web: www.candw.ky/users/cay3931. US PO Box 273781, Tampa, FL33688-3781; tel: 800 544 2722, 813 962 2236; fax: 813 264 2742
The only independent dive operator on the Brac, Brac Aquatics was established in 1978, the pioneer of diving on the sister islands. A family-run operation based behind Captain's Table restaurant in the southwest, they have two boats and take small groups of divers both to the sites around Cayman Brac and, once a week, across to Little Cayman. Snorkel trips are also operated around both islands.
Rates Two-tank boat dive US$70 (to Little Cayman US$90); Resort course US$90; Open Water US$350. BCD US$10, regulator US$12. Three-day, two-tank dive package US$65 per day; five days US$60 per day. Snorkel trips US$20–30. All-inclusive dive packages available in conjunction with nearby villas and condominiums.
Dive Tiara The dive school at Divi Tiara is exclusively for their own guests, although the dive and photo shops are open 8.00am–5.00pm to outsiders as well. The resort has five dive boats, covering both the sister islands. A five-star PADI centre, it offers all

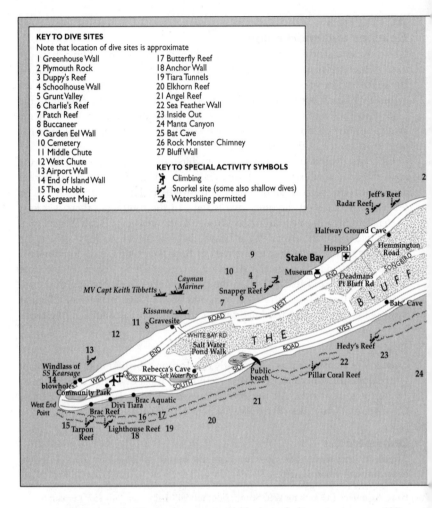

KEY TO DIVE SITES
Note that location of dive sites is approximate

1 Greenhouse Wall
2 Plymouth Rock
3 Duppy's Reef
4 Schoolhouse Wall
5 Grunt Valley
6 Charlie's Reef
7 Patch Reef
8 Buccaneer
9 Garden Eel Wall
10 Cemetery
11 Middle Chute
12 West Chute
13 Airport Wall
14 End of Island Wall
15 The Hobbit
16 Sergeant Major

17 Butterfly Reef
18 Anchor Wall
19 Tiara Tunnels
20 Elkhorn Reef
21 Angel Reef
22 Sea Feather Wall
23 Inside Out
24 Manta Canyon
25 Bat Cave
26 Rock Monster Chimney
27 Bluff Wall

KEY TO SPECIAL ACTIVITY SYMBOLS
🕴 Climbing
🐟 Snorkel site (some also shallow dives)
🎿 Waterskiing permitted

courses including nitrox. Dive packages are available through the resort (see page 198).
Reef Divers PO Box 56, South Side; tel: 948 1642 or 800 327 3835; fax: 948 1279;
email: reefdive@candw.ky; web: www.bracreef.com

A highly efficient outfit, geared to guests at the affiliated Brac Reef Resort, Reef
Divers also takes walk-in divers, space permitting. Be aware, though, that you will be
fitting in to the requirements of their own guests. Dive shop, with films, T-shirts etc,
is open 7.30am–12.30pm; 1.30–5.00pm.

Rates Two-tank dive US$75; Resort course US$100; Open Water US$450.
BCD/regulator US$12 each.

Live aboard

Little Cayman Diver II Tel: 948 1429; fax: 948 1527. US PO Box 280058, Tampa,
FL33682; tel: 800 458 2722; 877 L-CAYMAN; 813 962 2236; fax: 813 963 1925; web:
www.littlecaymandiver.com

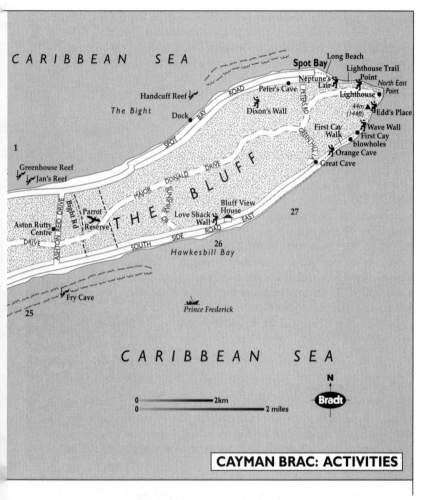

CAYMAN BRAC: ACTIVITIES

A live-aboard boat operated by Brac Aquatics, *Little Cayman Diver II* has four crew and a maximum of ten divers in five cabins, each with en-suite facilities.

Rates US$1,695 for a seven-night all-inclusive trip, with 24-hour unstructured diving.

Dive sites

There are plenty of sites to choose from among the Brac's 41 permanent dive moorings, which are for the most part concentrated in the western half of the island. Sites to the **north** are considered to be the most dramatic, with sudden drop offs as the wall plunges almost straight down from around 55–60ft (16.8–18.3m). It is the north, too, that has the best shore diving – in fact, there is no real shore diving to the southwest where the dive operations are based. Tunnels, crevices and narrow chasms characterise dives to the **south**, where you may come across any number of creatures as you turn a corner. Nurse sharks are often seen here under the overhanging rocks. At the other end of the spectrum, keep an eye out for the occasional exquisite air crab, or perhaps the extraordinary iron-shaped trunkfish. The swim-throughs at Tarpon Reef make it seem like fish city, with a central sandy clearing where you may spot a glittering silver tarpon just hanging in the water. Swim alongside or below it and you won't frighten it off. Less obvious, though, is the encrusted anchor that is suspended above a short tunnel at Anchor Wall.

Wrecks

One of the most visited wrecks in the islands was in fact deliberately scuppered as a dive attraction. The 315ft (95m) Russian frigate, originally known simply as #356, was bought from Cuba by the Cayman Islands government for US$275,000 and renamed the *Capt Keith Tibbetts*. The hull was cleaned out so that divers can swim through the cabins on the top three decks, then on September 17 1996 she was sunk 900yds (822m) offshore to the northwest of the island. Her bow rests in 80ft (24m) of water, with the stern at just 50ft (15m). As yet marine life is confined to angelfish, the occasional lobster and a lone moray. The wreck is usually dived from a boat, but can also be visited as a shore dive. Tanks may be hired for US$10 a day from Brac Aquatics, but you'll need transport to get them to the northern shore.

Just east of the frigate is the wreck of the 55ft (17m) *Cayman Mariner*, lying at a depth of 60ft (18m), while slightly inshore of that is the upturned hull of the 50ft (15m) steel tugboat, the *Kissamee*.

Other watersports

Aside from diving and snorkelling, there are few organised watersports on the island. Those with access to a boat can waterski 100ft (30m) offshore west of the junction of Kirkconnell St, Bay Font and Foster's Road as far as Sarah's Rock. Swimming and diving here are permitted within 100ft (30m) of the shore.

The two resort hotels have kayaks available to guests. Brac Reef rents their kayaks out to non guests at US$15 per person per hour.

Fishing

Fishing is extremely popular on the Brac, with bonefishing inside the reef, particularly along the coast to the southwest, and a variety of fish including snapper, grouper, tuna, marlin, wahoo and sailfish in the waters beyond. Boat trips can be arranged through the following:

Barefoot Watersports PO Box 78 WE, South Side; tel: 948 1299; fax: 948 1350; email: barefeet@candw.ky
Captain Steve Foster specialises in fishing, particularly deep-sea charters, in his 28ft (8.5m) boat, *Frayed Knot*. He also offers private guided diving charters and snorkelling trips. For more information, call in at Brac Distributors and ask for Steve or Debbie, or contact Dive Tiara.
Rates Half day US$350; full day US$600.

Captain Shelby's Tel: 948 0535; email: caymanislands@DOT (but use the phone to contact Captain Shelby when you're on the island)

A courteous and helpful Caymanian, Captain Shelby runs boat trips for all purposes around the island and over to Little Cayman. Bring your own lunch (except for picnic trips, of course!).

Rates Snorkel trips US$40 per person half-day (9.00am–1.00pm). Picnic trips to Point of Sand on Little Cayman US$70 per person, 9.00am–4.30pm. Diving charters only for those with their own equipment (including tanks). Deep-sea fishing US$350 half day (four hours); US$450 full day per boat (two–four people). Bottom or reef fishing US$300 half day; US$400 full day (up to six people). Bonefishing at Owen Island US$300 half day; US$400 full day.

Edmund Bodden GPO West End; tel: 948 1228

This fishing guide service boasts 'all tackle, all depths'. Specialists in bonefishing.

Gemini III Tel: 948 2517/2396; fax: 948 1676; email: the_rock@candw.ky

Steve Bodden of B&S Motorventures (see page 197) organises deep-sea fishing charters aboard this 30ft (9.1m) cruiser. US$350 half day; US$500 full day.

Nature and heritage trails

Cayman Brac has several designated heritage sites linked by walking and hiking trails, including attractions such as the Westerly Ponds, the bat caves and the lighthouse, all clearly marked. Interpretive signs give an overview of each trail and mention the species of birds, trees and other wildlife that you are likely to see during your walk. Visitors are asked to respect the trails, and to take nothing but mangoes – in season, of course! You are also advised not to touch cacti along the trail.

Wherever you go, remember to take plenty of water – there is nowhere on the south coast or on the bluff to get a drink – and to wear good strong shoes or boots. A basic first-aid kit would be sensible, too, if you're going up on the bluff, where the terrain is rocky and very uneven. If you're heading up here alone, it makes sense to tell someone of your plans before you set off. Most of the trails on the bluff, and the caves too (except Rebecca's Cave), require a degree of agility and are not suitable for the elderly, the disabled or the very young. And for all except Rebecca's Cave, take a torch, even if you're going with a guide (see page 213).

If you only have time for one of the trails, consider the three-hour Lighthouse Trail, which starts from Spot Bay and combines Peter's Cave with some magnificent views to the north and east and some tough hiking on the top of the bluff. See pages 215–16.

Tennis

The tennis court at Divi Tiara (tel: 948 1553) may be used by non-residents for US$2 per person per day.

Climbing

Many thanks to John Byrnes for this information

Cayman Brac's newest sport is something of a well-kept secret. The 144ft (44m) bluff rising almost vertically from sea level is an open invitation to climbers, with a variety of walls ranging from steep overhangs to sheer drops that will challenge even the most experienced, and with views to match. The best time of year to visit for climbing is from mid-November to early May.

Since 1995, a small group of has been working to establish various climbing routes on the eastern end of the bluff for the enjoyment of themselves and other visiting enthusiasts. Their house, Bluff View – otherwise known as the Climber House – is also used by climbers visiting the Brac. For details of renting the house, see page 199.

For the most part, routes on the bluff are suitable only for advanced climbers, with difficulty ratings ranging from 5.8 to 5.13 (UK 4c–7a). Many, particularly those around the lighthouse, involve a rappel (abseil) from the top of the bluff down to the sea, before climbing back up the sheer rock face.

Safety

If something should go wrong when climbing on the bluff, remember that, unless there are other climbers around, no-one else on the island can rescue you. It is therefore important that climbers understand and take the responsibility for self rescue. The emergency telephone number for fire department rescue is 911, but do be aware that this should be used only as an absolutely final resort.

Bolts

The stainless-steel bolts originally used on the Brac have started to corrode as a result of the constant exposure to salt water, and are no longer safe. In November 2000, a team of climbers began rebolting the various routes on the island with new titanium glue-in Tortuga bolts (see www.ushba.com for details). The new bolts are easily recognisable as grey rings about $1^1/_2$in (3.5cm) in diameter. They were developed specifically for marine environments and should provide safe climbing for many years to come. Climbers should not trust any of the old bolts, or any mechanical bolts you may encounter on the island. They are not safe, and about one in ten will fail without warning under body weight. By the end of 2000, 32 routes of every grade at four of the most popular areas had been rebolted, with more to follow. For the latest information, check with John Byrnes.

Equipment

For the approach routes to climbs at the Point (around the lighthouse) and Edd's Place, strong shoes or hiking boots that cover your ankles and a pair of leather gloves to protect your hands are strongly recommended – the terrain is pretty rugged. A foam pad to sit on when changing shoes or having a bite to eat is also an 'essential' luxury. Don't be put off by the sharp ironshore rock on the top of the bluff: once over the edge you'll find it much smoother.

There is nowhere on the island to rent climbing gear, so take everything you need with you, including quick draws, ascenders and prussiks. Climbers at the Point and Edd's Place will need two 165ft (50m) ropes, one for rappelling (abseiling) and one for leading.

If you have to bail from a climb (over land of course!), don't leave steel 'quick links' (quick draws or extenders) on any bolt, as they will rust shut in a day or two and have to be hacksawed off. As all of the new titanium bolts can be easily threaded, you don't need to leave any gear.

Recommended procedure

The rappel (abseiling) approaches present some unusual challenges for many climbers, especially since many of them overhang and you will be rappelling on a single rope. The group who climb regularly on the island have devised a system that they have found to be logical, safe and effective. For details, contact John Byrnes (see below).

Routes

Climbing routes on the Brac have been roughly rated according to a star-quality system. Since many of the routes have only had a few ascents, take difficulty ratings with a pinch of salt. Remember, too, that conditions on the Brac can change overnight. Whereas on a clear, crisp day a route may feel easy at its given grade, on a day with higher humidity the same route could well feel clammy and relatively difficult.

Before deciding on a route, it's worth checking surf conditions to be sure that your targeted belay stance isn't being drenched by big waves. If it is, consider one of the inland areas for that day. There are maps of the routes at Bluff View (see page 199).

Routes below are listed anti-clockwise around the island, starting at the westernmost point on the south side:

Love Shack Wall is 2.7 miles (4.3km) east of Ashton Reid Road (also known as the 'hump' road) on the south side of island, and a five-minute walk from Bluff View House. The wall, identifiable by its left angling crack, is a sweeping, steep, fantastic rock best climbed in cool or shady weather. You may want to wear mosquito repellent – and don't disturb the bats!
Six routes: 5.11d to 5.12c/d (UK 6b–7a); none rebolted
Orange Cave lies just past the Great Cave. Park at the end of South Road, then it's a pleasant ten-minute stroll further east. If you can tear your eyes from the ocean you'll spy the cave; a short hike takes you to the base.
Seven rebolted routes, 5.8 to 5.11b (UK 4c–6a), including Chum Buckets, which was the first climbing route to be established on the Brac.
Wave Wall is some 20 minutes' walk east of the Orange Cave. As you pass two huge boulders, keep an eye out for pieces of caymanite, but leave them where you find them – it's illegal to possess raw caymanite if you're not an islander. Go on through the rocks and traverse carefully along the seaside – big waves can make the approach dangerous or impossible if the surf is up. The route is shaded in the afternoon from about 1.00pm. Boots and gloves are recommended for the approach.
Eleven rebolted routes, 5.8 to 5.12a (UK 4c–6c)
East Bluff or **Edd's Place**, also known as **Crag 29**. Park at the lighthouse on top of the bluff and follow a faint path heading south. Continue southeast to the cliff edge, then to the right. The terrain ranges from tough ironshore rock to an easier concrete-

like surface; in general, walking is easier along the cliff edge. The total approach is only 0.7 miles (1.1km) but can take anything from 25 to 40 minutes.

Four routes, 5.10a to 5.12a (UK 5b–6c), none rebolted

Northeast Point Usually just called **The Point**, this offers a unique experience even for very experienced climbers. The rock drops straight down for over 100ft (30m) directly into the water. From the top of the cliff and belay ledges, turtles, dolphins and large fish can be seen in the crystal blue water. As for the East Bluff, park at the lighthouse, then follow the trail left approximately 100yds (275m) to the main wall. All routes require rappel access.

Twenty-eight routes, 5.9–5.12/13 (UK 5a–7a), nine rebolted

Neptune's Lair Park in the Spot Bay turnaround at the end of the road to the north of the island. Follow the trail east, then walk along the beach towards the huge Foreskin (or Penis) Rock (that's what the locals call it!) in the sea. It's best to stay along the shore when entering the boulder area. Continue to the steep sweeping limestone face, about 20–25 minutes from the car. Bring your snorkelling gear for a lunchtime break – there are some unusual corals in the sea here, and lots of other marine life too. Though the recently established routes may seem short compared to others on the island, the setting of Neptune's Lair is something of a 'must visit'. You may spot booby hatchlings on the cliff: please don't disturb them.

Seven routes, 5.11a to 5.12 approximately (UK 6a–6c), none rebolted

Dixon's Wall is located 2.1 miles (3.4km) east of La Esperanza on the north of the island, with access across private land. The wall is steeper than it looks and is of the finest quality. North facing, it's shady most of the year. Beware of rock fall in the stalactite zone, and ask locals to stand clear of the drop zone.

Five rebolted routes, 5.11a–5.12a/b (UK 6a–6c)

New routes

Climbers who are considering creating new routes should use the Tortuga bolts, but please let John Byrnes know in advance. Some specialised tools such as a glue gun may be available at Bluff View, where there are also detailed written instructions and pointers on installation. Be forewarned that glue-in anchors are in general much more tricky, time consuming and expensive to place properly than mechanical bolts.

For further information on climbing in the Brac, including technical descriptions of the above routes, and a copy of 'Bluff View Guide to Cayman Brac Climbing', contact John Byrnes on jbyrnes@frii.com, or check out the website, www.tradgirl.com/caymans.

TOURING THE ISLAND

There is no obvious tour of the island, since the road doesn't run right round. As many visitors stay in the area to the southwest, however, it makes sense to start from here and to treat it as two separate trips taking anything from an hour or two each to a full day, depending on your interests and the time you plan to spend walking. Obviously the two suggested itineraries could be combined. The bluff can be accessed from either the north or the south, so has been treated separately (see page 217).

Island tours are available from Maple Edwards, tel: 948 0395, mobile: 916 3714 (Miss Singer). A two-hour tour costs US$15 per person. Alternatively, round-the-island tours may be organised through one of the other taxi companies (see page 196).

For guided **nature tours**, contact the government department, tel: 948 2651, fax: 948 2506; email: bracdc@candw.ky. T J Sevik (known to everyone simply as TJ) is the government's tour guide and leads nature tours around the island. Not long out of school, his knowledge of the island is born of years of exploring both the bluff and the surrounding sea. He is passionate about his island, and his ability to spot the Brac's birds is excellent.

North side

Starting from the resorts to the southwest, head east along South Side Road, then turn left on to the Cross Road, with the end of the runway to your left. At the T-junction by Tibbetts Square, turn left again and follow West End Road all the way to the end. Here, the road appears at first to peter out, but if you continue on through what looks like a car park you can turn right into James Scott Road, then cross Georgiana Drive to the sea. On the beach to the right lies the windlass (ship's winch) from the *SS Kearsage* of 1860. When the sea is up you can see blowholes here as well. You can continue along the beach and return to the main road via Robert Foster Lane, possibly stopping for a swim at Buccaneer Barcadere. The snorkelling is recommended here, too, but watch out for the sharp drop off.

Return the way you came, and on the right you will see the **tourist office**, a pretty cottage-style building painted in pink and blue pastels (tel: 948 1649; open Mon–Fri 8.30am–midday, 1.00–5.00pm). Behind the tourist office is **Cayman Brac Community Park**, where a short nature trail leads the visitor through a succession of labelled trees that are native to the island. Although it was opened only recently, the park feels rather unloved. The playground with its climbing frames and wendy houses, and the woodland area with barbecue grills, deserve to be used; even the public toilets are clean!

Continuing east, pass the airport and Tibbetts Square. Shortly after this on your left is Pioneer Lane, a good place to stop for a short **walk**, or perhaps some time on the beach watching the birds. Follow the lane to the sea where there is a sandy beach to the west – a rare commodity on this northern side of the island, where the beach is for the most part ironshore. If you turn right along the hurricane boulder path, you can return on a track to the main road. A little further along the main road, again to the left, is White Bay Road, the site of a **mass gravesite** from the 1932 hurricane. Nineteen people died here when the house that stood on this spot was destroyed in the storm. The site is set back from the road on the left near the sea, but is so overgrown that it's not easy to find.

Opposite White Bay Road is the start of the **Salt Water Pond Walk**, which leads south across the island, coming out beside Rebecca's Cave (see page 216). Although the trail is only at the beginning of the bluff, don't be fooled into thinking that the terrain will be easy – it's pretty tough going, even here, so allow at least an hour and possibly more to get to the cave. With luck you'll be rewarded with the sight of several native birds, such as the vitelline warbler or the Caribbean elaenia, as well as a wide variety of tropical plants along the trail.

As you head further east along West End Road, the road veers inland until the bluff towers over it to the right. A little way after this, you enter Stake Bay, where a short loop with the rather grandiose title of **Stake Bay Walk** will take you along Ryan's Drive to Stake Bay Road on the coast. On the corner here is the J A Ryan cemetery, burial site of the descendants of W S Ryan, one of the Brac's most illustrious citizens, who died in 1910 having reputedly been the first Bracker to marry, the first to go to sea as a master mariner, and the first to become a justice of the peace. Here, too, is the site of the original harbour where the schooners came in. Pass the older houses overlooking the sea and return along Kirkconnell Street, which brings you out near the museum on the main road.

Cayman Brac Museum was opened in 1983, housed in the old government building in Stake Bay. The government's loss was the museum's gain, for the building is of typical Cayman construction, an attractive wooden house with a shaded veranda. The new government administration building, a faceless modern block housing the post office, immigration office and much else besides, lies behind the museum.

The museum collection, somewhat dusty but nevertheless of genuine interest, effectively tells the story of Cayman Brac before the '32 hurricane, when life on the Brac was changed forever. The scale model of a schooner with its cargo of catboats on board, ready to go out to the fishing grounds, is a visual reminder of the importance of the sea for the Brac. Personal and work-based artefacts and documents include some post 1932. Books are on sale. Open Mon–Fri 9.00am–midday, 1.00–4.00pm; Sat 9.00am–midday.

Just past the hospital on your right is the first of two trails that lie quite close together. **Deadman's Point Bluff Road** involves a climb up the steps on to the bluff, leading to a hike through endemic forest to Songbird Drive, which is effectively the backbone of the bluff. The path alternates between jagged karstic cliffrock, with its sinkholes and caves, and flat areas where grass overlies the rock. It passes through forest where several birds breed, including the loggerhead kingbird, the red-legged thrush, the white-crowned pigeon and the Zenaida dove. From August to May, you may also see migrant vireos, warblers and tanagers. Allow around an hour and a half for the return hike, or turn left along Songbird Drive and return to West End Road via the parallel **Hemmington Road**.

A little further east on the main road is one of the few signposted caves on this northern stretch of the island. **Half Way Ground Cave**, so called because it's halfway up the bluff, is home to a small colony of bats, but little else. About a mile further on, past the high school and Ashton Reid Drive, is the **Bight Road**, a trail of about a mile that was traditionally used to get from the settlements in the north of the island to the provision grounds on the bluff and thence to the south shore. Today, the trail follows the western boundary of the 197-acre **parrot reserve** through ancient forest across to the southern edge of the bluff. Note that no dogs are allowed into the reserve, no fires are permitted, and visitors should refrain from contact with any animals.

The best time to see parrots is during the summer in early morning, from 6.00am to 8.00am, although you are more likely to hear than see them. Even if you're unlucky – and the Cayman Brac parrot is a shy creature, not easily spotted – you'll have the opportunity to spot many other endemic birds and plants in an environment that could be miles from civilisation, rather than just a few hundred yards. Allow about three hours for the full return trip, or stop at the mid point on Major Donald Drive and come back from there. There is also a one-mile (1.6km) circular National Trust **nature trail** off the southern end of Bight Road, leading into the parrot reserve, where 15 species of orchid have been identified on the route. In addition to the Cayman Brac parrot, you may also see the red-legged thrush or the vitelline warbler, while in the winter there are numerous migratory birds.

Back on Stake Bay Road, continue east past La Esperanza (do stop for a drink or a meal on their pontoon) into Spot Bay Road. On the right is **Heritage House Interpretive Centre and Park** (tel: 948 0563), where you can get information on places to visit and book walks and hikes with a nature tour guide. Cultural events are also held here. The house was bought by the government in 1998 from the Lazzari family, who arrived from Cuba in 1870 and later settled in Northeast Bay. John Antonio Lazzari opened a tannery in the grounds, using freshwater from the six wells to cure the skins. The family also kept livestock on the bluff as well as tending their plantations. A series of ladder steps built up the face of the bluff to allow them access to their animals are still in use. Today, visitors to the elegant old house will also see some of the original thatched outbuildings and wells, while in the grounds tropical fruit trees – naseberry, soursop, tamarind, mango and custard apple – grow alongside other native species including coconut, sea grape and red birch. Books, maps and posters are on sale; refreshments available. Open Mon–Sat 10.00am–6.00pm.

Just before you come into Spot Bay, a path from the main road brings you to a set of historic steps up the north face of the bluff, leading up to the panoramic viewpoint known as Big Channel Road Outlook.

Spot Bay, in the northeast corner of the Brac, is a good starting point for some excellent walks. The picnic tables and natural shade at **Spot Bay Community Cove** would seem to make it a good spot for swimming (though there's a sharp drop off), but large notices currently indicate the contrary – presumably because construction is underway to build a small dock here. Shortly beyond the cove, the road ends. From here, follow the path through sea-grape trees to the shore and **Long Beach**. The walk beneath the bluff can be pretty dramatic; rough seas mean that only climbers should proceed further east beyond the end of the beach. Allow up to an hour and a half for the return walk back to the road.

Back in Spot Bay, follow Lighthouse Road on the bluff side to the Lighthouse Steps, which are the beginning of the **Lighthouse Trail** (allow up to three hours for the return walk from the bottom of the steps; strong shoes and water essential). Follow the steps up the northeast face of the bluff, and halfway up is the entrance to **Peter's Cave**, which has long been used as a hurricane shelter by the residents of Spot Bay. The cave is huge, with tunnels leading off in several directions, and it can get quite cold away from the entrance.

Continuing on up, you come out at the top to **Peter's Outlook**, with sweeping views across Spot Bay. There is a small car park nearby, at the end of Peters Road, so drivers up on the bluff can leave their vehicles and approach the caves from above. The trail takes you across uneven terrain through coarse shrubland. Halfway along the path, above the cay (large rock) on the beach, brown boobies breed in caves and ledges in the bluff. Eventually the path opens out into a stark area where the intermittent vegetation is regularly battered by the prevailing easterly winds. Seabirds wheel in the currents overhead, while underfoot the going remains tough. Here, at the easternmost tip of the island, stands the lighthouse, warning sailors heading west in the Caribbean of the imminent danger as they head for the bluff. In fact, there are at present two lighthouses, the first dating from 1930s, but these old beacons are soon to be replaced.

South side

The westernmost point of the island affords views across the strait to Little Cayman some five miles (8km) away. Here, you are on the edge of the **Westerly Ponds** which, despite their location close to the airport at the western tip of the island, remain peaceful and unspoilt, a haven for wildlife. Formerly a mangrove swamp that became cut off from the sea, the ponds that you see today are still affected by the tides via an underground connection with the sea. The result is that the water is at best brackish, becoming hypersaline by the end of the dry winter season.

Boardwalks and viewing areas enable observation of over a hundred species of birds on the wetlands, the majority on migration routes to Central and South America. West Indian whistling-ducks and the black-necked stilt are both in residence, as are several herons and egrets, their numbers augmented in winter by migratory species of heron. Of the other migrants, a small colony of least terns breeds on the edge of the lagoon in the summer, while up to 30 shorebirds have been spotted during the winter migration. Perhaps surprisingly, osprey, merlin and peregrine falcons nest in the surrounding red mangroves.

Following the road east from the ponds, pass the two resort hotels and the Cross Road, and you'll come to **Salt Water Pond** on your left. This small bird sanctuary attracts several species, and here, too, least terns breed in the summer months. There is talk of putting a boardwalk through this area for visitors.

Aunt Sha's, the florid pink building on the beach, is a pretty good place to stop for a snack at lunch time – the bar area overlooks the sea, and is much more pleasant than the restaurant in the daytime. It is also the last place on this stretch where you can get anything to drink, so stock up if you're planning a day out.

Not far from Aunt Sha's on the left is **Rebecca's Cave**, named in memory of 17-month old Rebecca Bodden who died nearby as her parents sought the shelter of the cave with her during an apparent lull in the 1932 hurricane. Tragically, the family was caught by the full force of the storm, and the little girl perished. Her tomb is in the cave, a sombre reminder of the island's past.

A wild fig grows at the entrance to the cave, and to the side is the southern end of the Salt Water Pond Walk across the bluff (see page 213).

Near the public beach (see page 205), on the other side of the road, the **Marshes Wetlands** spread out at the foot of the bluff. Up to 35 species of birds have been spotted here, in and around the mangroves, while high above, several pairs of brown boobies have their nests, part of a small colony that inhabits this southern stretch of the bluff.

From the name, you could be forgiven for thinking that **Bats' Cave**, a couple of miles further on, is the only one inhabited by bats. It isn't, but it certainly has a lot of them. Five species of bat live here, including the most populous, the Jamaican fruit bat. Shine your torch up to the roof of the cave and you'll uncover whole colonies huddled together in each of the high narrow recesses; come in the evening at around 9.00pm and you'll see the bats in flight.

The extraordinary spaceship-style building on the right as you continue east is known as the Bubble House, said to be designed to withstand hurricane-force winds. Be that as it may, its construction bankrupted the owner, and the half-completed building, now owned by the government, lies empty and desolate. Ashton Reid Drive, the only paved road across the bluff, leads off to the left, then shortly after is the southern end of Bight Road and the parrot reserve (see page 214). From here, the distance between the sea and the bluff narrows. Sea-grape trees line the road, and just a few small houses are dotted along the coast; otherwise, there is little to detract from the natural beauty of this southern shoreline.

The road ends abruptly at the **Great Cave**, a mile or so from the lighthouse that marks the eastern end of the island at the top of the bluff. The name is somewhat misleading, as there are in fact several caves up in the bluff, linked one to another by narrow and winding passages that are almost impassable in places. To climb up to the caves, you'll need to be reasonably agile as the steps are not completely even, and to have good shoes and a torch. It doesn't take much to imagine the terror of being holed up here in a storm, in total darkness, with bats darting about overhead, no water and very little air.

Continuing on foot from the Great Cave, **First Cay Walk** leads east along the beach, which is popular with local people for beach bonfires. The going is initially over rough shingle, which gradually gives way to ironshore where the sea rushes through blowholes and outcrops of caymanite decorate the otherwise uniform grey. Brown boobies and frigatebirds vie for the evening meal in the skies overhead, while from January to August migrant white-tailed tropicbirds may be seen. Beyond First Cay (the first large independent boulder on the beach) the seas can be pretty rough, and the area is not suitable for any but skilled climbers. Allow 1–2 hours for the return walk from the Great Cave, or bring a picnic and stay longer.

The Bluff

Although there are several access points up on to the bluff, there is only one paved road, Ashton Reid Drive, which crosses the island more or less in the centre. Once at the top, most of the roads are unpaved, so although scooters or even bikes (if you're fit, that is!) will get you up there, they are not particularly suited to the terrain, and hire companies ask customers not to use such vehicles on the bluff. Wherever you go, remember to take plenty to drink. It's a great place for a picnic, particularly near the lighthouse. The nearest telephone in case of emergency is at the Aston Rutty Centre on Ashton Reid Drive.

By car, you can take Ashton Reid Drive straight up to Songbird Drive from either side of the island. Alternatively, take the more scenic route from West End, which runs parallel to the edge of the bluff until Stake Bay, then winds on and up until it eventually meets Songbird Drive off to the left (if you miss this junction, you'll find yourself on the southern side of the bluff heading for Ashton Reid Drive). Continue on the unpaved Major Donald Drive towards the lighthouse, past Bight Drive hiking trail and the parrot reserve. Much of this area is forested, interspersed with small areas of open pasture where cattle graze. The road is for the most part fenced off with colourful posts of red birch, which in time will regenerate to create a living hedge. In the forests, all sorts of fruit grow wild, including the vine pear, with its sweet yellow fruit, and the red, equally sweet, prickly pear.

Towards the end of Major Donald Drive, take a brief detour to the right down Green Hill Lane. At the end of the road, the view over the southern side of the bluff is spectacular, though definitely not for those without a head for heights – it's a sheer drop to the sea far below. Backtrack, then continue east a little while – the turning to the left is Peters Road, which brings you to a small parking area and the steps above Peter's Cave (see page 215). Straight on, Major Donald Drive brings you out on to the eastern point of the bluff, which is also the end of the Lighthouse Trail (see page 215). Even if time is not on your side, savour for just a few moments this wild and windswept spot, watched over year round by the lighthouse beacons that guard H C Dixon's 'Little Rock', before heading back.

Appendix 1

ACCOMMODATION

The following is an at-a-glance summary of the various places to stay detailed in this guide, put together as an aid to planning your holiday. For details of each venue, see the page number given.

Name	Location	Type	No rooms/ units	Page
Adams Guest House	George Town	guesthouse	6	116
Anchorage Condominiums	Seven Mile Beach	condominiums	15	117
Annie's Place	George Town	guesthouse	2	116
Avalon Condominiums	Seven Mile Beach	condominiums	14	117
Beach Club Hotel & Dive Resort	Seven Mile Beach	resort hotel	41	114
Caribbean Club	Seven Mile Beach	villas	18	117
Cayman Diving Lodge	East End	dive lodge	11	166
Cobalt Coast	West Bay	condominiums	18	148
Coconut Harbour	George Town	dive lodge	35	115
Comfort Suites	Seven Mile Beach	medium hotel	110	112
Coral Sands Resort	Seven Mile Beach	flats/townhouses	12	117
Driftwood Village	North Side	cottages	4	163
Eldemire's Guest House	George Town	guesthouse	13	116
Grand Morritt's	East End	timeshare	20 in 1st phase	167
Grand Caymanian	North Sound	golf resort	132	113
Harbour View	Seven Mile Beach	apartments	9	118
Holiday Inn	West Bay Rd	luxury hotel	231	111
Hyatt Beach Club	Seven Mile Beach	condominiums	50	111
Hyatt Regency	West Bay Rd	luxury hotel	239	111
Indies Suites	West Bay Rd	medium hotel	40	113
Marriott	Seven Mile Beach	luxury	309	111
Morritt's Tortuga	East End	timeshare	177	168
Nautilus Apartments	West Bay	townhouses etc	4	148
North Side Surf Inn	North Side	hotel	10	163
Plantation Village	Seven Mile Beach	apartments	71	118
Retreat at Rum Point	Rum Point	condominiums	23	165

Royal Reef	East End	timeshare	82	168
Sammy's Airport Inn	Airport	medium hotel	60	113
Seaview Hotel and Dive Centre	George Town	dive lodge	15	115
Seven Mile Beach Resort	Seven Mile Beach	condominiums	38	118
Sleep Inn	Seven Mile Beach	medium hotel	115	113
Spanish Bay Reef Resort	West Bay	resort hotel	66	149
Sunset House	George Town	dive lodge	59	115
Sunshine Suites	West Bay Rd	medium hotel	132	114
Treasure Island Resort	Seven Mile Beach	medium hotel	281	114
Turtle Nest Inn	Bodden Town	apartments	9	158
Villas of the Galleon	Seven Mile Beach	condominiums	78	118
Westin Casuarina	Seven Mile Beach	luxury hotel	343	112
Wild Orchid	Bodden Town	guesthouse	4	159

Little Cayman (all in southwest of island)

Conch Club Condominiums		condominiums	20	180
Kingston Bight Lodge		apartments/rooms	10	180
Little Cayman Beach Resort		resort hotel	40	176
Paradise Villas		villas	12	180
Pirates Point		resort hotel	10	177
Sam McCoy's Dive Lodge		dive lodge	13	177
Southern Cross		resort hotel	11	179
Suzy's Cottage		house	1	180
Village Inn		efficiencies/ apartments	11	180

Cayman Brac

Almond Beach Hideaways	Spot Bay	villas	2	199
Beacon Harbor	Stake Bay	condominiums	2	199
Bluff View House	South Side	self-catering house	2	199
Brac Caribbean Beach Village	Stake Bay	apartments	16	199
Brac Reef Beach Resort	South Side	resort hotel	40	198
Carib Sands	South Side	condominiums	35	200
Cayman Cottage	South Side	house	1	200
Coconut Palms	Spot Bay	villas	2	200
Divi Tiara	South Side	resort hotel	71	198
La Esperanza	Stake Bay	apartments/houses	6	200
Southern Star	South Side	townhouses	5	200
Stake Bay Villas	Stake Bay	villas	2	200
Turtle Nest	Stake Bay	house	1	201
Walton's Mango Manor	Stake Bay	guesthouse	5	198

Appendix

FURTHER READING
History

Bingner, Alice Grant *A Brief History of the Cayman Islands*, 1982

Hirst, George S S *A Handbook of the Cayman Islands for 1908* Kingston, Jamaica, 1907

Hirst, George S S *Notes on the History of the Cayman Islands*, 1910. The most detailed of Hirst's books includes a fascinating account of life on the islands at the turn of the century.

Kohlman, Aarona *Under Tin Roofs* Cayman Islands National Museum, 1993

Mitchell, David *Pirates* Thames and Hudson, 1976

Our Islands' Past Introductions by Philip Pedley. Cayman Islands National Archive and Cayman Free Press. A series of three books, bringing into the public domain some of the material currently held by the National Archive in George Town:
Volume I: *Edward Corbet's Report and Census of 1802 on the Cayman Islands*, 1992
Volume II: *The Wreck of the Ten Sails* Guest ed Dr Margaret E Leshikar-Denton, 1994
Volume III: *Traditional Songs from the Cayman Islands*, 1996

McLaughlin, Heather R *Cayman Yesterdays* Cayman Islands National Archive, 1991. A compilation of transcripts.

McLaughlin, Heather R *The '32 storm* Cayman Islands National Archive, 1994

Ross, H E *Love's Dance – The Catboat of the Caymanes*. An illustrated account of Cayman's seafaring tradition, with plenty of reminiscences from former catboat sailors themselves.

Williams, Neville *A History of the Cayman Islands* Government of the Cayman Islands, 1970. Published to coincide with the tercentenary of the 1670 Treaty of Madrid, this is a readable account of Cayman history.

Biography

Dixon, H C *Cayman Brac, Land of My Birth*. A brief but affectionate account of the Brac written in the 1950s by a man who left the island to become a preacher.

Jackson, Will *Smoke-Pot Days* Cayman National Cultural Foundation, 1997. This biographical account of Cayman since the 1920s gives a pretty good insight into life both on land and at sea in the years when the islands were almost completely cut off from the outside world. It also tells of the effects, good and bad, of rapid developments wrought by tourism and development since the 1960s.

Tibbetts, Elsa M *The sea of bitter beauty*, 1984 An autobiographical tale of life on Cayman Brac.

Culture

Barnett, Dr Curtis L E *Toes in the Sand: Caymanian Tales and Thoughts*, published by the author, 1995. A rather worthy but nevertheless interesting collection of stories and essays investigating traditional Cayman values and culture and their effects on the population today.

Fuller, Robert S *Duppies Is* Cayman Artventures, 1981. Real ghost stories of the occasionally spine-chilling variety, based on first-hand accounts of this peculiarly Cayman phenomenon, and with an impassioned introductory diatribe against the modern world and its effect on Cayman's duppies.

Meekings, Brian *The Storyman* Storyman Publishing, 1997

Muttoo, Henry with 'Jerry Craig', Karl *My Markings: The Art of Gladwyn K Bush* Cayman National Cultural Foundation

Poupeye, Veerle *Caribbean Art* Thames & Hudson, London, 1998. Although Cayman art is only touched on, almost in passing, Poupeye's book offers an interesting overview of art in the Caribbean as a whole.

Our Islands' Treasure volume 1, Pirates Week Commitee, 1980

Natural history

Bradley, Patricia *The Birds of the Cayman Islands* Checklist number 19, BOU. The definitive record of all the birds on the Cayman Islands.

Bradley, Patricia, and Rey-Millet, Y-J *Birds of the Cayman Islands* Caerulean Press, 1995. An excellent field guide to Cayman birds, with useful information on habitats as well as detailed descriptions of endemic birds, and good colour photographs.

Brunt, M A, and Davies, J E (editors) *The Cayman Islands: Natural History and Biogeography* Kluwer Academic Publishers, 1994. A series of academic essays on a range of natural history subjects, including climate and tides, by individual writers who are each experts in their field.

Burton, F J, and Clifford, P *Wild Trees in the Cayman Islands* National Trust for the Cayman Islands

Greenberg, Idaz and Jerry *Corals & Fishes: Florida, Bahamas & Caribbean* Seahawk Press, 1999. A handy four-colour pocket guide to 260 species of fish, coral and other marine wildlife that inhabits the waters around Cayman.

Ground, Richard *Creator's Glory: Wildlife of the Cayman Islands* National Trust for the Cayman Islands

Humann, Paul *Reef Fish Identification* New World Publications, Florida. Probably the best (but at around US$40 also the most expensive) of the fish identification books available. In the same series are guides to coral and creature identification and fish behaviour.

O'Keefe *Sea Turtles: The Watchers' Guide* Larsen's, Florida, 1995

Proctor, George R *Flora of the Cayman Islands* HMSO, London, 1984

Sauer, Jonathan D *Cayman Islands Seashore Vegetation: A Study in Comparative Biogeography*, University of California Press, Los Angeles, 1982

Diving guides

Cohen, Scholmo & Roni *Cayman Divers Guide* Seapen Books, Israel

Frink, Stephen and Harrigan, William J *The Cayman Islands Diving Guide* Swan Hill Press £16.95

Humann, Paul *Cayman Underwater Paradise* Florida, 1979
Humann, Paul *Cayman Seascapes* Florida, 1986
Pierce, Jean *Diving and Snorkelling: Cayman Islands* Lonely Planet Pisces
Wood, Lawson *Dive Sites of the Cayman Islands* New Holland, London

General guides and photographic books

Boultbee, Paul G *Cayman Islands* Clio Press (World Bibliographic Series, vol 187), 1996
Humann, Paul *Beautiful Isles Cayman*
Driver, Jenny and Dilbert, Leonard (introduction) *Cayman Islands* Caribbean Publishing
Oliver, Ed and associates *The Postcards of the Cayman Islands* EDO Ltd, 1993. The combination of old and new postcards and attractive line drawings makes this an appealing souvenir.

Business

Doing Business in the Cayman Islands Price Waterhouse, World Firm, 1993

Fiction

Matthiessen, Peter *Far Tortuga* Vintage Books, 1988. A tale of the sea that gives a close-up account of life for the Cayman turtlers. The *New York Review of Books* compared it to 'the best of Conrad or Stevenson'.
Meekings, Brian *The Storyman* Storyman Publishing, 1997. A collection of short stories based in Cayman and introducing several aspects of the islands' culture and natural history. Ideal for children of around primary school age.

WEBSITES

www.caymanislands.ky   Department of Tourism website
www.divecayman.ky   Department of Tourism's dive website
www.caymanbrac.com   A useful site dedicated just to Cayman Brac

Royal palm

Index

Page numbers in bold indicate major entries, those in italics indicate maps.

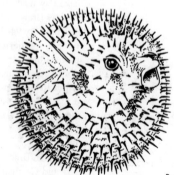

Porcupine fish